D1395398

THE LAST OF THE LAST

THE LAST OF THE LAST

The Final Survivor of the First World War

Claude Choules

MAINSTREAM
PUBLISHING

EDINBURGH AND LONDON

Copyright © Claude Choules, 2010
All rights reserved
The moral right of the author has been asserted

With thanks to Karen Farrington
for additional historical material

First published in Great Britain in 2010 by
MAINSTREAM PUBLISHING COMPANY
(EDINBURGH) LTD
7 Albany Street
Edinburgh EH1 3UG

ISBN 9781845966317

Originally published in Australia and New Zealand in different form
by Hesperian Press, Western Australia

No part of this book may be reproduced or transmitted in
any form or by any other means without permission in writing
from the publisher, except by a reviewer who wishes to quote
brief passages in connection with a review written for
insertion in a magazine, newspaper or broadcast

The author has made every effort to trace copyright holders.
Where this has not been possible, the publisher is willing to acknowledge
any rightful copyright owner on substantive proof of ownership

A catalogue record for this book is available
from the British Library

Typeset in Baskerville and Optima

Printed in Great Britain by
Clays Ltd, St Ives plc

1 3 5 7 9 10 8 6 4 2

Bedfordshire
County Council

9 39381200	
Askews & Holts	940.45941 CHO

To Ethel and our family

Acknowledgements

First, I must thank my family for their encouragement and help at all times. This kept my nose to the grindstone and made me realise that this was something really worth doing; for Claude himself, for his large family, for the navy and for the world.

I am very fortunate to have Peter Bridge of Hesperian Press in Australia and Mainstream Publishing in the UK as publishers. I am most grateful to Howard Willis for his editorial suggestions and wish to thank Cally and Celene Bridge for their input.

Above all, I thank my father for writing this memoir, which is a wonderful legacy. We are all very, very proud of him.

Daphne Choules Edinger

Contents

	Introduction	11
ONE	A Childhood in Wyre Piddle	13
TWO	I Join the Navy	35
THREE	Going to War	51
FOUR	Scapa Flow	71
FIVE	The Guns Fall Silent	77
SIX	Cock and Bruce Stories	87
SEVEN	Leading Torpedoman	95
EIGHT	With the Royal Australian Navy	113
NINE	Delivering HMAS *Canberra*	123
TEN	Exploits Aboard the *Canberra*	133
ELEVEN	Homecraft and Bushcraft	141
TWELVE	Another World War	153
THIRTEEN	The Yanks Arrive	165
FOURTEEN	Kimberley Frontline	173
FIFTEEN	Fremantle at War	179
SIXTEEN	Peace	191
SEVENTEEN	Gone Crayfishing	201
APPENDIX	Claude Choules' Ships and Shore Bases	213

Introduction

IN HIS 80S, MY FATHER RECORDED HIS MEMOIRS FOR THE sake of his many grandchildren and great-grandchildren. However, the manuscript acquired considerably wider significance when, in July 2009, at the vast age of 108, he became the only surviving First World War combatant – and the last man in the world to have seen active military service in both World Wars.

Claude's story was originally handwritten in a variety of old school exercise books. Later, in what spare time I had from my busy life as a survey botanist, I began to type the memoir into my computer. As I proceeded, I was fascinated to learn about his naval life, many aspects of which I was never aware of. I was amazed, too, at his powers of recall after so many years. (There were some lapses, however – I'm pretty sure we ate those 'two lovely little nanny goats' Claude claims were given away.)

In transcribing, I sometimes found it desirable to break up the occasional overly long sentence. When Howard Willis became involved, he helped create a better chronological and thematic flow and undertook some necessary fact-checking.

Claude was a strict but loving father, who has continued to influence me tremendously throughout the course of my life. He taught me to swim and instilled in me a great love of the sea and of boating, diving and fishing. These passions I have, in turn, passed on to my own four children during our holiday visits to Garden Island.

As children, we spent our summer holidays under canvas at Coogee Beach, south of Fremantle. Claude sewed the tents himself, a skill he learned as a boy in sailing ships. At Coogee, we sailed our little dinghy, *Titmouse*, which he and I built on the side verandah of our Holland Street house.

Claude loved the Australian bush. Growing up in our household meant travelling out to the hills or someplace down the coast to camp out and hunt kangaroo and ducks, which we enjoyed eating. On weekends, we would walk into the bush to admire and learn about the wild flowers and birds. Claude taught us the names of all the birds we saw.

My father was an outgoing man who loved people. My mother, Ethel, was more reserved. She discouraged him from seeking promotion to officer status in the RAN because she did not wish to subject herself to the social commitments that would entail. He never held any resentment on this account.

When asked the secret of his longevity, Claude will intone 'cod liver oil'; if he's feeling a little devilish, he might advise: 'keep breathing'. At heart, he believes it was our family that kept him going and that a stable and loving family has been his most important asset in life. This feeling is no doubt influenced by his having lost contact with his mother at a tender age.

After his retirement, Claude continued to live an active life. He swam in the sea on a regular basis. When he reached 100 years of age, I remember suggesting to him that perhaps he should invest in a new pair of swimming trunks. 'Oh, I don't know,' he replied. 'If I thought I had another ten years in me it might be worth it.'

Ethel died at the age of 98, in 2003. They had been married for 76 years. Claude is now in his 110th year. He has three children, 11 grandchildren, 23 great-grandchildren and two great-great-granddaughters – 39 direct descendants.

Daphne Choules Edinger
September 2009

CHAPTER ONE

A Childhood in Wyre Piddle

ON 3 MARCH 1901, SIX WEEKS AFTER QUEEN VICTORIA died, with the country still in full mourning, I was born in Pershore, Worcestershire. At that time, Pershore was a town of about 2,000 people and I was christened in its famous abbey. Choules is an Anglo-Saxon name, meaning 'fisherman'. The name appears in the Domesday Book in Salisbury Cathedral and has remained unchanged since before the Norman Conquest of Britain in 1066.

There were seven children in our family: Douglas, Leslie, Gerald, Phyllis, Hartley, Claude and Gwendoline. Unfortunately, Gerald died as a baby and Hartley died aged four or five, of appendicitis. I can only just remember him. Many infants died before getting close to adulthood in that era before penicillin and vaccinations.

Before I started school, we moved to 'The Cottage' in Wyre Piddle, a village on the banks of the River Avon, between Worcester and Evesham, in the beautiful Vale of Evesham. Its population of between 200 and 300 nearly all lived in thatched cottages. There was one pub, the Anchor Inn, one store, one bakehouse, a butcher's shop and a beautiful Norman church. At that time, local market gardeners and farmers brought their produce to be sold at the market cross in the centre of the village. That cross must have been very old, because the stone steps at the base were worn down by long use.

The Cottage lay half a mile out of Wyre Piddle. It was the only house in Anchor Lane, which petered out amid various orchards and farm meadows. Two miles across the meadows was the village of Throckmorton. I well remember the day we helped fight a fire in a thatched house there, which fortunately stood alone. The fire engine, drawn by six horses, passed our house on its way to Throckmorton from Pershore. All assistance was welcome because the pump was operated by hand, with about eight or ten people on each long handle at either side of the engine. It was hard work and frequent changes of volunteers were required. Despite our efforts, the house was destroyed, as a fire in a thatched building is very difficult to contain. This tragedy occurred when I was only eight or nine years old. We children thought it a most exciting event, as we were allowed to help with the pumping.

The fire service that rushed past Claude's cottage to combat a thatch fire was one of hundreds of small outfits operated individually by municipal authorities. Until the 1900s most tenders were steam-powered. As he lived in a rural environment, it seems likely that it was this kind of machine that was being used, as innovation was slow to reach rural areas. However, it was about this time that steam-powered appliances were being superseded by those driven with an internal combustion engine. It wasn't until 1938 that a national fire service was formed, unifying fire fighters across the country.

Another excitement for us was the first motor car to travel through Wyre Piddle. A man was trotting along in front with a red flag and all the villagers turned out to see this great novelty.

Our family had a dog of mixed pedigree called Sooner because he would sooner sleep on the sofa than in his own kennel. I was learning to play the mouth organ, and whenever I played it within hearing distance of Sooner he would put his head back and howl. This caused me much amusement but it greatly annoyed anyone else nearby.

We also had a black cat called Smut. Smut was quite a character. When we went down into the village she would usually accompany us, walking in front with her tail in the air. On reaching the first house, she would jump through the hawthorn hedge and remain there until our return – then she would hop out and lead the way home. She was a great hunter and would often bring home rats and mice, and leave them on the front doorstep for us to admire. On occasion, she brought in a hedgehog. I thought she had magical powers. When I was left alone in the evenings, as sometimes happened, I used to lie on the sofa with the cat on my chest, feeling sure she would protect me from any harm.

My mother, Madeline Winn, a Welsh actress, left home when I was five. At the time, I was told she had died. In fact, she went back on the stage but I never saw her again. My sister Phyllis went to live with Uncle Leonard Choules and his family of four girls, and my baby sister Gwendoline was adopted by my father's sister, Adeline Rawlins, and her husband, Herbert, who had no children of their own. Uncle Herbert was a very successful farmer at Pewsey, in Wiltshire, and used to ride around his 600-acre farm on a beautiful horse.

That left my father, my two older brothers Douglas and Leslie, and myself. We were looked after by Mrs Savage, who used to walk over to The Cottage from her home in Pershore each day. She was an excellent cook and cared for us very well. My two brothers went to the Pershore National Boys' School, a walk of two and a half miles each way. After attending the Infants' School in Wyre Piddle, I joined them at Pershore.

On my way home from Pershore School, I used to pass under the railway bridge over Anchor Lane. This bridge carried the London to Birmingham Express, which passed our village each afternoon. I would watch in awe as the speeding juggernaut sped over the bridge, rattling its rivets. One day my cousin Frank and I climbed the embankment and discovered that there was enough space for two small boys to squeeze into the point at which the great steel H-bar girders which carried the weight of the bridge entered the buttresses of masonry. Next day we hid there to feel what it was like when the express passed over. We could both see and hear the train for some time before it reached the bridge. It looked like a monster swaying towards us. We huddled together in fear, trembling like leaves, almost deafened by the roar, wondering if the bridge would collapse through the terrific vibrations set up by the train. When she

THE LAST OF THE LAST

had passed, we emerged none the worse for wear and vowing it was the greatest thrill we had ever known. We kept news of this episode to ourselves and afterwards quite often enjoyed the same thrill. If we had told our brothers and sisters, and word got to our parents, that would have put paid to any further such adventures.

The last half of the journey to school took me past a flourmill on the Avon operated by a waterwheel. After winter flooding, the water meadows alongside the river would often be frozen over. In frosty weather, we used to carry our skates slung around our necks. As soon as we struck the meadows, we would strap them on and skate to the jam factory on the outskirts of Pershore, where we would change into our boots and proceed to school.

Just before we reached the jam factory, we had to pass over a low bridge spanning a drainage channel. One foggy morning, I was out in front of the others. Thinking I was heading for the bridge, I skated over the bank and landed on my forehead on the icy surface of the channel. I woke up some time later, in the home of a family friend in Pershore High Street, with the lady of the house putting butter on a large lump on my forehead. I remained there for the rest of the day, until my brothers and sister called to take me home.

My brother Douglas was born in 1893 and Leslie a year later. As they were quite a lot older than me, I made my friends among the village lads. There was no organised sport at school but out of school we often played football. I was keen on running and used to practise doing circuits of the field where we played football. In winter, we often played ice hockey, which was great fun.

Fishing I also enjoyed very much. My friends and I used to cut our rods from withies, a type of willow. A withy rod was considered equal to a cane one, which had to be bought. Our favourite spot for fishing was the Wyre Brook, which joined the Avon near the watermill between Wyre Piddle and Pershore. The catch usually consisted of eels, gudgeons, roach, perch and bream. Sometimes we took them home to cook but often we cooked and ate them at the brook.

This was where I learned to swim, though for a long time I could only swim with my head underwater. By taking a deep breath I could swim across the brook, about 15 or 20 feet. Luckily, I learnt to get my head up before joining the Royal Navy's training ship *Mercury* in April 1915.

One of our favourite pastimes was to lie on our backs in the hay meadows and watch the skylarks in their ever-ascending spirals, bursting their little hearts in urgent song. We could still hear them when they had gone up so far they were out of sight. Then they would reappear, descending in long glides, and land in the grass some way away from their nests. By following carefully, we could track their nests, which were hidden in dense clumps of grass. The skylarks did not sing as they descended, probably so as not to disclose the whereabouts of their eggs or young. Or maybe they had run out of breath!

In one of the meadows alongside the brook was an old elm tree with a hole about 20 feet up. One evening, at dusk, I thought I saw a bat fly out of it. On the summer evenings, we saw lots of bats flying around. I climbed the tree, put my hand in the hole and pulled out a bat. After a good look at it I put it back again. Sometimes friends would ask me to show them a bat, which I gladly did, although I always insisted that they didn't hurt it and that I should put it back afterwards. I think the bats got to know me because I was never once bitten, though there were quite a number of them resident in that hollow tree.

Another exciting thing occurred one day while I was trying to catch minnows from the landing stage of the Anchor Inn, where the pleasure steamers taking tourists to Stratford-upon-Avon used to come alongside. Unfortunately, I fell in.

A lady who was lazing in the sun screamed and fainted. My Uncle Dick, the husband of my mother's sister, Annie, as well as being the publican, came running down, dived in and fished me out. They pumped the water out of my lungs, gave me a brandy bath and laid me down to sleep in a large double bed at the inn. When I came round, they asked me if I'd like a drink of something. I said lemonade, and insisted that my cousin Frank come to share it. My only sensation whilst in the river was of wonder that everything around me was yellow. I later realised that this impression was caused by the sun shining through the mud particles in the water.

My early education was at the village infants' school, under the kindly guidance of Miss Bridgewater, who was in charge of the school for 42 years. As I have mentioned, after this I went on to Pershore National Boys' School where the headmaster, Mr W.T. Chapman, was a strict but fair man who did not enjoy particularly good health. He nevertheless did a fine job as secretary of the Pershore Cooperative Fruit Markets for many years after he retired.

As I could not run as fast as my two older brothers, they would not let me accompany them when they went down to Wyre Piddle. They said that if we were chased, I'd be caught, and they'd be caught out in any wrongdoing that had occurred. One of their pranks was called 'tip-tap-the-spider', played with a pin, a reel of cotton and a button. It has to be remembered that the village was very dark and quiet at night; the local houses were lit with kerosene lamps or candles and traffic consisted of the occasional horse-drawn carriage or bicycle.

For tip-tap-the-spider, the pin was stuck into the woodwork of a windowpane, with the button fastened about a foot away. Unreeling the cotton as they went, Doug and Les would position themselves across the street, from where slight tugs would cause the button to knock on the windowpane. When the door opened, the owner would look around and, seeing no one, return inside. That's when the boys would start knocking again.

Guy Fawkes Night was a red-letter date for us. We used to save up our pennies for months beforehand to buy fireworks, which were placed in the warm oven for several nights to make sure they were thoroughly dry for the 5th of November. We'd set off our fireworks in the village, much to the annoyance of some residents. I remember one man doing a mad dance to dodge a Jumping Jack, then chasing furiously after the village kids, who all ran off. I couldn't keep up, so I climbed up into a stack of empty fruit hampers to hide. But the man spotted me, hauled the hampers down, took off his belt and gave me a good walloping, which I still believe was undeserved, as I hadn't lit a single firework. My brothers and I made sure that man did some more dancing that night! When Les and Doug emigrated to Western Australia in 1911, I'm sure most people in Wyre Piddle heaved a huge sigh of relief.

Australia in 1911 had spent a decade as a country rather than a colony, and was proud to call itself part of the Commonwealth. Before 1901, Australia consisted of four colonies: New South Wales (which included what are now Victoria, Queensland and the eastern part of the Northern Territory), South Australia, Western Australia and Van Diemen's Land (now Tasmania). Each had its own system of government, of which it was fiercely protective. For a while, it seemed inter-state rivalry might scupper plans to bring everyone under one Australian umbrella. New South Wales was particularly belligerent on the issue.

The Victorian era had ushered in numerous changes in Australian society. New communications technology had a unifying effect, bringing the major cities into closer contact than ever before, even though they were thousands of miles apart. There were some obvious advantages to federation: the states could operate a unitary defence force and it would put an end to much administrative duplication. Tariffs could be scrapped. After two referendums, federation was finally agreed. A census carried out in 1911 revealed there were 4,455,005 people living in Australia, parts of which were still unexplored.

Les and Doug Choules left for Western Australia just as it embarked upon an unprecedented period of growth. Before the twentieth century its population was about 46,000, just under a quarter of whom lived in the capital, Perth. The discovery of goldfields at Kalgoorlie in 1890 had changed all that. Although the gold boom began to decline as early as 1905, Western Australia's economy remained strong thanks to the riches generated by the wheat and wool trades. The war caused a blip in its growth, however, as it did elsewhere in the country. About 40 per cent of the male population of Australia aged between 18 and 44 fought in the First World War, and about two-thirds of them became casualties.

Once, when I was about halfway to school, a sudden thunderstorm developed and I saw lightning strike a cow in a field. She bellowed and fell over, then struggled to right herself. I went to the farmhouse to tell the farmer, Jimmy Partington. He came over to look at the stunned cow and said his son would soon be back from Pershore, where he was delivering a load of wheat. 'He'll help me get her into the house yard,' he said. He thanked me and asked his daughter Alice to call the school to let them know I'd be late. The school was already mustered for assembly when I arrived, so the head told everyone there about my mishap. Jimmy was so grateful he told me, 'If ever you want a job, Tommy Boy, come and see me.'

He called me 'Tommy Boy' because I was born during the Boer War, when British soldiers were called Tommy Atkins, and my nurse christened me Tommy. This I was known as till I met and married Ethel Wildgoose. She always called me Claude, my given name, and so I remained from then on. I was given the nickname 'Chuckles' in the Australian navy.

In fact, British soldiers had been known as 'Tommy Atkins' as far back as the mid-eighteenth century, although one anecdote has the Duke of Wellington using the term after being impressed by the conduct of a soldier of that name. In 1794, during the Flanders Campaign, the Duke approached a wounded private who had acted with valour in the field. 'It's all right, Sir. It's all in a day's work,' the soldier murmured, before breathing his last. The Duke often used this cameo to illustrate the dutiful courage of the British soldier.

Another story emerged from the Sepoy Rebellion in 1857, when army chaplain Reverend E.J. Hardy recorded how a man called Tommy Atkins remained at his post despite the hopelessness of the battle and eventually died there. Reverend Hardy wrote: 'Throughout the Mutiny Campaign, when a daring deed was done, the doer was said to be "a regular Tommy Atkins".'

There's also a claim that 'Tommy Atkins' was included on military forms, particularly when the recruit was unable to write. However, it should also be noted that the name Atkins means 'Little son of the red earth'. Perhaps for this reason the name at the time was understood to be a generic one, adopted for British soldiers.

Whatever the reason behind the name, it was used affectionately in relation to British soldiers. During the Boer War one Private Smith, of the Black Watch, wrote the following poem after the British defeat at the Battle of Magersfontein:

> *Such was the day for our regiment,*
> *Dread the revenge we will take*
> *Dearly we paid for the blunder*
> *A drawing-room General's mistake.*
> *Why weren't we told of the trenches?*

Why weren't we told of the wire?
Why were we marched up in columns,
May Tommy Atkins enquire . . .

More famously, Rudyard Kipling (1865–1936) wrote a poem in 1892 intended
to illustrate a hypocritical attitude that prevailed in Britain, particularly among
the middle classes.

For it's Tommy this, an' Tommy that, an' 'Chuck him out, the brute!'
But it's 'Saviour of 'is country' when the guns begin to shoot;
An' it's Tommy this, an' Tommy that, an' anything you please;
An' Tommy ain't a bloomin' fool – you bet that Tommy sees!

Soldiers themselves lost their love for the name in the First World War when the
enemy used it in cries and taunts that echoed around the trenches.

A fruit and vegetable market was held each weekday in Broad Street, Pershore, a very broad road indeed – about 30 yards wide. Horse-drawn wagons, drays and carts brought the produce there and it was laid out in regular rows so that the auctioneer could pass along each lane and sell the goods. During my first years at school, Pershore Cooperative Fruit Market was built. Here, the produce was all under cover and the lanes were raised about 18 inches, which reduced the amount of lifting required during handling. Offices were provided for the use of the auctioneer and his staff.

Subsequently, I came to own some shares in the market and used to get the quarterly newsletter, which kept me in touch with all that was going on in the district. The way in which I became owner of the shares was strange.

Whenever anyone was sick, the local midwife Gran Rose was called, as she was credited with great healing powers. She was a grand old lady with 12 children and was, I'm sure, loved by all who knew her. Her husband worked as a ganger – or foreman of a group of workers – for the Great Western Railway Company. The Rose family also ran a smallholding of about ten acres and grew fruit and vegetables. All the necessary labour was supplied by the family.

They also ran poultry, which Gran used to take to the Worcester kerbstone market ten miles away.

Our family lore has it that Gran Rose once saved our father's life when he had double pneumonia by forcing some brandy between his lips after the doctor said he was dead. Our father always felt great indebtedness and affection for her ever after. I also had first-hand evidence of her healing skills for, after Doug and Les had gone to Western Australia, I was riding Dad's bike down Wyre Hill and came a cropper. I managed to hobble into school the next day, but my bruised knee was giving me so much pain that the headmaster decided to take a look but could not pull my knickerbockers over it due to the swelling. Being lunchtime, he took me home on the carrier of his bike, which I think was very good of him.

The doctor pronounced: 'He has a blood clot on the knee due to a damaged vein and will probably have a stiff leg. He must lie up and have hot poultices applied.' I went to Gran Rose's place for 14 weeks to be nursed and, thanks to her care, I made a full recovery.

Towards the end of the First World War I was on leave and, as usual, visited Gran Rose and her family. She told me that things were not too good and asked if I could lend her twenty-six pounds. I said of course I could. She then said, 'I will only accept the loan if you take my 26 one-pound shares in the Pershore Coop Market in exchange.'

'Keep your shares, Gran, and pay me back when you can,' I told her.

But she insisted and duly transferred the shares to my name, where they remained till 1966, when I redeemed them at current prices. The shares had earned a 5 per cent dividend each year during all that time.

I can only just remember my paternal grandmother, Betsy Anne White. Our great-grandparents were horse-breeders and lived in a lovely old place called Broad Oak in Hampshire. I went there as a child with my father's sister, Aunt Nellie. It was then occupied by a cousin of my father's, Annie Fencott. My grandfather, whom I never saw, and grandmother lived at Hartley Wintney, in the old rectory where my father was born. A small sidelight on the times was that my grandmother always addressed her husband as Mr Choules. When I was a small boy, grandmother Betsy Anne lived with my father's sister, Adeline, at Pewsey, on the farm run by Aunt Addie and her husband, Uncle Herbert Rawlins. Grandmother dressed like Queen Victoria in her later years and looked quite like her. She would sit in an armchair by the fire with her hands in her lap looking into the flames and not saying anything, nor moving, no matter what was going on around her. It reminded me of the old saying, 'Sometimes I sits and thinks and sometimes I just sits!'

My maternal grandmother, Sarah Winn, lived at Kidderminster, which was about 30 miles from Wyre Piddle. Her family was Welsh and came from Llandudno.

After Doug and Les emigrated, The Cottage was too big for my father and me, so we moved into rooms with Mrs Charlie Bradley at Wyre Hill, near Gran Rose's place.

My father and I would go fishing together on the river in one of the light clinker-built boats. I would take the oars and pull up and down the stream, while he trolled for pike or cast a fly for trout. For about three or four weeks of the summer holidays, I would pull him down the river to the Wyre flourmill and we would land up near the waterfall that carried the excess water past the mill. On the stones of this fall grew a green weed, like tufts of hair about three or four inches long. This was a great attraction for roach, which waited at the bottom of the fall for any that washed off. We used to break off a small amount and wrap it round our hook (about the size of a herring hook) and cast it into the swirling water. Invariably, we would have an immediate strike. Roach are fatter than herring and make very nice eating. I don't remember ever seeing another fisherman doing this, so maybe it was a well-kept secret of my father's.

My father also took me fox hunting, following the Croome Hounds owned by the Earl of Coventry. We would often call in to one of the country inns around Pershore or Evesham and buy our lunch of two pennyworth of cheese – about three to four ounces – and the top of a wholemeal cottage loaf, for one penny. It was a good, tasty meal for the grand total of threepence! Beer in those days was twopence a pint and cider a penny-halfpenny a pint. Prices remained stable until well into the First World War. I remember going on leave from the training ship HMS *Impregnable*, when my pay was sixpence per day. I'd visit the Anchor Inn to renew acquaintance with the villagers of Wyre Piddle and for two or three shillings I could shout for all hands.

At the time of Captain Scott's preparations for his expedition to the South Pole, I was a schoolboy. The tremendous interest taken by the general public in this activity intensified after Scott and his companions so tragically lost their lives on their return journey. Throughout Britain and the Empire, the feeling against his Norwegian rival, Roald Amundsen, became very bitter indeed. Amundsen reached the Pole a month before Scott, after a smooth-running expedition; whereas Scott's journey was fraught with difficulties and ended in disaster. The boys in my school were told to write an essay on Captain Scott's expedition. As my father had each day read the news to my family, I was well versed in the story and was lucky enough to win the prize.

Later in life, I received first-hand information about the expedition from Edward R.G.R. 'Teddy' Evans, who, as a young lieutenant, was second-in-command under Scott and who later wrote *South with Scott*. Evans became famous during the First World War as commander of the destroyer HMS *Broke*. He took his ship alongside a German destroyer in the English Channel at full speed one night and gave the order 'Boarders away'. That signalled members of his ship's company, armed with cutlasses and pistols, to jump aboard the German ship. They captured her in hand-to-hand combat. This operation called for superb seamanship and extraordinary courage. It was the first time this kind of action had been carried out since the days of sail. His consort, HMS *Swift*, sank a second German destroyer of three in this action.

Both Evans and Scott became heroes of the age for their 'against all odds' courage. Robert Falcon Scott (1868–1912) was a naval officer invited to join the National Geographic Society's expedition to Antarctica between 1901 and 1904. Having gone further south than anyone before, Scott was one of a new breed of polar explorers elevated to the status of celebrity. Immediately, he set about raising funds for another expedition, this time with the South Pole as his goal. His ship Terra Nova finally departed from Britain for the snowy south in June 1910 and hopes of a record-breaking trip were high. Only after he left Britain did he hear that Amundsen was also heading for the South Pole. The men were now locked into a race.

While Amundsen used Eskimo know-how to get ahead, Scott was constrained by some preconceived ideas that ultimately proved impractical. Plans to make use of mechanical sledges and ponies were scuppered by the extreme weather. On 17 January 1912 a diminished team reached the South Pole, only to find Amundsen had beaten him there. Dejected and exhausted, the British party turned around in a futile attempt to reach safety.

When the bodies of Scott and two colleagues were found in 1913, a letter to his wife Kathleen was discovered. It began by acknowledging that he was in 'a tight spot'. He urged her to marry again and went on: 'You know I have loved you, you know my thoughts must have constantly dwelt on you and oh dear me you must know that quite the worst aspect of this situation is the thought that I shall not see you again. The inevitable must be faced — you urged me to be leader of this party and I know you felt it would be dangerous — I've taken my place throughout, haven't I?'

Scott had invited Evans to join the ill-fated expedition. Although Evans was eminently qualified, Scott's agenda was in fact to prevent him leading a rival expedition. All the men in Scott's team were left vying for a place in the group that would make the final push for the Pole. Failing to make the cut and being sent back by Scott was a monumental disappointment for Evans. Even without undertaking the last leg of the expedition, he nearly perished. During his return journey, he was devastated by an attack of scurvy and survived only thanks to his companions, Tom Crean and William Lashly, who pulled him back on a sledge, in direct contravention of Evans's order to abandon him in the wilderness and save themselves. Evans was, wrote Lashly, 'turning black and blue and several other colours as well'. All three were in danger of dying. Crean went for help, walking for 18 hours non-stop to reach a camp. Evans made a full recovery and returned to Antarctica in 1913 to fetch surviving support staff from the expedition. Evans readily related his Antarctica adventures to fellow seamen during the remainder of his illustrious naval career. One of his favourite anecdotes was how men would pee on their own feet to prevent frostbite.

In 1929, Teddy Evans became rear admiral in command of the Australian squadron, and used to give us most interesting lectures about the Antarctic, showing slides of penguins, seals, whales and so on to companies on RAN ships. Later still, in the Second World War, he was the first admiral to become commander-in-chief Combined Operations. Between the wars, as captain of a British cruiser on the China Station, he took his ship to the rescue of a British passenger liner that had run aground in a gale and swam to the ship, taking a line which enabled the rescue of all passengers and crew. For this, he was awarded the Albert Medal in gold. It was stories of men like Scott and Evans that attracted me to navy life. I didn't know many other sailors during my childhood.

The only Wyre Piddle villager in the Royal Navy was Dick Goddard. He was the eldest of twelve children. His family lived in a thatched cottage near the Anchor Inn, whose gardens also ran down to the river. Dick was unmarried, and when he was on leave we would see him as he walked through the village on his way from the Pershore Railway Station, carrying his gear in a black silk handkerchief in one hand with a canary or parrot in a cage in the other. Each forenoon he would go to the inn and take up his customary place on the left side of the chimney base in the tap room, where he would sit and smoke his pipe. Anyone occupying this spot would vacate it for him. It was known as Dick's seat. There was always a crowd of kids around Dick while he drank his beer – restrictions on children in public houses were not in existence then. He could tell the most wonderful yarns. Dick was a real hero to us kids, and he proved himself to be so to the Service for in the Battle of Jutland on 31 May 1916, he was serving in HMS *Warrior*, an armoured cruiser. She was so severely damaged that she was taken in tow back across the North Sea, but foundered just before reaching the east coast. Dick was then a stoker petty officer.

I think that knowing Dick Goddard influenced me to join the Royal Navy, plus the fact that when I was fourteen, the First World War had been in progress for seven months. I had intended to emigrate to Western Australia as soon as I could leave school (at 14). The war made that impossible. The letters sent home by my brothers were very interesting and my father allowed me to take them to school for the headmaster to read to the senior boys. Western Australia was on the other side of the world, in the most isolated part of the island continent, and Mr Chapman would point out on the map exactly where they were.

Douglas had been driving a camel team out of Coolgardie, taking supplies out for the construction of the Trans-Australian Railway. Leslie had been driving a camel team from Nyabing, down the Rabbit Proof Fence to Point Anne on the south coast as a boundary rider. His job was to keep the fence in good repair; the trip lasted seven days each way. It was very lonely, as there were no settlements between Nyabing and Point Anne in those days. He used to talk to his dog and even to the camels. He said he once met the man who was inspecting the telegraph line from Adelaide to Albany and they spent a whole day together – yarning!

The Choules brothers became involved in two of the major construction projects of the age in Australia, with the merits of one far outweighing those of the other.

The Trans-Australian railway line was a vital artery to link isolated Perth with the rest of the nation. Funded by all the states of Australia, it had been one of the major inducements offered to bring Western Australia into the federation of 1901 when six states – New South Wales, Victoria, Tasmania, Queensland, South Australia and Western Australia – were formed into one nation. Prior to the advent of the railway, there was no road for travellers to take, nor watering holes along the way. For those that wanted to get from one side of Australia to the other, the only option was a sea voyage, which took eight days. If Australia was isolated, then Western Australia was particularly so. A railway was seen as a tonic for the economy of both sides of the country.

But building the railway across vast tracts of waterless desert was a mighty undertaking. It took two years to survey the site of the railway, which was to run from Port Augusta in South Australia to Kalgoorlie in Western Australia, a track distance of 1,063 miles (1,711 km) to be built at a cost of some £4 million. Legislation passed in 1911 signalled the start of the project and it began from both ends, heading towards the middle. Keeping the construction workers supplied with food, water and materials proved to be one of the greatest challenges. Fleets of camels proved the most effective method of supply. The project continued throughout the First World War until both ends met on 17 October 1917 at Ooldea, 621 miles east of Kalgoorlie. Five days later the first transcontinental train left Port Augusta, cheered by 1,500 people. The carriages were fitted with electric fans and a fridge but were still uncomfortably hot as they toiled through the emptiness of the Nullarbor Plain, where at one point the track runs for 309 miles without a curve.

Curiously, the rail link was also built in no fewer than three different gauges, which meant numerous changes for passengers.

Meanwhile the rabbit-proof fence was, in retrospect, one of the most perplexing projects of the century. Rabbits, not native to Australia, had been introduced by early settlers, to provide hunting and food. Possessing an astonishing capacity to breed, rabbits had become a major pest. Where rabbits were abundant crops and grazing were at risk. A fence was suggested as a way of keeping rabbits out of Western Australia. When it became clear that one fence was insufficient, fences two and three were built.

By 1908 the three fences were complete, running to a length of 1,864 miles (3,000 km) in total. Unfortunately, rabbits were already running freely within its boundaries in places, although farmers insisted the fence provided some protection from the unwanted attentions of dingoes and emus.

As early as 1903 there were boundary riders employed to help maintain 200-km lengths of fence. Working in pairs, their duties were to repair damaged sections, remove dead animals or debris from the wire, repair erosion, keep its gates operational and check the rainfall gauges.

At first they used bicycles for transport, then switched to camels and, later, a motor vehicle. Finally, the most durable option was a buckboard buggy drawn by a pair of camels. Of course, camels were not native to Australia. They had arrived in 1860, having been recruited on a trip to India, after Australians realised that horses and mules had a limited capacity for desert life. Camels and their owners were the unsung heroes of many expeditions into Australia's unknown interior.

By the time of the Coolgardie gold rush, which began in 1894, the Afghan cameleers were swift to spot the opportunity that awaited them. The goldfields were isolated in harsh terrain. Workers could not have continued without the food and water transported by the camels with comparative ease and at low cost. By 1898 there were 300 Muslims in Coolgardie, the main focus for the Muslim community in Australia at that time. It comprised only men who eventually relocated from Coolgardie to Perth, the new capital of Western Australia. Although they did not exploit the mineral riches of Coolgardie themselves, the cameleers ran a profitable business, which stirred some jealousy among other workers. Racism towards anyone who was not of white, British stock was prevalent at the time. It is thought that a few of the cameleers were murdered while their animals were, in some instances, tortured. There was little that could be done to seek proper justice. This was starkly drawn into focus by legislation passed by the newly federated states at the beginning of the twentieth century, as politicians sought to keep Australia free of non-white immigrants. Cameleers were hard hit by taxes that discriminated against camels in favour of horses. As they were considered foreign workers – no matter that many had spent years in the country – the Afghans could not travel freely between Australian states without being hard-hit by the hindrance of red tape. Nor were they permitted to become citizens to free themselves of the burden. When cameleers could no longer make a decent living many returned to Asia, leaving their animals in the hands of Australians.

The rabbit-proof fence was lauded by some. In 1907 one rabbit inspector declared: 'I went along portions of the R. P. fence to the north of Burracoppin recently on the outside (east) and there was not a blade of grass to be seen, not even enough to feed a bandicoot. On the west side there was grass from three to six inches high and any amount of old feed.'

But by 1935 the experiment was seen as an unmitigated failure, not least because the fence's security had soon succumbed to the elements. David Stead, a former rabbit commissioner for the New South Wales government, wrote: 'There is one thing outstanding very clearly in the matter . . . whatever effective work the fence did . . . it absolutely failed in an effort to prevent the movements of Rabbits [sic] from one part of the state to another. From the beginning it was largely a gigantic make-believe – a danger, too, inasmuch as it, like other large fences, lulled the landholders most concerned, into a false sense of security which numbed his own endeavours and really assisted the spread of the Rabbit [sic].'

The fortunes of Coolgardie went into decline in the twentieth century as the supply of gold became scarce. In 1898 it had been the third-largest town in the colony, as hundreds flocked there to make their fortunes. It had an urban population of 15,000 while a similar number lived in its neighbourhood. At its peak there were 700 mining companies registered there, supporting numerous other businesses from hotels to newspapers. Its streets were among the first to be *lit by electric lamps. Within a quarter century everything about Coolgardie had diminished – even its street lights had disappeared, replaced by ancient hurricane lamps. Hardly surprising perhaps that when the First World War broke out an estimated one person in every ten in Western Australia enlisted for service overseas, drastically curtailing the boom that Perth and its surrounding area had been enjoying.*

Much of that country is still unsettled and untrammelled, as my elder daughter, Daphne, found when she spent eight days on an exploration trip, under the auspices of the Australian and New Zealand Scientific Exploration Society, to the lower reaches of the Fitzgerald River. She went to Point Anne during the May school holidays in 1981, nearly 70 years after her Uncle Les was there.

We had received letters from my two brothers saying that they had joined the Australian Imperial Force (AIF) in the first month of the war. Les wouldn't join Doug's battalion, the 11th, as he said that if one of them got skittled they both probably would, so he joined the 16th. Both were entirely Western Australian battalions. After training at the Blackboy Hill Camp in the Darling Range, near Perth, they then sailed from Albany with the first large convoy. On the way across the Indian Ocean, one of the escort ships, HMAS *Sydney*, was detached to attack and destroy the German raider *Emden*, a light cruiser which had just destroyed the Cable Station at the Cocos (Keeling) Islands.

My brothers were landed in Egypt, where their training continued, and from there were taken in convoy to Gallipoli for the landing at Anzac Cove on 25 April 1915. They fought there until the evacuation, almost a year later. This was one of the most disastrous campaigns ever undertaken by the British, though, had it succeeded, it would probably have shortened the First World War considerably. Their occasional letters home were very exciting and I couldn't wait until I was 14 so I could leave school and join up.

The name Gallipoli came to signify an iconic episode in Australian history. For most it was welcomed as an opportunity for the federated states to prove their worth, as the Melbourne Argus *revealed on the day of the Gallipoli* landings. Australia had, it said, 'in one moment stepped into the world of great manhood'.

Also known as the Dardanelles campaign, it was the brainchild of future British prime minister Winston Churchill and would have undoubtedly cut months or even years from the war had it succeeded. Unfortunately, it failed, with the loss of thousands of lives on both sides either during the attack or the subsequent painful stalemate. Gallipoli was the name of the peninsula troops were sent to capture, while the Dardanelles is the name of the waters by it.

The campaign's aim was to capitalise on the weaknesses of the Ottoman Empire, an ally of Germany and an enemy of the Allies. If the empire, centred on Constantinople (present day Istanbul), were contained or knocked out of the war, then supply routes to Russia – also teetering on the brink of collapse – could thrive without harassment. Further, the stretched Russian front would be relieved when enemy troops were diverted to the defence of Gallipoli. Initially, its architects believed that one decisive naval action would have the desired effect.

The Gallipoli campaign began on 19 February 1915, when the British attacked Turkish forts defending the Dardanelles. But after the Turkish defenders withdrew from the outer forts, Royal Navy ships' gunnery could make little impact. In March, another abortive raid by the Royal Navy, supported by the French navy, took place, this time with the loss of more than 700 men after three ships were sunk and three severely damaged.

When it became clear that the navy alone was not going to win the battle, the army was drawn in, forming an invasion force. Lord Kitchener (1850–1916), Britain's Secretary of State for War and the face of a famous poster recruitment campaign, was advised he would need 150,000 troops. He decided a far leaner force would suffice for the April assault. The chosen soldiers were the British 29th division, who would fight alongside troops from Australia, New Zealand and the French colonies.

The Turkish commander not only had advance information about Allied troop movement but also had the landscape in his favour. His defenders adopted superior positions on coastal heights, while the incoming Allied troops would have to scale cliff faces. This was especially true after unkind currents in the Dardanelles swept the invaders past the bay that had been earmarked for action, to the foot of sharp inclines. Hopes that the Gallipoli peninsula would be swiftly raked through by Allied soldiers were soon dashed. Turkish defenders were fired up by a tide of nationalism that was sweeping the country. By the end of August,

Allied casualties amounted to 40,000, with Kitchener reluctant to plug the gap left by the dead and wounded with fresh troops.

By the winter of 1915, the plight of the soldiers was bleak. Withdrawal was the only option and here, at last, there were belated signs of sound leadership. Remaining troops were covertly evacuated without further loss of life.

However, the toll taken at Gallipoli was grim. The British suffered 205,000 casualties, including 43,000 dead. There were more than 33,600 ANZAC (Australian and New Zealand Army Corps) casualties, a third of whom were killed. French casualties amounted to some 5,000, while the Turks saw 250,000 men killed or wounded.

Later, the joint Australian and New Zealand forces chose 25 April, the day of the landings at Gallipoli, as a memorial day for the fallen.

I tried to enlist in the army as a bugler boy, but the recruiting officer knew our family so he was reluctant to sign me up when he realised I was under-age. He said: 'You come back and see me in a year's time.' When I told my father of my disappointment, he said he might be able to get me into the Royal Navy instead. He did this through the naval school TS *Mercury*, whose commanding officer was Commander C.B. Fry, an athlete, an Oxford Triple Blue and a famous English cricketer.

Charles Burgess Fry (1872–1956) was a true sporting 'great'. Best known for his cricketing skills, he was also an accomplished athlete and played football for Southampton and England. When he chose to play for England in the tour of South Africa in 1896 it meant the national athletics team was deprived of its most promising long jumper and sprinter for that year's Olympic Games.

But it was on the cricket pitch that Fry was in his element. He captained a Sussex side and the England team, taking pride in the fact that England never lost a test match while he was in charge. He scored more than 30,000 first-class runs, with an average of more than 50 runs per innings, and scored 94 hundreds during his illustrious career.

He also forged a reputation away from the sports fields after standing as a Liberal candidate at three elections – always unsuccessfully – and allegedly being offered the crown of Albania. This was among his fondest anecdotes, although proof that the small nation turned its face to Fry when it was seeking a suitably qualified candidate for the throne is hard to come by. He claimed the reason behind his refusal of the prestigious post was his lack of personal financial means. For many years his party piece was to jump backwards onto a mantelpiece from a standing position.

It seems he was no less proud of his work with training ships than he was of his sporting prowess. He and his wife Beatrice devoted almost 40 years to the Mercury *and he was ultimately awarded the rank of captain in the Royal Naval Reserve. One observer commented that, in later life, he would stride about in his uniform looking 'every inch like six admirals'.*

CHAPTER TWO

I Join the Navy

I JOINED THE *MERCURY*, A THREE-MASTED SAILING SHIP, IN April 1915, a month after my 14th birthday. My number was 1392. She was anchored at the mouth of the Hamble River, which empties into Southampton Water. We boys used to see the great Atlantic liners such as the *Mauretania* (holder of the Atlantic Blue Riband for 26 years), *Aquitania*, *Lusitania*, *Laurentic*, the original *Majestic* and scores of other wonderful ships travelling through Southampton Water. We could only imagine the luxury of cruising in liners like that, for life in the *Mercury* was tough.

On entry into the school, the first thing we submitted to was a haircut – all over, with short clippers – then we had to bath and kit up. We weren't allowed belt or braces, so one could always identify a new boy by the fact that every few paces he would stop and hoist up his bell-bottomed trousers. We soon got used to letting them rest on our hips.

We slept aboard every night, in canvas hammocks with no mattresses. These hammocks were slung between wire gantlines, stretched athwart-ships and set up by bottle screws. Each hammock was allowed 18 inches of space. After a general muster, the hammock-stowers served out hammocks, which were then slung by head and foot lanyards to the gantlines, each boy having his allotted place. We were then directed to the clothes lockers for our issue. At the order 'Turn in', the instructor set his stopwatch going, and at the end of one minute, we all had to be in our hammocks with our clothes off and folded in our lockers. Any boy not off the deck had to spend an hour doing blanket-edging, that is, stitching along the top and bottom of a blanket. This was how sailors learned to sew.

We were never allowed in a boat or on board ship with our shoes on. They had to be left in the shelter at the end of the pier where we embarked in the boats, 12-oared cutters, that would take us to the *Mercury*. In winter we sometimes had to hop into these boats with several inches of snow on the thwarts and bottom boards. The oars were double- and treble-banked; that is, there were two or three boys to an oar for the quarter-mile pull-off to the ship. In the summer months, we had to swim ashore each morning.

Boys were classified as non-swimmers until they could swim from the ship to the pier. A penalty for non-swimmers was that they did not receive a slice of cake each week. This slice was about four inches square and one inch thick, of a mixture something like a rock cake – it was so hard it was called 'a brick'. The non-swimmers also had to pull the cutters ashore with the swimmers' clothes, all folded neatly, and lay the clothes out in the shelter on the pier. Towels were also laid out in this shelter but there were not enough to go round, so some had to do the best they could with a towel which had already been used. We had to swim ashore for five or six months of the year. In the colder months, we took the boat.

The non-swimmers went aboard the ship each day for their lessons. They would strip off on the upper deck and go down the gangway onto the boat landing platform, a wooden grating about 20 feet long and four or five feet wide, where the instructor was standing with a six-feet-long boat-hook stave in one hand and a cane in the other.

He would ask, 'Can you swim, boy?' If the answer was 'No, Sir', he would ask, 'Have you ever been in the water before?' On receiving a negative answer, he would give the order, 'Jump in.'

If a boy who had not been in the water before was afraid to jump in, the instructor would say to two of the senior boys, 'All right, fist him and chuck him in!' This they would do, probably with great delight. The boy would struggle on entry into the water and rise to the surface, whereupon the instructor placed the end of the stave within reach. The boy would grab it, hoping to use it to climb up out of the water. But then he'd receive a cut with the cane on his fingers to restrain him. The instructor would talk to him and draw him through the water as he hung on grimly to the end of the stave. After a while the order would come: 'Now, let go of the stave.' And when the boy did, he'd move it a few inches from his hands and say, 'Reach out and grab it!'

In this way the boys were taught the essentials of breast stroke. It certainly got good results, though it was a cruel way to treat youngsters who had never seen more water than the amount in their bath in front of the kitchen fire at home. Luckily for me, I could swim before I joined, though I couldn't swim a quarter mile (400 m), but I soon learned and, in the annual regatta and swimming sports, I took part in the mile race.

In the eighteenth and nineteenth centuries, Britain had command of the world. One of the primary tools at her disposal was the Royal Navy, renowned internationally as the most powerful in existence, and the best. Of course, the navy wasn't the only reason why Britain blossomed. Although small, the island nation had superior internal communications, was a major tariff-free market and did not have to maintain a large standing army, thanks to the navy's flexibility. Britain, thanks to its lucrative empire, was also financially stable and open to technological innovation.

But for nearly a century after defeating rival France, British global dominance – hailed as 'Pax Britannica' – depended on her battlefleets and merchant navies, the crews of which were notoriously rough and ready, initially good for hauling sail and later stoking coal.

At the start of the twentieth century a new world order was dawning with Germany, the US and Japan shaping up to challenge British pre-eminence. The role of ships, merchant and military, was evolving. Merchantmen were dealing with the impact of commercial competition stemming from the onset of railways, the combustion engine and even radio. In terms of weaponry for military vessels there was the development of aircraft, submarines, tanks and improved artillery that needed a response from the Royal Navy. Oil would soon replace coal as the fuel of choice for Royal Navy ships, which could then refuel at sea, thereby substantially extending naval embrace. Simple engineering in the bowels of a ship was soon making way for sophisticated equipment that needed skilled operators. A new breed of sailor was needed in great numbers for this evolving scenario. More than that, a fresh approach was required in Royal Naval training.

In 1896 the Windsor Magazine *carried an article by Archibald S. Hurd that outlined how sailors were trained.*

> *. . . after they leave the training ship, blue-jackets in these days of steam seldom handle canvas or make or shorten sail. Every bluejacket is now trained from boyhood to use the cutlass and rifle and lay a gun with precision.*
>
> *Whereas it used to take several years to build a wooden battleship, one of our modern leviathan vessels can be built in less than two years; but it takes twice as long to train efficient bluejackets to man it . . .*
>
> *Now we are able to man the largest fleet the world has ever seen with men who volunteer for service and the navy in this year of grace, when we are not at war with any of our neighbours, consists of about 60,000 seamen, thus disproving the statement that is sometimes heard, that the British are no longer so eager for life on the sea as they were in the good old times. This is one of the many popular fallacies about the navy. They never die.*
>
> *It must not be supposed that our navy stands at 60,000 men because more could not be obtained. Unlike the army, the navy has no need of recruiting officers. Continuous streams of boys daily present themselves on the various training ships seeking to join the navy. So great is the number of would-be sailors that of every ten boys who leave the shore in watermen's boats to be examined by the officers of the training ships, nine are returned to their parents . . .*
>
> *Moreover, not only have the boys to show their physical fitness for sea-service but they must satisfy an examiner in reading, writing and arithmetic. Every year, of the many thousand boys examined, about 4,000 are taken on to one or other of the training-ships and commence the course which eventually results in their winning the proud distinction of A.B.*

The magazine outlined the procedure that recruits like Claude would have experienced:

> *Having satisfied the surgeon and chaplain as to their physical and mental fitness each boy signs a contract endorsed by a parent or guardian to serve*

in the navy for twelve years from the time that he reaches the age of eighteen years. When a boy has satisfied all these requirements he is taken . . . [to the training ship] where he is bathed and fitted out with a complete equipment of clothes, a combined prayer and hymn book, and what is known as a 'ditty' box, in which he can lock away his letters and personal trifles. The boy is now ready to go on board the training ship where he is vaccinated and placed with other newly entered lads, known as novices, under the charge of a kindly petty officer who, during the first week of his new life, acts in the capacity of father. Despite this very wise separation of the boys from their future companions, who would be likely to take advantage of their 'greenness', many of them suffer keenly from home sickness and a general feeling of forlornness.

The life of the boys is vigorous and thoroughly healthy. The instruction as at present carried on is the result of long experience and the aim is to enable the lads to acquire as much general, educational and seamanlike knowledge as can be assimilated in about fifteen months – the length of time occupied in transforming a novice into a first-class boy ready for sea service. But to the newly entered lad the life . . . is full of strange surprises. He begins his training, not by learning how to handle a sail, wield a cutlass or lay a gun, but by being taught how to hold a needle and to put his clothes away neatly. His first duty is to mark his kit and to pack his clothes and other belongings into the long, capacious bag which serves as his portmanteau in his future travels over the seas.

There is a field within a few hundred yards of the training ship and here boys can play cricket, football and other games. The dull evenings are beguiled by magic lantern entertainments and concerts when the lads themselves sing and recite, while a good library, bagatelle and draughts fill up other odd half-hours. In this way the boys' lives pass very pleasantly, never lacking in interest and even excitement.

After about nine months the young seaman is able to handle a gun, pull an oar, and swim, and, having passed through the necessary classes in seamanship, becomes a first-class boy and his drills become more intricate.

It was this kind of training that Claude would have undergone on the Mercury.

Before we left the ship in the morning, we had to scrub the decks, and after getting ashore we put our shoes on and were marched up to the house and lecture rooms, where we cleaned out the rooms then had our bath. This took place in a communal shower room, where the boys stripped off in the anteroom and then entered the shower room, naked. A senior boy slapped a small amount of soft soap on their hands as the boys passed him, each one taking their toothbrush from the rack and dipping it into a container of pink, precipitated powder. Once the instructor gave the order to clear the bathroom, we filed out, halting in front of him, pulling down our bottom lips to show our teeth were properly cleaned. We then turned round to show our backs and he would say, 'Carry on.' Only then could we proceed to dress. In summer the water would often be too hot and in winter too cold. But we dared not complain aloud.

After breakfast in the dining hall, we went to Divisions, a general muster, where the ship's band played the national anthem, followed by the anthems of all the British Allies. After Divisions, we went to instructions, comprising seamanship, gunnery, rifle drill, signals, Morse and semaphore, and physical training. Lunch was at noon and there was more schooling during the afternoon. Tea was at 4 p.m., then there were evening classes in seamanship and signals, after which, having each been issued with a hard ship's biscuit, we were mustered again and marched down to the pier. There it was 'off boots' and down into the cutters to pull off to the ship, where the night officer again mustered us and ordered us to 'turn in'.

We had a church service every day, twice on Sundays, conducted by the chaplain. It was very high Church of England, with the burning of incense and carrying of banners, which I did not care for very much as I was used to our low church in Wyre Piddle. However, I was made a choirboy and enjoyed the singing.

On weekends we played sport – football or cricket – with occasional walks through the countryside escorted by an instructor. On Sundays, we turned out a half-hour later than on weekdays, at 0615.

Our mail, both inward and outward, was read, and any money sent to us was retained and given back to us when we went on leave for 14 days, twice a year. We were not allowed to be idle, so in our spare time most of us learned to do macramé work. All we needed was a piece of board about the size of a foolscap sheet, half an inch thick, and some macramé twine which we could buy from the ship's stores. It came in two thicknesses and various colours. We used to make ladies' handbags, fringes for mantel pieces (very fashionable in those days), belts and wall hangings. New boys learned from the old hands. The work was fascinating and helped us in our seamanship, knots and splices.

TS Mercury *was one of more than 30 training ships established during Victorian times to respond to the increasing demand for seamen for both the Royal Navy and merchant fleets. The first, HMS* Implacable, *put down its gangplank for boys at Devonport in 1855. A French ship captured shortly after the Battle of Trafalgar (1805), it was far from luxurious.*

In fact, most of the ships used for training were best described as hulks. (Similarly old or broken-down ships were used to imprison felons.) Standards rose somewhat during the last half of the nineteenth century.

Boys with parents sufficiently wealthy to pay fees had a choice of ships. Those too poor to meet the costs were either paid for by the local authority or found themselves on one of the reformatory ships. TS Mercury *was established by a wealthy London banker, Charles Hoare, to help boys that fell between the two extremes. Tuition on* Mercury *was either free or almost free and extended to boys aged from 12 – when formal education finished – to 15, the minimum age for joining the navy.*

Mercury *was initially housed on the barque 'Illovo'. After it was moored permanently on the Hamble outside Southampton* Mercury *grew to include some accommodation on shore and on other vessels, primarily HMS* President. *Before moving to Southampton it had been a drill ship moored in West India Docks in London. Prior to that, she was better known as HMS* Gannet, *a veteran of the war with Sudan.* President *was a dormitory ship for* Mercury, *which was where lessons were conducted.*

Fry took over at Mercury *in 1908 after the death of its patron, Hoare. Fry's wife, Beatrice, had helped Hoare to found the establishment and played a prominent role in its administration until her death in 1946.*

In the house of the Commanding Officer, C.B. Fry, was a magnificent collection of old ship models housed in two large rooms, which we called the museum. On 'clean ship' days, I was one of the boys detailed to scrub the floors and dust around the museum. We were all fascinated by the lovely models. This collection was sold to the nation between the two world wars and, last I heard, was housed in Greenwich Maritime Museum.

On Sundays, 'clean ship' routine was in a minor key and No. 1 uniform was worn. We had Holy Communion first, after the padre had held his parish service at 0900, followed by breakfast. This meant no food until 1000, by which time we were all starving. I'm sure we didn't appreciate the theological benefit of this. Church was preceded by Captain's Divisions. This was often the only occasion of the week when we saw the captain. He sometimes appeared on the playing field and played cricket with us. Sunday afternoon and evening were spent in organised outdoor activities, but less strenuous than other days, for it was our day of rest.

Our 'walks' were really route marches without packs. We were allowed to march at ease, but only when out of sight of the ship. Our instructors were nearly all ex-Royal Navy chief petty officers and we were sometimes treated to fine yarns, depending how their livers were, as most were hard drinkers and had been out on the town the previous evening.

Discipline was very strict, and punishment harsh, mainly consisting of extra rifle drill, which meant marching up and down on gravel, barefoot, carrying a rifle at arm's length. Sometimes we were required to do muscle drill, that is lifting the rifle overhead and out in front of the body. On rare occasions, such as flagrant disobedience to a direct order from the captain or instructor, a boy was caned in front of the ship's company. He was stretched over a vaulting horse placed on a grating, with straps on wrists and ankles passed through the grating and hauled taut. The cane, about five feet long, was wielded by the biggest instructor.

If one was not very successful at music, there was the dancing team. This involved learning Morris dancing, hornpipes and the eightsome reel. Not being very musical, but keen on dancing, I was in the team. We used to perform at the ship's concerts and the prize day before Christmas leave, when the ship's company put on a show for parents and friends. It was always very nautical in flavour. Nearly all the ship's company took part and all were mentioned in the programme. On several occasions, the dancing team was taken to Netley Hospital, near Southampton, reputedly the largest military hospital in Britain, to entertain wounded servicemen.

Netley Hospital in Southampton was one of Queen Victoria's pet projects and it was she who laid its foundation stone on 19 May 1856. Southampton was chosen for its site for the ease of transporting soldiers there by ship from foreign battlefields.

The need for a modern military hospital was highlighted by the well-publicised plight of soldiers during the Crimean War. It was built not only to care for injured soldiers or those suffering from tropical diseases but also to help train army medics. From 1870, there was an asylum attached to the hospital. Netley grew to be the largest military hospital in the world, with one building extending for a quarter of a mile, with 38 wards and 1,000 beds. However, its design was criticised by Florence Nightingale, the nursing campaigner famous for her care of the wounded during the Crimean War. She soon realised that the lack of light and ventilation would prove a problem but worked to ensure nursing standards were high.

During the First World War the hospital's capacity was doubled. An estimated 50,000 patients were treated there before the end of hostilities, among them the poet Wilfred Owen.

It was similarly used during the Second World War, with patients from the evacuation of Dunkirk and the D-day invasion among the admissions. By 1958, the enormous hospital was proving too expensive to run. Its closure was followed 20 years later by that of the asylum. The only reminders of the building to escape the ravages of fire and demolition are the chapel and the cemetery, which functioned throughout its life.

These outings to Netley Hospital were red-letter days for us because of the appreciation shown and the excellent spread of food put on for us at the end of the show. The food was the main attraction, as there never seemed to be enough at mealtimes in the *Mercury* and any that could be scrounged was keenly sought after by growing boys. Maybe this food shortage was always in evidence, or perhaps it was simply owing to the war rations.

The scholastic training was good, with the emphasis being on navigation. The boys in A classes were destined for the Royal Navy and those in B classes for the Merchant Navy. As I was signed up for the Royal Navy, I was in the former and the training I received here enabled me to pass for Advanced Class in HMS *Impregnable*, the collective name for ships acting as a training school in Devonport, near Plymouth. The general training in the *Mercury* also assisted me in passing for sub-instructor boy in the *Impregnable*. This was like being a head prefect and carried with it many perks. If the instructor was called away from his class for any reason, the sub-instructor boy carried on the instruction and was responsible for the class until his return. This was good experience in taking charge.

I was a pretty good oarsman when I joined the *Impregnable* and soon after I was selected as one of the captain's galley crew. A galley was the captain's private boat, a beautifully built, lightweight craft, and the fastest pulling and sailing boat carried in capital ships in the Royal Navy. It was kept in a perfect and spotless condition by the captain's galley crew – consisting of the coxswain, a petty officer and six of the best and smartest oarsmen in the ship – who also kept the captain's quarters clean – that is, the day cabin, sleeping cabin, galley and pantry situated aft below the quarterdeck, and his sea cabin on the bridge, where he slept when the ship was at sea. They did not have to answer any bugle calls or pipes except 'clear lower deck' (which means everyone except men actually on watch muster on the upper deck) or 'action stations'.

The six boys under the coxswain pulled the galley, using spoon-bladed oars, or sailed it wherever the captain wished to go. When the captain was aboard his galley, his crew pulled in a special way: at the end of each stroke, as the oars were feathered, there would be an appreciable pause before the next stroke commenced, which required a considerable amount of training with 16- and 17-foot oars. However, it was most impressive when viewed from other ships in the fleet.

Sometimes on Sunday, the captain would take the tiller and would sail out of Plymouth harbour and round the Eddystone lighthouse, 14 nautical miles to seaward. The first time he took us out there, and I saw the big seas running, I was scared, but soon gained confidence when I saw how well he handled the boat and how easily she climbed over them. He had broom handles secured under the thwarts for us to tuck our toes under so that we could lay out to windward. After the first fright, this was a most exhilarating experience.

Claude was rowing around the fifth and most enduring of the Eddystone lighthouses. Otherwise known as Douglass's Tower, it was completed in 1882 after cracks began appearing in the rock beneath its predecessor, Smeaton's Tower. Using a more robust foundation on rocks to the south-east and the innovations of engineer Robert Stevenson, James Douglass of Trinity House supervised construction of the new lighthouse using large stones dovetailed to fit each one of those around it. Its oil-powered lamps were not replaced by electrics until 1956. Two years after a helicopter pad was installed on its roof in 1980 it became fully automated.

We went ashore each day for sport and exercise in pulling boats called launches. They were open boats 42 feet long, weighing 184 cwt (9,347 kg), propelled by 18 oars, 16 or 17 feet in length, with three boys to an oar. It used to be funny watching the boats going ashore from a distance; one would see the boys' heads appear above the gun'le then the blades of the oars would dip, the boys' heads would disappear until the end of the stroke. This would be repeated until they reached the shore. It was difficult to 'toss the oars' as they were so heavy, being made of ash. This was always done when going alongside. I observed the same phenomenon some years later, when serving in the *Revenge*, watching the Turkish caiques being pulled up and down the Bosphorus from Constantinople, as it was then called. I suppose it would have been much the same watching the triremes in the Mediterranean Sea 2,000 years ago.

We had much more freedom in the *Impregnable* than in the *Mercury* and, instead of our families having to pay fees for us, we were paid wages. A boy second class was paid sixpence per day, a boy first class a shilling per day and a sub-instructor boy one shilling and sixpence per day.

Payday was once a week. Each boy in turn placed his cap on the pay table and the paymaster placed a sixpence on it. The remainder of our pay was held over and given to us when we went on leave. To spend our sixpence, we walked several miles on Saturday afternoons to a small village called Cawsand in Cornwall. In those days, sixpence went quite a long way. For instance, a packet of five Woodbine cigarettes cost only one penny. It was quite an event deciding what to buy but our sixpences were soon spent and it was an unwritten rule that no one took money back aboard ship.

If boys were caught fighting, the instructor who saw them would take their caps and order them to appear in the boxing ring at 5 p.m., or 1700, when they would put on the gloves and fight it out under the eye of the PT instructor.

In the navy, boys were forbidden to smoke, and one remained a boy till the age of eighteen, when he was promoted to ordinary seaman. Those boys recommended for accelerated advancement were 'specially rated' ordinary seamen at the age of 17½ years, which meant that they could commence the classes in torpedo, gunnery and seamanship for able seamen – but they were still not allowed to smoke until they were 18. Boys caught smoking were taken before the commander and given six strokes of the cane. Some of the instructors punished the boys themselves instead of taking them before the commander. This was done with their 'stonicky', as it was called, a length of one-and-a-half-inch tarred hemp, back spliced about ten inches long, with a loop to fit around their wrist. It was much preferred to the humiliation of being caned.

Although smoking was banned among boys in the navy, it was widely seen everywhere else in society at the time. The modern history of the smoking habit usually starts with the Crimean War (1853–56). It was a Scottish veteran of the conflict, Robert Peacock Gloag, who opened the first cigarette factory in England in the year Florence Nightingale returned home a heroine for the advances she and her team had made in nursing care.

Smoking was an inexpensive vice. As early as 1888 five 'Wild Woodbine' cigarettes cost a penny, while a loaf of bread cost six times as much. Moreover, it was generally considered a harmless or even a healthy habit. Although the

British Medical Association helped to raise concerns about its long-term effects in the early years of the twentieth century, there was little popular appetite for its message. Indeed, it was the era that women as well as men began smoking in vast numbers.

In 1923, scientists in Paris claimed that smoking was healthy because the chemicals in cigarettes warded off bacterial infections. At a subsequent exhibition – albeit one hosted by the tobacco companies – a doctor declared there was 'no risk of cancer from tobacco'. In the thirties, an advertisement for the Chesterfield brand of cigarettes asserted they were 'just as pure as the water you drink . . . and practically untouched by human hands'. Cigarettes were established as something of a 'must' from Hollywood film stars and royalty down to working men and women.

Not until after the Second World War, with soaring rates of lung cancer among Britons and Americans, was there a concerted attempt to discover the cause. Studies by Sir Richard Doll and Sir Austin Bradford in 1949 and 1951 pointed to a link between lung cancer and smoking. It still took decades before the idea that smoking was harmful to health was popularly accepted.

When ships from the fleet which had been in action with the enemy entered harbour, we used to 'man ship' and cheer them as they passed. To man ship, boys were lined around the bulwarks, standing on the yards holding hands with arms outstretched. This was an old custom, a survival from sailing-ship days.

One of the things we were taught was to use the boatswain's pipe – spoken thus, 'bo'sn's pipe'. This was made of electroplated nickel silver (EPNS), and was held in the palm of the hand with the stem in the mouth. While blowing hard, the fingers were opened a certain amount to produce various notes. The tongue also played its part on the stem. This call was used to attract the attention of the ship's company to a verbal order which was sung out by the bo'sn's mate, or call boy.

Some orders such as 'piping the captain aboard' or 'piping dinner' comprised an elaborate series of notes. When we passed out of the piping class, those boys who had obtained 90 per cent or more were rewarded with a bo'sn's pipe and chain. Those with 75–90 per cent, with just the pipe; and those below 75 per cent were not recommended as call boys when they joined the Grand Fleet on completion of their training in the *Impregnable*.

The duty call boys spent their watch with the quartermaster of the watch and when it was necessary to pass an order from the officer of the watch or commander, each boy had certain mess decks or parts of the ship to traverse while 'piping' the order. In a battleship of 30,000 tons, there were many mess decks and compartments. Call boys were later done away with when loudspeaker systems came into being.

The *Impregnable* was the largest three-decker line of battleship ever built, nearly 5,000 tons displacement, mounting 140 guns on three gun decks. Her ship's side was so thick that I could sit in one of the square gun-ports with my legs outstretched and my heels were still not outboard. Roughly three feet of solid oak – no wonder the forests of Britain were so depleted of their beautiful oak trees. The reason for this great thickness of wood was to prevent enemy shot from penetrating the crowded gun decks and causing havoc among the gun crews. Her mainmast was so large that two boys standing on opposite sides, where the mast passed through the upper deck, with their chests against the mast and reaching round with arms outstretched, could not make their fingertips meet. The great oak beams running athwart-ships, supporting the deck above, were about 15 inches square, and the oak knees supporting these at the ship's side extended from the deck head to the deck below.

There were two other old ships used in conjunction with the *Impregnable*, moored head and stern with her, and a third one moored abeam. We could walk over a gangway constructed from the bows of the *Impregnable* onto the stern of the *Black Prince*, which was used as the gunnery ship, and from her bows by a similar gangway onto the stern of the *Inconstant*, which contained schoolrooms and a lecture theatre. The third one was a smaller ship called the *Circe*, which contained the swimming pool where the non-swimmers were taught to swim – by a method more humane than in the *Mercury*. The boys here were supported in a canvas belt with a rope attached, running through a leading block attached to a traveller overhead; the instructor held the rope and gave the boy instructions on how to move his arms and legs.

Our chaplain on the *Impregnable* had served on HMS *Invincible*, Admiral Sturdee's flagship in the Battle of the Falkland Islands on 8 December 1914. Here the British squadron sank Admiral von Spee's squadron ships, *Scharnhorst*, *Gneisenau*, *Nürnberg* and *Leipzig*, while only the German light cruiser *Dresden* managed to escape to the south in fog. The British casualties were very light, ten killed and about a dozen wounded, while the German losses were almost 2,000 killed or drowned. The British ships were only able to save about 200 from the sea, although all boats were lowered and every endeavour was made to rescue men clinging to wreckage or swimming. Thus did Sturdee avenge the loss of the *Good Hope* and *Monmouth* to von Spee's squadron at the Battle of Coronel on 1 November 1914. Among the awards and honours for the battle, Sturdee became the first officer to receive the traditional baronetcy for a successful action at sea for more than a century.

My cleaning station each morning was to clean the chapel and the chaplain's quarters along with other boys, and sometimes he would talk to us about the battle. In our eyes, he was a hero. The *Invincible*, which bore the brunt of the enemy fire, had no man killed or wounded. Though struck by 22 shells, the majority of 8.2-inch calibre, her efficiency was barely affected. There was only one 4-inch gun out of action, and one coal bunker flooded. The *Inflexible*, on the other hand, only received three hits, which caused no significant damage but which killed one seaman and wounded two others. This was just reward for Sturdee's decision to engage his opponent at long range.

Physical training was considered highly important in this training ship and every day we went to the PT instructor for classes. This was usually very enjoyable, especially the vaulting horse exercises. Advanced-class boys received extra schooling, especially in electrical measurements, magnetism, geometry and trigonometry. This was to stand us in good stead later on in our careers in the Service.

CHAPTER THREE

Going to War

AT THE AGE OF 16, I WAS CONSIDERED FIT TO JOIN THE Grand Fleet. To do this, I was taken in a special train filled with sailors, from Plymouth to Thurso in the north of Scotland, and from there by special ferry across the Pentland Firth to the Orkney Islands. Here I joined HMS *Revenge*, flagship of Vice Admiral Sir Charles Madden. She was flagship of the First Battle Squadron, which included her sister ships *Royal Sovereign*, *Royal Oak*, *Resolution* and *Ramillies*. Each ship had mounted eight 15-inch, twelve 6-inch and four 4-inch anti-aircraft guns. These were mighty ships of 30,000 tons and boasted a top speed of 23 knots.

It was a wonderful sight to see this Grand Fleet of five squadrons of battleships, with their attendant squadrons of cruisers and flotillas of destroyers all assembled in one fleet anchorage. It was more wonderful still to go to sea with them all, and see our C-in-C manoeuvre them at high speed, like pieces on a chessboard.

Admiral Jellicoe had gone to the Admiralty as First Sea Lord at the end of November 1916. He then turned the Grand Fleet – 'the most efficient fighting machine the world has ever seen' – over to Admiral Beatty, who was its commander-in-chief at the surrender of the whole German High Seas Fleet to the Grand Fleet on the morning of 21 November 1918.

When at sea, the boys were stationed 'aloft and a-low' as lookouts, to report any ships or submarines sighted. I suppose this was because their young eyes were considered sharper than those of the older men.

One of our greatest thrills was to see our destroyer submarine screen change station each evening. Imagine a line of battleships stretching for miles, steaming at 20 knots, with lines of destroyers out on either beam doing the same speed. A signal flying from the flagship is hauled down, the destroyers out on the starboard beam at a distance of half a mile turn slightly towards the line of battleships and increase speed as they approach, finally passing between them with the distance between the battleships only two cable lengths, i.e. 400 yards, apart. It was most exhilarating to look astern along the line of battleships, and see these greyhounds of the sea passing through the line in perfect formation. The starboard destroyers would take up their new station outside the port submarine screen when a new signal would be hauled down from the flagship. Then the port screen destroyers would repeat the manoeuvre just carried out by the starboard screen and pass through the line of battleships to take up their new position as the starboard screen. This spectacular movement took place every evening, weather permitting. I witnessed it many times and always marvelled at the superb skill of the commanding officers of the destroyers in not scraping one of our battleships as they passed through the line, in perfect formation, at a speed of 30 knots.

Another occasion when ships were skilfully handled was when the battleships entered harbour at Rosyth, in the Firth of Forth. The destroyer flotillas, comprising 15 to 19 vessels of approximately 1,000 tons each, would approach their pens at 12 knots, reach their appointed position alongside the jetties, go full astern on their engines and have their mooring lines secured in a jiffy. The next ship would follow on in quick succession until the whole 50 or so vessels were safely ensconced in their harbour positions. It was just as exciting to watch them reverse the procedure the next time the fleet was ordered to sea.

The *Revenge* had the highest mast in the fleet. In consequence, we were the only ship that had to strike our top-gallant mast when passing under the Forth Bridge, which carries the railway north over the river. One might think this strange given there were four other ships of the same class in the First Battle Squadron, but it may have been that she was given a slightly higher fore mast to carry the admiral's flag. It was weird standing on the quarterdeck looking up to the foremost truck or masthead as it approached the great arch of the bridge, feeling that it must collide, then as it got close the bridge seemed to rise up and up and the mast to slip under. As soon as she was clear, the foretop men would hoist the foretop-gallant mast and secure it again.

To assist the Grand Fleet in spotting the enemy when patrolling in the North Sea, each of the flagships of the battle squadrons was provided with a kite balloon, similar to those used for air raid protection in Britain during the Second World War. This was a vast sausage-shaped envelope of silk with a large number of securing ropes hanging from it and three bulky fins on the after end to give it some stability. This supported a basket carrying two observers and various instruments, including a telephone whose leads ran through the core of the flexible wire cable which passed through the quarterdeck to a powerful electric winch on the main deck below. These were towed out to the various flagships on lighters or barges just before the fleet proceeded to sea. As may be imagined, they were most unmanageable in bad weather, which often occurred in those northern waters.

It was not so bad when the balloon was being sent up but when it was being brought down to relieve the observers, and neared the ship, it was caught in air currents caused by the superstructure of the battleship. The hot smoke and fumes from the funnels didn't help. She would swing across from side to side, with the balloon well clear of the ship on each swing, and this increased as she was hove down closer to the ship. When this action was being carried out, the commander would have the quarterdeck men and all the boys piped onto the quarterdeck 'to secure balloon'. This was because the boys could leap higher than the older quarterdeck men. The object of the exercise was to leap up and grab the ropes and hang on while being carried out over the ship's side by the swaying balloon. As she swung back again it was important to lift legs clear of the guardrails or risk a tumble. The securing ropes had figure-of-eight knots tied in them at intervals to prevent everyone's hands from slipping. In bad weather, the first few boys to grab lines risked being dipped in the sea on each side, but this only happened once or twice. Each time she swung, more and more boys and men grabbed ropes, so controlling her until the basket was finally landed safely on the quarterdeck abaft Y turret's 15-inch guns. On these occasions, our commander would reward the first boy to grab a rope with an item from the canteen. He would invariably select something to eat, such as a tin of fruit or fish, so there was great rivalry between the boys, numbering about 100 in each battleship to be the first. The total ship's company would be between 1,100 and 1,300, depending on the class of ship. I sometimes won the commander's canteen award during this thrilling operation.

On one occasion, we lost our balloon at sea during a thunderstorm. I was commander's messenger when it happened, at about 0645, that we ran into a violent thunderstorm. The commander was on the boat deck when the ship was struck by lightning. He looked up and a trickle of sparks travelled up across the nose of the balloon. It was raining heavily when he sent me to get the chief bo'sun's mate. I also had to collect his oilskin coat and mine. He ordered the chief to pipe the quarterdeck men and boys onto the quarterdeck in oilskins. Luckily there was no one in the balloon so the commander ordered the winchman to 'heave in'. When she was at about 500 feet, she burst into flames and fell into the sea off our starboard quarter. The basket, acting as a drogue, reversed the motor, burning it out, and all the wire was run off the drum and went overboard. While this was happening, the wire cut through the guardrails of the quarterdeck and carried away some of the stanchions. One of our attendant destroyers was ordered to salvage the basket and wire, which they did forthwith.

While carrying out North Sea patrols, the commander-in-chief often formed the Grand Fleet into red and blue fleets and exercised special tactics in preparation for meeting the German fleet, should it come out again. The C-in-C assumed command of one fleet and our admiral, Sir Charles Madden, being second-in-command, was in charge of the other. They would then carry out fleet manoeuvres against each other in the North Sea and, at completion, the admirals and captains would assemble on board either the *Queen Elizabeth* or the *Revenge* for a conference. Here they would assess the value of the strategy and tactics adopted by each side.

We asked the petty officer in charge of the boys' mess deck if we would be afraid when going into action. He replied: 'Everyone is afraid whilst waiting for the action to commence, but once in action, you are too busy doing your job to be afraid.' He was one of the senior petty officers in the ship and had served in her at the Battle of Jutland. We later realised that he was correct in his assessment.

We also carried out battle practice gunnery and torpedo exercises, with both day and night firings. These were sometimes against a towed battle practice target and sometimes against our own ships, using what was called 'throw-off firing'. In this case, the director was 'thrown off' so many degrees so that the shells landed a certain distance astern of the target ship and the fall of shot could be accurately estimated. During these practices, the ships' companies would be at action stations.

The first time we carried out full calibre firing after I became commander's messenger, he walked for'ard along the upper deck until he was under the guns of B 15-inch turret. I hung back because I was scared of the gun blast, so he called me and asked: 'Messenger, have you ever seen 15-inch shell in flight?'

I replied in the negative.

'Then watch up there,' he replied, pointing to a position in the sky well above the area of flash and smoke. Sure enough, when the next broadside was fired, I could see the shells, like two black discs, rising in the sky and rapidly getting smaller on their way to the target, 10 to 15 miles away. The heat, the shock and flash for anyone on the receiving end of these guns can be imagined when you realise that the firing of a broadside causes a 29,000-ton ship to roll 10 degrees away from the engaged side due to the recoil of the guns. It needs some punch to propel eight 15-inch shells, each weighing nearly one ton, over such a distance.

Big guns were still the weapon of choice for Royal Navy ships. At this time the Royal Navy was still getting to grips with the potential of torpedoes, a comparatively new option in its arsenal. The term 'torpedo' had been used loosely for many years to describe weapons that we would know better as mines.

It wasn't until the 1860s that a British engineer, Robert Whitehead, working in Austria, pioneered the development of a self-propelled bomb powered by compressed air that could be fired just beneath or just above the waterline. It managed a speed of 6.5 knots for a distance of about 200 yards. Measuring 11 feet 7 inches in length, it had a pointed nose and a cylindrical body.

It was thought torpedo targets would be stationary in harbours and it was for this use that improvements were developed. Torpedoes would introduce an element of stealth and surprise – something that was considered unsporting by some British and US commanders in its early days. And they were aimed below the waterline, at a ship's weakest point.

However, if torpedo-firing devices were introduced near the bow of a ship then it would render another time-honoured naval technique obsolete, that of ramming the opposition. Nonetheless, naval staff rightly guessed that this was the future and began manufacturing torpedoes at Woolwich in London for the fleet.

Whitehead continued to work on the finer points of his design, extending its range and changing its shape from sharp- to blunt-nosed to increase the amount of explosive it could carry. He introduced a gyroscope to assist its tracking, a device that the Royal Navy was compelled to introduce to torpedoes across the fleet at the turn of the twentieth century.

Meanwhile, the Americans invested in designs of their own, none of which knew the outstanding success that Whitehead experienced. He established factories in Britain and France and sold his product across the world.

In the early twentieth century, there were a series of improvements in the torpedo detonator. In Germany, the technology of electric torpedoes was racing ahead but it wasn't sufficiently advanced to fire during the First World War. However, during the Second World War, German torpedoes were unleashed against the British, with terrible consequences.

By 1914, the role of torpedoes in warfare and their place in preference to shells was subject to some debate, as the following excerpt from the Naval Review of that year reveals:

> *Until lately it was a generally accepted maxim that the torpedo could not play any part in a fleet action until one side had established a definite*

superiority in gun-fire, and that then its function was merely to complete, in the shortest possible time, the work begun by the guns.

The introduction of the long-range torpedo has changed these conditions entirely and rather suddenly. Its range approaches equality, and its effective range may in circumstances prove superior to that of the gun; it is quite conceivable that some future fleet actions may commence with torpedo fire.

This change in conditions does not appear to be fully recognised yet, and, even among those who realise it, there is considerable divergence of view as to how best to deal with the new state of affairs.

The following ideas are put forward not with any claim that they provide a solution of the problem, but with a view to starting a discussion which may lead to a crystallisation of opinion and assist the Service generally to a right appreciation of the possibilities of torpedo fire in action.

Now that the ranges of guns and torpedoes are comparable, a comparison between the two weapons in other respects may be of assistance when considering the use of the latter.

The torpedo may be regarded as a slow-moving projectile with a flat trajectory; the gun fires a projectile the time of flight of which is comparatively very small and the trajectory not flat.

Consequently, the characteristic error of the gun is a range error, while that of the torpedo is a lateral or deflection error.

Hence, at long ranges, if the gun projectile is to hit, the range must be known within narrow limits, and, in most circumstances it will either hit the ship aimed at or miss altogether – it is unlikely that it will hit any other ship in the same line.

As regards the torpedo, however, the lateral error, which causes it to miss the ship aimed at, may very possibly cause it to hit another ship in the same line.

We frequently exercised night action stations during this period, using star shells and searchlights, which was very spectacular. The contingency of night action had not been seriously considered prior to the Battle of Jutland.

A very disturbing occurrence took place on board *Revenge* soon after I joined her. The fleet had been taken to sea by Admiral Beatty, our commander-in-chief, to carry out night exercises, which we frequently did in order to frustrate a possible repetition of what happened at the Battle of Jutland, when the German High Seas Fleet escaped from the clutches of the British Grand Fleet during the night.

On the night in question, *Revenge*, flagship of the First Battle Squadron of five battleships, was leading the blue fleet with all ships at action stations. It was a dark night and all our ships were darkened when we received a report, saying: 'Enemy in sight bearing green 60.'

Instantly, the captain ordered: 'Burn all searchlights.'

We carried eight 36-inch searchlights, each of one million candle power, and they could be burned behind their steel shutters without showing a squint of light outside. When the crews switched on their searchlights, nothing happened and reports fired back into the bridge: 'No. 1 light won't burn', 'No. 4 light won't burn', and so on, until it was obvious that none of our eight lights were about to illuminate.

The torpedo officer immediately ordered a message to be passed down to know if the searchlight generators were running correctly. On receiving a reply that they were, the *Revenge* was ordered out of the line to investigate the cause of such a serious failure of her equipment.

The captain ordered everyone to remain at action stations and called all heads of departments to the compass platform, also the commander, his second-in-command, whose messenger I was. The captain, in company with these senior officers, did the rounds of the ship from truck to keel, visiting every nook and cranny. During this time, an investigation was being carried out to see why the searchlights would not burn. It was found that the main cables to each searchlight had been cut just below the pedestal. We returned to Scapa Flow, in the Orkney Islands, and next day some new marines joined the ship. They were secret service personnel.

The ship's company had the jitters, with everyone watching everyone else. And if one turned out during the night to go to the lavatory for'd, there would be heads looking round every corner to see what one was up to. The following day we were sent to action stations and a complete search was made of everyone's kit locker and kit bag. A pair of heavy wire cutters was found in the kit of one of our torpedomen and he left the ship under escort for Thurso in company with the new marines. We never saw or heard of him again, but the general belief was that he was shot by a firing squad. No wonder it caused such a flap, because it was soon after HMS *Vanguard*, a battleship, was blown up at anchor with the Grand Fleet in Scapa Flow, through the efforts, it was believed, of an enemy agent who had been working on board as a dockyard artificer.

HMS Vanguard *was one of three Royal Navy ships to explode mysteriously in home waters during the First World War.*

The first loss was a 1902 battleship, HMS Bulwark, *which blew up when she was moored off Sheerness near the mouth of the River Medway on 14 November 1914. The death toll was in the region of 740, with only a dozen survivors, all of whom sustained terrible injuries. A naval court of inquiry held shortly afterwards decided the haphazard storing of shells was to blame for the internal blast.*

On the afternoon of 30 December 1915, more than 400 people were killed when HMS Natal *capsized following a series of explosions in the Cromarty Firth. The dead included children and guests at a Hogmanay party being hosted by the captain and his wife, although half the crew was away from the ship, which pegged back casualty figures.*

Although sabotage was initially thought to be the cause, a later report pointed once again to unstable cordite on board the ship, which was launched in 1905 and boasted six 9.2-inch guns and six-inch thick armour plating. As with the Bulwark, *disaster wartime reporting restrictions largely kept the tragedy under wraps, although, until the end of the Second World War, Royal Naval crew were called to salute every time they passed the upturned hull of the* Natal, *still visible above the water.*

HMS Vanguard *blew up at 11.20 p.m. in Scapa Flow, with only two saved of a crew numbering more than 900. Among the dead were two visiting Royal Australian Navy stokers and an observer from the Imperial Japanese Navy.*

The explosion left the ship smothered with acrid smoke. When it had cleared, there was no trace of the vessel, other than assorted debris floating on the water. Once again, the spotlight fell on the unplanned detonation of cordite, perhaps sparked this time by an unreported fire.

Ernest Moroney, a sailor from nearby HMAS Melbourne, reported what he had seen:

> A great explosion occurred in the midst of the Grand Fleet, a terrible detonation took place, lighting the whole fleet as if it were daylight. There was a crash and one of the big boats went sky high with a crew of 900 men. All searchlights were switched on immediately but not a thing was to be seen.
>
> A trawler which was close by got smothered in blood and pieces of human flesh, and afterwards picked up half the body of a marine, the only body recovered up to date. I happened to be on watch and saw nearly everything. No one knows how she went up, but seeing she had a new ships' company it is surmised that it was the work of German spies.

The loss of all three ships was blamed on the work of German agents by those in the immediate vicinity. Theories about a saboteur at work and a wartime cover-up persisted through subsequent decades.

However, those who don't believe it was the work of Germany point out that none of the ships involved were state-of-the-art targets — they were all older than many ships in the British fleet. The same security measures applied to all Royal Naval ships, so enemy action would more likely have been directed at a modern flagship that would have presented a far greater threat to German vessels at sea.

As a result of the loss of HMS Vanguard, the Admiralty demanded more awareness in the handling of explosives aboard ship and regular recording of temperatures near magazines. Accordingly, new guidelines for improved storage and handling of cordite were issued.

Two days after the loss of HMS Vanguard, the Admiral of the Fleet, Lord Beatty, wrote to his wife, breaking news of the incident:

> A terrible calamity has befallen us and one of my fine old battleships blew up at anchor at 11.30 p.m., Monday night — the poor old Vanguard with over 1,000 men on board, in 25 seconds it was all over.
>
> The explosion was terrific, two men and an officer were picked up, and the latter died soon after. Luckily, 15 officers were out of the ship on board another at the time. A boat's crew was away and three officers and 50-odd men had been sent away on leave to make room for Admiral Sturdee and his

staff who were going to Vanguard, *while his ship, the* Hercules, *was undergoing a refit.*

But fortunately for him and his staff I sent them on leave instead, or else he and his staff would have been among the victims. It is an overwhelming blow and fairly stuns one to think about. One expects these things to happen when in the heat of battle, but when lying peacefully at anchor it is very much more terrible.

Not long after I joined the *Revenge*, I had my first taste of action. On 16 November 1917, the First Battle Squadron, led by the *Revenge*, went to sea, accompanied by our battlecruisers and two squadrons of light cruisers with their attendant destroyers. That night, we went to action stations on receiving reports of enemy ships from our light cruisers. The next morning, we heard gunfire and received reports that our scouting forces were in action. Soon after this, *Revenge*'s foremost turrets, A and B, opened fire and later claimed they had shot down a German Zeppelin.

As usual, the Germans scuttled back into the safety of their minefields, so this action resulted in little appreciable damage, except to HMS *Caledon*, flagship of Admiral Cowan. She got such a punch in the ribs from a 13-inch shell that I thought she would drop in two halves. The *Königsberg* stopped two 15-inch hits that reduced her speed to 17 knots, but too late in the battle for the British ships to catch her and complete her destruction. The German forces had been sent out to protect their minesweepers, which, on sighting the British forces, had slipped their gear and fled but not before several of them had been sunk. In this case, the enemy used a smokescreen to aid their escape, a tactical method of defence used by both sides in the First World War. The amount of smoke normally created by ships steaming at high speed, using coal for fuel, was fairly great. Towards the end of the war, quite a few of our ships were built to consume oil instead of coal, or had been converted to oil fuel, which considerably reduced the amount of smoke created. It also gave them a greater range of travel without refuelling.

Some months later, the First Battle Squadron proceeded across the North Sea as covering battleships for our light forces escorting the aircraft carrier *Furious* on a raid on the Zeppelin sheds and base at the island of Tondern. Again, the Germans retreated behind a smokescreen once action was joined, but not before our forces had severely damaged their Zeppelin base.

The German objective was always to trap a small section of our fleet with a superior force and then retreat before our main body of ships could get into action. After the enemy had, in 1917, decimated two of our Norwegian merchant convoys from Bergen to Lerwick, Beatty used to send a division of dreadnoughts to cover them. These convoys between Norway and the Shetlands had previously only been protected by a couple of destroyers.

Another preparation, made for covering all contingencies of war, was our carrying out of what was called general drill. This was performed every Monday, weather permitting, by all battleships and battlecruisers at anchor in Scapa Flow, our Grand Fleet base. The drills were initiated by signal from the flagship and performed competitively between ships in each squadron. In the signal book there is a general drill table, where suitable tasks are entered against the flags which initiate them. The tasks, which demanded prodigious feats of seamanship from large bodies of men, were carried out at full speed and full pressure, with points awarded to each ship according to performance. They included: 'Sway all boats pull round the fleet'; 'Take next ship in the line in tow'; 'Out collision mat, port or starboard side'; 'Drop second anchor'; 'Send fire party to flagship'; and 'Send demolition party to flagship'.

There were many others but the one I liked best was 'Weigh anchor by hand'. At that, we boys had to dash down to the capstan engine flat below the foc'sle and fist the capstan bars from their racks. We would then rush these wooden bars, each about 15 feet long and steel shod, up onto the foc'sle, and ship them into the slots in the head of the centre-lying capstan. We held the outer ends up while the shipwrights 'passed the swifter', a special rope supplied to secure the outer ends of the bars to each other, thus forming the rim of the wheel, the bars serving as spokes. While this was being done, the chief stoker disconnected the capstan from its machinery. The marine band, mustered in the foc'sle abaft the capstan, played lively music while as many men and boys as possible clapped on to the bars and swifter, heaving around the capstan until the cable and the five-ton anchor were aboard.

The general drill signal table is designed to cater for all tastes. For example: 'Secure captain in straitjacket and send him to flagship'; 'Chaplains paddle round their ships in Carly rafts'; 'Land all heads of departments, next seniors take over'; 'Chief cook to report on board flagship with fried eggs'; 'Out kedge anchor, two cables on port or starboard bow'.

We trained and worked hard, but some tasks required more resolve than others. Coaling ship was, of course, hard and dirty work – but it was the clean-up afterwards that was especially daunting. The mess tub, a hogshead barrel cut down to about 15 inches, was filled with warm, fresh water, as were all the other mess tubs in the ship, and placed on the upper deck. Fresh water was at a premium, especially as our ship's company comprised 1,200 men. All hands were very dirty after emptying two colliers into our bunkers. The first man to wash himself was the leading seaman in charge of the mess, then the senior AB and so on down the list of 18 or 20 men; the junior ordinary seamen were last to use what was left of the tub of water. What dirt we couldn't get off using this goo, we did our best to remove under the saltwater three-inch hose, with the aid of saltwater soap. Needless to say, we didn't stay long, as this water was pumped straight out of the sea and was especially cold in Scapa Flow and at the fleet anchorages at Invergordon on the Firth of Cromarty and Rosyth on the Firth of Forth. For about a week after coaling ship, we looked like the modern miss with her black eye shadow.

As a relaxation from the monotony of training and waiting for the German Fleet to come out, the men were sometimes given a few hours ashore on the Island of Flotta, where they could present their two coupons at the canteen and receive two pints of beer. We boys were occasionally given a couple of hours' leave on a Sunday afternoon on Mainland, the largest island in Orkney. We would go to the crofters' houses and buy fried eggs and oatcakes baked on a griddle for a few pence, and much appreciated they were.

The German High Seas Fleet made a sortie from their base at

Wilhelmshaven in the Jade estuary, near Bremerhaven, on 22 April 1918, to intercept a large homeward-bound convoy from Norway, escorted by the Second Battlecruiser Squadron and Seventh Light Cruiser Squadron. The Admiralty and Beatty didn't know that the German Battle Fleet was moving further afield than it had dared to do for the past four years, until it was far enough north to be in a position west of Stavanger. Fortunately for the convoy, the German intelligence was 24 hours in error. It had already crossed the North Sea and entered the Firth of Forth, when Admiral Reinhard Scheer ordered Rear Admiral Franz von Hipper's battlecruisers to search for it. The *Moltke* chanced to lose a propeller, which flooded an engine room and brought her to a standstill. This disabling accident obliged Scheer and von Hipper to break wireless silence, which was enough for the Admiralty to order Beatty to sea from Rosyth with 31 battleships, 4 battlecruisers, 26 cruisers and light cruisers and 85 destroyers, early in the afternoon of the next day.

However, the High Seas Fleet was already retiring to the south, with the *Moltke* in tow of the *Oldenburg*. By nightfall, it had crossed ahead of the Grand Fleet's line of advance, reaching the Jade estuary the next morning without incident, excepting the near loss of the *Moltke* to a torpedo fired by the British submarine *E42*, which had been patrolling near the northern edge of the minefields guarding the Heligoland Bight. This was the last occasion the German Fleet ventured to sea before the end of the war.

Scheer was given complete control of the German navy in August 1918 and conceived a plan for the High Seas Fleet, covered by all Germany's submarines, to make a final desperate effort by offering battle to the Grand Fleet. But when the German ships were ordered to sea, the majority of their ships' companies mutinied. Hundreds of men were marched ashore, preferring arrest rather than being sacrificed in a hopeless battle, and von Hipper had to cancel orders for the sortie. The German U-boats had already sailed on 25 October and, three days later, *U-78* was torpedoed and sunk by the British submarine *G2*.

Another German submarine that failed to return was *UB-116*, which, on leaving Germany was ordered to enter Scapa Flow and attack the British Battle Fleet during the night of 28 October, in order to weaken the enemy as much as possible before the decisive battle. The German U-boat commander, Lieutenant Emsmann, was advised to enter the Flow by Hoxa Sound because U-boats passing through the Pentland Firth had reported this to be in regular use by British vessels and therefore, unlike the other entrances, it would not be blocked by mines, nets or sunken ships. This assumed that the British had abandoned their once common method of defending a harbour entrance with moored mines. These mines could be electrically fired from the shore, but were only of use against an identified enemy vessel that was seen to cross them. British scientists had overcome this deficiency and by 1918 the mines moored across Hoxa Sound had been augmented by magnetic loops of cable on the seabed connected to galvanometers in an observation station ashore. These were sensitive enough to record the induced electric current caused by a vessel crossing over them.

When, at about 2230 on 28 October, our hydrophones picked up the sound of approaching engines and no friendly ship was expected, a possible U-boat was reported. A few minutes later, Emsmann continued his approach and surfaced momentarily to check his position when he was heading straight for the entrance. A few seconds later, the hull of *UB-116* moved the galvanometers on Flotta Island and the moored mines across Hoxa Sound were fired. When the sound of their detonation had died away, there was nothing to be heard. Daylight revealed patches of oil and a German naval watch coat. Finally, divers identified the crushed remains of *UB 116*. The other 23 U-boats returned to Germany without firing their torpedoes at the Grand Fleet.

The German C-in-C ordered his ships, assembled in the Jade estuary, to raise steam on 29 October 1918. Several of their crews, demoralised by the same seeds of unrest that had affected them in 1917, refused to obey orders. They had no intention of falling in battle when the end of the war was near. Attempts to quell the mutinies failed and soon all the German warships were flying the red flag of rebellion. The British Fleet was not required to put to sea but there is no doubt that, had it been necessary, it would have gained an annihilating victory. At that time, the Grand Fleet was the greatest naval force the world had ever known – we had 43 battleships and battlecruisers to Germany's 24. Our ships' magazines were protected from cordite flash, our ships' shell rooms were filled with effective, armour-piercing shells, and our ships' companies, raring to go, were led by admirals and captains who would seize every opportunity the enemy offered.

In 1918, German sailors in the High Seas Fleet were swept up in the Kiel Mutiny, a staging post on the road to revolution. It was sparked by secret plans drawn up by German naval top brass to mount one final and desperate attack on the British at the end of October 1918. The naval hierarchy was frustrated by its lack of results in the First World War, a conflict conspicuous for its lack of major sea battles. The most significant confrontation, at the Battle of Jutland in 1916, resulted in both sides claiming victory. The High Seas Fleet appeared to shy away from clashes with its enemy but was in fact acting on the orders of Germany's Kaiser Wilhelm II, who was keen to preserve it.

This time the German admirals sought to keep their bold plans away from political leaders. Unfortunately for them, the sailors in the key ports of Kiel and Wilmershaven got wind of what was happening and furiously refused to cooperate. With the end of the war beckoning, it was their belief that the plans were folly and would end in an entirely avoidable catastrophe. Sailors either slipped away from their ships, refused to accept orders, or took 'leave'. Ultimately, all plans for action were abandoned.

However, by now all the sailors of the German navy, alongside industrial workers in the docks, were sucked into activities that ranged from disobedience to rebellion. As the unrest spread like wildfire among major cities, it became clear the government's position was untenable and it was compelled to sue for peace.

There had been buzzes – or rumours – going around our ships for some time that the Germans would ask for an armistice and, on 11 November, when the Grand Fleet was in the Firth of Forth, we received a signal that, at 11 a.m., it had been granted. There was much rejoicing and Admiral Beatty ordered the famous signal, 'Splice the mainbrace', which meant an extra tot of rum was to be served out. This only happens to mark occasions such as victories at sea or major feats of endurance, such as rescues from shipwreck.

This tradition originated in sailing ships, when the greatest feat of seamanship the men were called upon to perform was to 'splice the mainbrace' on the main yard – when this was successfully carried out, they were rewarded with an extra tot of rum.

On 15 November, the German cruiser *Königsberg*, carrying Admiral Meurer, arrived at Inchkeith in the Firth of Forth, as directed by the British Admiralty, to receive the terms of armistice from Admiral Beatty. The German admiral presented his credentials to Beatty on board HMS *Queen Elizabeth*. He said: 'I must inform the Herr Admiral that plenipotentiaries of the Sailors and Workers Soviet of the North Sea Command have made the voyage in the *Königsberg* and have been authorised by the Provisional Government to attend all conferences.'

Beatty replied bluntly, in English, 'Tell them to go to hell!'

This pleased the German, who then entered the conference and was informed that the High Seas Fleet was to be handed over to Britain, plus all their submarine fleet.

Before dawn on 21 November 1918, the Grand Fleet got under way in the Firth of Forth and proceeded to sea to meet and take the surrender of the German High Seas Fleet. The first ships out were the destroyer flotillas: 150 'greyhounds of the sea', followed by the light cruisers, then the battlecruisers, and finally the battleships. At daybreak, the fleet of five squadrons of battleships, two squadrons of battlecruisers and seven squadrons of cruisers headed by a hundred and fifty destroyers, were formed into two columns six miles apart, each about fifteen miles long, steaming eastwards at twelve knots. At sunrise, the buglers sounded 'action stations'. The Germans had been ordered to sail without ammunition and with reduced crews, but we could not be sure they would not attempt some last-minute treachery.

The *Queen Elizabeth*, Beatty's flagship, led one column, while the *Revenge*, Madden's flagship, led the other. There was no sign of fight left in the Germans as they came out of the mist at about 10 a.m. in the forenoon. The Germans were led by HMS *Cardiff*, a light cruiser, and comprised five battlecruisers: *Seydlitz*, *Moltke*, *Hindenburg*, *Derfflinger* and *Von der Tann*. Then came *Friedrich der Grosse*, wearing the flag of Rear Admiral von Reuter, *Grosser Kurfürst*, *Prinzregent*

Luitpold, Markgraf, Bayern, Kaiserin, Kronprinz, Kaiser and *König Albert*, all battleships, followed by seven light cruisers and 49 destroyers. They were led between the two British columns until the *Queen Elizabeth* and *Revenge* were abeam of the German flagship. At this point, the two columns wheeled outwards, onto the course to the west being steered by the Germans. The *Queen Elizabeth*'s column, now to starboard, comprised nineteen battleships, five battlecruisers and four squadrons of cruisers. The port column, led by the *Revenge*, had fourteen battleships, battlecruisers, an aircraft carrier and three squadrons of cruisers. These columns were followed by our 150 destroyers. When I looked astern from the *Revenge*, there were warships as far as the eye could see, and much further. What an inspiring sight! Overhead there were a couple of British airships to add to the spectacle.

The German fleet was taken to Aberlady Bay, where they anchored. Among the ships in the Grand Fleet were the battleships *Canada* and *Malaya*, battlecruisers *Australia* and *New Zealand*, light cruisers *Sydney* and *Brisbane*, and the five US battleships in the Sixth Battle Squadron with the flagship USS *New York*. The French navy was represented by a cruiser and two destroyers. Once the German ships were anchored, the tension was relaxed, and the ships' companies of each Allied ship, as they passed the *Queen Elizabeth*, cheered our victorious C-in-C. Just before sunset, Beatty made the signal, 'The German flag will be hauled down at sunset today and will not be hoisted again without permission.'

So ended the most momentous day in the annals of naval warfare – a fleet of ships surrendered without a shot being fired.

Picked units of men inspected the German fleet the following day, to make sure they had complied with the orders for armistice: all guns to be immobilised; all magazines and shell rooms to be empty; and no torpedo warheads or demolition charges to be present. While this inspection was carried out, the German crews were mustered on deck. Every compartment was searched to make sure there were no reserves of shell and cordite, bombs, or drums of poison gas for a final, desperate venture. Nothing was found that violated the terms of the armistice.

The next day, Admiral Beatty came aboard the *Revenge* and addressed our ship's company, together with representatives from other ships in our squadron. He told us that we were to be given the privilege of escorting the German fleet to Scapa Flow, and there to look after them until their fate was decided. One of my messmates took down this speech in shorthand and later made copies, one of which I obtained. It was a memorable speech and very prophetic, as later events showed.

A British wireless service report, dated 3 December 1918, reveals the contents of a speech given by Admiral Beatty to the crew of the Lion *before they departed for Scapa Flow to escort the surrendering German navy into British waters. Like many seamen of the day, Beatty was unhappy that he had not been able to triumph against his German counterparts in open seas. Although it may not exactly replicate the speech heard by Claude and his shipmates on* Revenge, *the sentiments would have been similar:*

> *We expected them to have the courage that we look for from those whose work lies upon the great waters, and I am sure that the sides of this gallant old ship, which have been well hammered in the past, must have ached as I ached and as you ached to give them another taste of what we had intended for them.*
>
> *His humiliating end is a proper end for an enemy who has proved himself so lacking in chivalry. At sea his strategy, his tactics and his behaviour have been beneath contempt and worthy of a nation which has waged war in the manner in which the enemy has waged war.*
>
> *We know that the British sailor has a large heart and a short memory. Try to harden the heart and lengthen the memory and remember that the enemy which you are looking after is a despicable beast, neither more nor less.*
>
> *He is not worthy [of] the sacrifice of the life of one bluejacket in the Grand Fleet and that is the one bright spot in the fact that he did not come out.*

CHAPTER FOUR

Scapa Flow

THERE WAS MUCH UNREST AMONG THE GERMAN CREWS, with mutinous sailors and bitter officers angry at their treatment by both the Germans and the British. At the end of January 1919, Rear Admiral von Reuter, who had returned to Germany after he had completed his internment, came back to Scapa Flow and took over command from Captain Oldekop, his chief of staff. His prison-bound men and his fleet of 74 ships were dirty and dilapidated. They were certainly not enjoying our northern winter (but then, neither were we). A drifter took von Reuter to the *Friedrich der Grosse* and the cabin he had left 43 days before.

'How have things gone?' he asked of the officers who welcomed him.

'We have endured it as best we could,' replied Captain Oldekop. 'Three hours of daylight, gales from the North Pole, constant English vigilance. The bleakest exile in the world for the German temperament.'

'The crews?'

'Toothache, grippe, dirt and rebellion. Their quarters are filthy. They refuse all authority.'

It was a tale of inflamed tempers, drinking bouts, invasions of the officers' quarters, red guards, proletarian wrangling and mob brutality. If the men had possessed firearms, they would have been shooting at each other and us after the first fortnight. *Friedrich der Grosse* had dismissed her captain and elevated a deck officer to command.

71

After 12 hours of rioting, they reinstated the captain. Things got so bad aboard the German ships that von Reuter requested an audience with our admiral and was told that, if he wished, the mutineers could be imprisoned on board a British battleship. He was pleased with this reply but could not bring himself to hand over his sailors to British imprisonment. He said he would send all the dissidents back to Germany at the first opportunity. Our admiral agreed to this arrangement and, when the next supply ship arrived, the transfer of 2,000 rebellious men from the German ships onto it was conducted under the watchful eye of one of our destroyers, cleared for action.

This left only a handful of trusted men and officers aboard the German ships, which delighted von Reuter, who had no intention of allowing Britain to use any German ship. To this end, he issued a secret order that when the flagship made a certain signal and hoisted the German ensign, all his ships were to be scuttled by opening the seacocks, portholes, hatches and submerged torpedo tubes.

The time came for him to put his plan into action on 21 June 1919, a Saturday. Early that week, the weather had appeared to be clearing up and, on Wednesday, 18 June, we were prepared to do long-range torpedo running. But Thursday and Friday turned bad, as it so often does in that windswept, desolate place. Saturday dawned a beautiful morning, so the Battle Squadron, with our destroyer flotilla, proceeded to sea to carry out the exercise. This and full-calibre 15-inch firing were the only exercises we could not do in the Flow.

Submerged torpedo tubes were carried for'ard in the *Revenge*-class battleships. My action station was in the starboard submerged torpedo flat. The port torpedo had been fired. The ship was turning under maximum helm to bring the starboard tube to bear and we were expecting to fire at any second, when the captain's 'cease fire' gong sounded. The gong is only used in emergencies, so I thought that one of our own, or a merchant ship, must be in the line of fire. But in the next few seconds I could tell from the vibrations that our engines had increased to full speed. We received the order to 'secure', which meant that the water from the flooded torpedo tube had to be drained into the flat, pumped out and the deck swabbed dry, the torpedo removed from the tube, air-vessel pressure blown down, fuel and water bottles drained, pressure from firing reservoir blown down, and so on. This is most disheartening to the tube's crew after being in the ready position and on the brink of firing. All sorts of rumours were passing as to why we had to 'secure' and had increased to full speed.

When we had secured the submerged torpedo flat, we were ordered on deck and the boarding parties were mustered. These consisted of marines and seamen other than the 15-inch guns crews who had been training for months to board the German ships and subdue their ships' companies, should it have been necessary. Our rifles, bayonets, ammunition, webbing gear and water bottles were stowed in the 6-inch battery, all ready to slip on in case of necessity.

We arrived back at Scapa Flow at about 2 p.m. to a most amazing sight. Most of the German capital ships had already sunk and, in all directions, others were sinking. The Flow was filled with German ships all flying a white flag and carrying the internment crews. All our boats were lowered and we were rushed aboard any of the German ships still afloat in an attempt to close portholes, watertight doors and such, but this proved useless, as they were too far gone. Nine Germans had been shot and killed as the British tried to stop them scuttling the ships. Our demolition crews managed to blow up the cables of the *Hindenburg* and she finally settled on the bottom on an even keel, with her upper turrets awash at high tide. It was a disturbing sight; a whole fleet had almost disappeared.

When our lads saw what had happened, an involuntary cheer went up and they said: 'Thank God, now we'll be able to go south and receive our war service leave.'

The German boats were towed alongside our battleships by our picket boats and the Germans were herded into the 6-inch batteries with armed sentries in charge. Von Reuter was brought on board *Revenge*, where Vice Admiral Sir Sydney Fremantle, who had taken over from Admiral Sir Charles Madden after the armistice, informed him he was a prisoner of war. Fremantle had stern words for the German:

By your conduct you have added one more to the breaches of faith and honour of which Germany has been guilty in this war. Begun with a breach of military honour in the invasion of Belgium, it bids fair to terminate with a breach of naval honour. You have proved to the few who doubted it that the word of the New Germany is no more to be trusted than that of the old. What opinion your country will form of your action I do not know. I can only express what I believe to be the opinion of the British navy, and indeed of all seamen except those of your Nation. I now transfer you to the custody of the British military authorities as prisoners of war guilty of a flagrant violation of Armistice.

All the next day, our lads worked like Trojans to raise any of the German ships they could. Our divers went down and closed portholes and watertight doors, while working parties manned pumps. Our ship's company managed to raise the light cruiser *Emden*, which von Reuter had made his flagship when he left the turbulent *Friedrich der Grosse* at the end of March. A day after the scuttling, the First Battle Squadron proceeded to Invergordon, where we turned over our several hundred German prisoners to one of our Scottish Regiments, the Gordon Highlanders, where they were kept until repatriated at the end of January 1920. At Invergordon, all senior German officers were taken aboard the *Revenge*. While Admiral Fremantle again told them they were a disgrace to their service and that they had broken faith, von Reuter stood with his head bowed but on being accused of breaching naval honour, he broke his silence to say, 'I am convinced that any English naval officer, placed as I was, would have acted in the same way.' His disarming response got him off the hook and no charges were brought against him.

Concerning the weather uncertainty in this part of the world, I recall that on one Sunday in Scapa Flow that started off as a fine day with a good sailing breeze, the captains of our battleships decided to hold a sailing race against each other in their galleys. Early in the afternoon, many of the ship's company were walking up and down the foc'sle, yarning and smoking, when McCarthy, a leading seaman of the quarterdeck division, happened to glance across towards Kirkwall only to see all the galleys suddenly capsized by a terrific squall. He said to the two able seamen with whom he was walking: 'Hop down into the admiral's barge with me.' Just a few minutes before, the barge had returned the admiral aboard and been secured to the lower boom. The coxswain and crew had come inboard but the stoker was still in the engine room.

As soon as they were aboard, McCarthy ordered cast off and full speed to rescue the captains and crews of the capsized galleys. Picket boats, 15-knot steamboats, were sent from other ships, but our admiral's barge was first on the scene, since she was faster than the picket boats and we were lying nearest to the scene of capsize.

Later, McCarthy was taken before the commander to explain why he had taken the barge without orders. In ordinary circumstances, this would have been regarded as a heinous offence. However, he had rescued most of the captains and their crews. When this was finally reported to the Admiralty, they ordered that McCarthy be promoted to petty officer forthwith. He was therefore what is known as 'Admiralty Promoted' and could not be dis-rated without Admiralty sanction. This form of promotion is only carried out in exceptional circumstances. Normally, a leading seaman has to pass examinations in education, all branches of seamanship and signals before his name is placed on the roster for petty officer.

CHAPTER FIVE

The Guns Fall Silent

IN JULY 1919, WE WERE AT SOUTHEND FOR THE PEACE assembly of the fleet. We were put through our paces with rifle drill and marching, then the gunnery officer selected about 100 men who were to take part in the Victory Parade in London. I was lucky enough to be chosen. We went in special trains up to 'The Smoke' where we lived in tents in Kensington Gardens for one week and had a marvellous time. We were given leave every day and were entertained right royally.

We *Revenge* lads were invited to lunch as guests of the Gold and Silversmiths in their hall. All the utensils were of gold and silver, and a waiter was stationed behind each two sailors to supply their every wish. After the meal, we were entertained by some of the best artistes of the day. During the week of the peace celebrations, the ships in the fleet were illuminated at night by having their waterline, decks, masts, yards, forestays, backstays and triatic stays outlined by thousands of electric light globes; the admirals' flags were also outlined to show the flagships. Hundreds of thousands of people flocked to Southend to see this magnificent sight.

The guns of the First World War fell silent on 11 November 1918. The conflict's death toll made horrific reading, 1,700,000 Russians having perished alongside 1,357,800 Frenchmen, 1,774,000 Germans, and 910,000 Britons. Although it is hard to record the numbers with pin-sharp accuracy, there were about 37.5 million wounded. Now the nightmare had come to an end.

There were celebrations across the country. The Daily Mirror *reported that: 'Bells burst forth into joyful chimes . . . bands paraded the streets followed by cheering crowds of soldiers and civilians and London generally gave itself up wholeheartedly to rejoicing.' In Plymouth, soldiers, sailors and wounded servicemen celebrated together in the streets. According to the* Western Morning News, *there was a commendable measure of restraint:*

> *This was perhaps in large measure owing to the restrictions on the opening of public houses and the sale of liquor, restrictions which in Plymouth were wisely and patriotically extended by the licensed victuallers themselves, many of whom at the mayor's request closed at the early hour of 7.30 p.m.*
>
> *Hence, while there was plenty of noise and jubilation there was very little to which reasonable objection could be taken. To most people, indeed, the declaration that hostilities had ceased came with a sense of relief too deep for light manifestations of joy and for too many homes the occasion was saddened by the thought of dear ones through whose sacrifice the glorious victory of right over wrong, of liberty and justice over slavery and tyranny, had been brought about. Never, surely, were the thanksgiving services so widely held more fervent and sincere. On the whole, the entire nation and not least the people of the West Country have received the news in the manner which does them credit from the personal and patriotic point of view.*

But many felt that wholehearted celebrations would be best left until the end of the peace negotiations. The Treaty of Versailles was finally signed on 28 June 1919 and it gave the green light for a Peace Day, which was held on 19 July.

As one of the lucky ones picked to attend the formal gathering in London which was the focal point of the Peace Day activities, Claude marched among 15,000 servicemen led by eminent commanders. The route was lined with countless thousands of people, many of whom made extraordinary efforts to attend.

He marched past the Cenotaph, at the time made from wood and plaster but already dedicated to 'The Glorious Dead'. At its base there were numerous floral tributes made from all kinds of flowers, as the poppy had not yet become the official armistice bloom. It wasn't until later in 1919, on the first Armistice Day, that the two-minute silence was introduced. This suggestion by Australian journalist Edward George Honey, in a letter published in the London Evening News, *was taken up by King George V. By 1920, the Cenotaph was replaced with a version made from Portland Stone, in time for the burial of the Unknown Soldier at Westminster Abbey, a ceremony intended to honour all the dead of the Great War. Poppies came later still, an idea inspired by war poetry and initially popularised in the USA.*

In July 1919, London was filled with concerts and shows during the afternoon, while in the evening a lavish firework display in Hyde Park triggered the lighting of bonfires nationwide.

A four-day event was on the cards until organisers realised there was considerable public feeling against what some perceived as frivolous spending. The Manchester Evening News *commented: 'Perhaps, after the Manchester and Salford Corporation have celebrated this "peace" and incidentally will have wasted the thousands of pounds which it will cost, they will devote their spare time to alleviating the "bitterness" and "misery" which exist in the body and mind of the unemployed ex-soldier.'*

In Norwich, the Ex-Servicemen's Federation chose to boycott celebrations altogether, for fear that it would encourage militarism. In Luton, where the town council refused permission for ex-servicemen to hold their own memorial service, a riot began and the town hall was burnt down. Police and soldiers arrived to find rioters having a sing-song around a stolen piano.

The revelry – or rioting – was taking place between waves of 'Spanish flu', a pandemic which ultimately claimed an estimated 50 million victims, as compared with the First World War death toll of about 16 million. This devastating outbreak of influenza was named Spanish flu because its effects were first broadcast in neutral Spain, at a time when censorship prevented publicity about it among Allied countries.

The first wave of the illness, which began in America, came early in 1918. A second, causing serious loss of life, occurred between September and November 1918. Troop movements and transport improvements hastened the progress of the disease around the globe. The pandemic finally subsided in mid-1920.

Rather than targeting the old or frail, Spanish flu was capable of swiftly killing young, previously healthy men and women. Symptoms including bleeding from the nose, ears or lungs, and a blue pallor, were followed by blood loss or pneumonia. Within 24 hours of showing symptoms, about one in five victims died. It was sometimes mistaken for dengue fever, typhoid or cholera, other diseases prevalent in that era.

At the end of July, we went to Devonport, then, in mid-August, to Invergordon. That summer, the navy visited the towns and ports it had defended. In September, the *Revenge* went from Devonport to Portland, Folkestone, Ramsgate, Yarmouth and Scarborough. In each port, the ship was open to visitors every day and thousands came aboard. In October, we went back to Invergordon, Scapa Flow and Rosyth to recover from the festivities, then to Devonport in December. In mid-January, we joined the Atlantic fleet off Plymouth for the spring cruise, planned to include Arosa Bay in northern Spain, Pontevedra, Palma, Algiers and Gibraltar and to finish two months on at Berehaven, one of the Treaty Ports in Ireland. But for the First Battle Squadron, the cruise extended to more than a year and they were to see Trebizond (Trabzon), Batum, Sinop, Samsun, Sebastopol, Constantinople, fire and famine and slaughter before they returned to their home ports again.

In 1919, there was much turmoil in the Middle East. From the Aegean Sea to Tartary, peoples and governments were in a state of war and revolution, principally those of Turkey and the USSR. Many men in the navy saw more death and desolation in 1919 and 1920 than they had seen in four years of major war. United States ships patrolled in the Mediterranean into 1920, and Britain and France kept powerful squadrons active in Near East waters until 1923, when peace was at last made with the new Turkey under Mustapha Kemal Atatürk, who led the Turkish Nationalists finally to power.

The fall of the once-potent Ottoman Empire had a ripple effect around Europe and Asia. Slowly accrued, the empire at first centred on Anatolia, the heartland of the Turkish people, then the mostly Christian Balkans and finally, in the sixteenth century, Muslim and Arab provinces in Africa and Asia. Its capital was Constantinople, renowned as being a tolerant and educated society shaped by numerous international influences that flourished without aggressive dominance of one creed or culture. It proudly oversaw trade routes between Europe and Asia and became wealthy as a result.

The Ottoman Empire was ruled by a caliphate, which inspired unquestioning loyalty from its Muslim populations but which did not unduly trouble those from an entirely different religious or ethnic background. The sultan, or caliph, was a religious figurehead who claimed legitimacy from the prophet Muhammad. At its zenith the Ottoman Empire controlled all the religiously significant sites of Islam.

Still, there was no compulsion on Ottoman citizens to convert to Islam, not least because Christians and other religious denominations paid taxes that didn't apply to Muslims. Most of its subjects were reconciled to the empire at some level.

But despite the relative harmony of its sprawling territories, Ottoman power began to stagnate, then decline, as early as the sixteenth century. By the late nineteenth century, it was figuratively on its knees, crippled by debt and vulnerable to other imperial powers hoping to increase their own empires. The ideologies which once sat in relative harmony under the Ottoman umbrella were now competing, and the empire's borders were no longer strong enough to contain them.

During the early years of the twentieth century the caliphate had another troubling issue with which to contend. A new political movement was gaining ground. Nicknamed the 'Young Turks' and led by Enver Pasha, it was fuelled by nationalism, which did not sit comfortably alongside Islam. By 1908, it was pressing for a part in government.

As the Ottoman authorities wrestled with domestic problems, there were skirmishes at distant points of the empire as rival powers swooped in to steal regions.

Having joined the Germans in the First World War, the fate of the Ottoman Empire was sealed with the defeat of the Axis powers. In 1920, the Treaty of Sèvres drawn up by the Allies had the region divided into numerous states. Inevitably, there was further conflict as this was announced and enforced, with Turkish nationalists seeking to keep the integrity of at least one part of its homeland. One universal feature of the region at the time was unfettered violence set against a fluid political landscape that lacked clarity. It was to this hot spot that the Royal Navy was dispatched with the aim of imposing security.

During this time, sailors and soldiers of the Allies struggled with horrors from the Black Sea to the Persian Gulf. They rescued refugees fleeing from massacres. They warred with pirates and brigands. They policed ammunition dumps left in the wake of war, which had become a temptation to every local politician and freebooter. They settled quarrels between local sheikhs, or, if they failed, subsequently gathered the remains. They watched Smyrna burn. They rescued stranded survivors of White Russian armies and Armenian villages. They blew up Caspian forts, fed babies and rescued Christian girls. The ships' crews saw miseries beyond belief and did more to mitigate them than all the outer world's philanthropies. The sailor's job was to struggle with man's inhumanity to man and to provide at least some element of order and stability in the chaos of those times and places.

Navies have other uses than battle. On the voyage of the *Revenge* down to Arosa Bay, we had the unique experience of seeing father and son, both full admirals, on the bridge of a battleship: our admiral, Sir Sydney Fremantle, took his father, also an admiral (retired), as his guest for the trip. Sir Sydney Fremantle was a grand-nephew of Admiral Sir Charles Howe Fremantle, after whom the port city in Western Australia is named, and the fourth successive admiral in that family, whose service lasted from 1777 to 1928.

At Arosa Bay, the First Battle Squadron was exercising or sending its officers and men ashore to visit Villagarcia or Santiago. We were due to spend most of February based on Gibraltar, but on the first of that month, we were suddenly ordered to Malta. On the way we exercised night action. We arrived on 4 February and the ship's companies were given a steady course of small-arms practice and field exercises ashore. The air was filled with buzzes as to our destination, when, on the 17th, the squadron was ordered to Constantinople. On the 20th we saw Gallipoli, where my two brothers had served in the AIF. They were at the landing on 25 April 1915 and served right through the campaign until the evacuation at the end of the year. We saw wrecks along the beaches and the causeway that was built out to the *River Clyde*. We could also see graveyards among the hills.

The next day we saw Constantinople, with its vast mosque of Hagia Sophia and all its minarets. *Revenge* anchored astern of Admiral de Robeck's flagship *Ajax* off the sultan's winter palace. Our first days in Constantinople were occupied with landing parties of Seamen Battalions and Royal Marines parading through the streets. The Turkish Nationalists under Mustapha Kemal were carrying out appalling massacres of Armenians in Anatolia and ships were sent up the coast to do what they could for the thousands fleeing from the hills.

The First Battle Squadron exercised in the Sea of Marmara and the *Emperor of India* was ordered to Novorossiysk, where Budyonny's cavalry were riding down the last resistance of isolated Cossacks. Turkish guards in and around Constantinople were seizing or refusing to give up ammunition dumps and the First Battle Squadron again anchored off the Golden Horn. British and Allied ships anchored in the Bosphorus, cleared for action.

In the middle of March, British and Allied troops marched in to take over the city. Four thousand bluejackets and marines were landed from the British ships. I was in the *Revenge*'s Seaman Battalion and we marched through the main streets with fixed bayonets. Some of our seamen occupied the War Office, Post Office and all public buildings, while others were put into trenches around the perimeter of the city. *Revenge* troops were alongside a Highland regiment on one side and a Punjabi regiment on the other. We fraternised with them and I remember sitting around in a circle with the Sikhs and them passing around their hubble-bubble pipe, or hookah.

Around the Sea of Marmara, the Turkish Nationalists blew up railways and bridges and burnt villages, but in Constantinople, only two British soldiers and nine Turks were killed. Our Gurkha troops acted as traffic police in the city and we were impressed by the way they enforced their orders on the populace with their 'single sticks'. The city was dirty, but some of the buildings were magnificent. The sultan was deposed and our sailors escorted his harem up the Bosphorus to his summer palace. He had many scores of wives.

Our squadron then went up the Gulf of Ismid, an arm of the Sea of Marmara. Here we saw the ex-German warship *Goeben*, whose escape to Constantinople at the commencement of the war was not prevented by the British Mediterranean Fleet and was responsible for Turkey entering the war against Britain. The landing parties had much exercise ashore during this time, supporting General Ironside's patrols if Nationalists or brigands got out of hand.

Soon after this, we were ordered into the Black Sea, where we struck the tail end of a gale. The next morning, the gale had blown itself out and we found the ship aloft festooned with birds of all kinds, which had taken refuge in our rigging. They had been exhausted trying to fight the winds, and found our ships suitable resting places. There was even an eagle on our foretop gallant yard, while alongside it were smaller birds that would normally have been scared of it, but at this time their only thought was rest. I suppose the reason for the great number and variety of birds was the fact that the Black Sea is an inland sea of vast extent, 300 by 600 miles, so its waters can become very turbulent in a gale.

We went to Batum, which was the oil pipeline outlet from the Baku oilfield. The place was in turmoil, with Georgia and Armenia struggling for the town, so marines and seamen landing parties were put ashore. We embarked refugees fleeing from the terror ashore and a few days later we left for Trebizond, where we blew up the fortress guns and ammunition dumps. Before the demolition, all the inhabitants were ordered indoors by the landing parties. As an acting seaman torpedoman, I was in the demolition party. From there we went to Kerassunde, then to Samsun and back to Constantinople.

After some months of pretty arduous service trying to quell the Turkish Nationalists in the Sea of Marmara, the Bosphorus and the Black Sea, the First Battle Squadron was ordered to Malta for stores and ammunition. While there, we were granted 72 hours' general leave, going ashore one watch at a time. I was in the starboard watch, which was the first to proceed ashore. After a look around Valetta, the main city in the vicinity of Grand Harbour, a couple of hundred men, mainly from the *Revenge*, decided to travel on the train from Valetta to Città Vecchia to view the catacombs, the underground dwellings where the inhabitants used to live many hundreds of years ago when they were invaded by Moors, Phoenicians, Greeks, Romans and others.

After an escorted tour, we returned to the station to find we would have to wait over an hour for the train's departure for Valetta. We hung around for a while, then a smart laddie sang out: 'What are we waiting for? Who can drive an engine and who can fire one?'

A couple of stokers from our ship said, 'We can!'

'Then let's go!'

So we all hopped aboard and the stokers started her up. The stationmaster was going berserk at seeing his train pinched but away we went along the single-rail track. A few miles down the line our engine crew managed to stop her on the outskirts of Valetta and we all jumped out and disappeared in all directions. As can be imagined, it was not long before reports of this escapade reached our admiral. Sir Sydney Fremantle ordered special patrols ashore to round up all *Revenge* libertymen and order them back aboard. At noon, the captain had these men paraded on the quarterdeck. He announced that if he found the culprits, he would make it really hot for them. Next morning, the libertymen were again paraded on the quarterdeck and the stationmaster from Città Vecchia walked up and down along our ranks trying to identify the two stokers, but he failed to do so. Thus our 72 hours of general leave sadly amounted to only a few and we had to spend the rest of the day doing extra work aboard.

Chapter Six

Cock and Bruce Stories

AFTER A SHORT STAY IN MALTA, WE RETURNED TO Devonport to give 28 days' foreign service leave to each watch. The ship was to be 'paid off' prior to going into dockyard hands for a refit. This meant that all hands left the ship and went into their depot ship; on completion of refit, the ship would re-commission with a complete new ship's company, except for a few who may have volunteered to re-commission her. I was drafted to HMS *Defiance*, the Torpedo School at Devonport, to carry out the confirmation course for Seaman Torpedoman. I had already been promoted 'acting ST' in the *Revenge*. The *Defiance* consisted of three old wooden battleships, which had been converted into lecture rooms, workshops and living quarters for the staff and men under training. These ships were moored head and stern at Saltash, which was on the Cornish part of Devonport harbour.

The opportunity for men like Claude to progress in the Royal Navy had never been greater. Those that managed their appointed tasks well could now expect to progress to officer class, an unthinkable notion just a few short years before. When unemployment was high in civvy street, it made any choice about staying in the navy an easy one to make. Frank C. Bowen's The King's Navy, *which appeared in 1925, amply illustrates the point:*

> *All would-be recruits have to come up to a high standard of conduct, intelligence and physical fitness, as is clearly shown by the figures for a recent year in which only 7,000 were accepted from 42,000 candidates.*

Apart from the definitely skilled ratings, the rank and file of seamen, Royal Marines and stokers are in their everyday duties constantly handling mechanisms of the greatest complexity and delicacy, and handling them with skill and assurance.

Knowing the qualities of their men, it was not surprising that naval officers were disgusted with the tone of the report made by a committee of businessmen which in 1923 inquired into the pay of the fighting services. So far as the navy was concerned, the committee seemed almost to think that it was still manned by the sweeping of jails and the press-gang, or at any rate, that the bluejacket was on a par with the lowest unskilled labourer.

On completion of our course, my class was, as usual, drafted into the Devonport Naval Depot, HMS *Vivid*, which is a shore establishment adjacent to Devonport Naval Dockyard. This was my first time in there and the only men who wanted to stay there were those whose homes were in Devonport or Plymouth, the discipline being very strict. I had no fancy at all for a stay there. All I wanted was to get back into a ship, so I said to a mate of mine, Wyn Thomas: 'I'm getting out of this. Let's go to the drafting office, and see what we can do.'

We tapped on the shutter at the drafting office, which was opened by a burly chief petty officer.

'What do you want?' he asked.

'A ship, Chief,' we said.

'There's a cruiser commissioning in a couple of weeks for the West Indies Station,' he told us, 'and the *Valiant* is commissioning today.'

We liked the sound of *Valiant* and so we were told we'd be mustered on the parade ground at 1400 hours. That afternoon, we were marched to join HMS *Valiant* in the fitting-out basin of Devonport Dockyard. We were very relieved to get out of the stone frigate, as sailors called HMS *Vivid*, where they lived in great barracks built of cold stone. The dockyard was divided into two by a high ridge of rock and to provide access between North and South Yards, as they were called, there was a tunnel cut, carrying railway lines and a road. The *Valiant* was in the North Yard and in the South Yard basin was the aircraft carrier *Argus*, carrying out a refit.

'Cock' Alders, a Cockney able seamen, had an old shipmate on board the carrier whom he used to walk through the tunnel to meet. On one of these visits, he learnt that their ship's mascot, a Great Dane bitch, had a litter of pups that were available as mascots for other RN ships. Cock, being a dog lover, put in a request to see the commander and he asked if we could have a pup as our mascot. The commander said: 'Yes, providing you will look after the dog.' Cock readily agreed and off he went to the *Argus*, armed with a permission slip from our commander. As may be imagined, he had difficulty in taking the dog through the tunnel and so far away from its mother. However, he eventually got him on board the *Valiant* and down to his mess, where he gave him some food. Cock would not chain him up because he said that would be cruel, so warned the quartermasters to see that he did not go down the gangway onto the dockyard. We named the pup Bruce, a noble name for a noble dog, and he soon became a great favourite with the ship's company.

We had to spend a couple more weeks in dockyard hands to complete our refit and every chance Bruce got he would be down the gangway and off through the tunnel, back to his family. Cock Alders certainly knew his way through that tunnel before we finally got to sea, on our way to join the Mediterranean Fleet for the next two years. Once we were away from Devonport, Bruce quickly settled down to shipboard life. He loved to grab a rope's end with a sailor on the other end and have a tug-of-war. One of his favourite tricks was to watch a sailor carefully cheese down a rope on the upper deck after 'scrub decks' in the morning. As soon as the lad turned his back, Bruce would go to the centre of the coil, seize the end and run with it along the deck. The sailor would promptly grab the rope to prevent him running out the lot and a nice tug of war would ensue, with Bruce finally being sent below to Cock Alders' mess deck. This performance never failed to cause great merriment to those who witnessed it.

When we had a 'make and mend' session, Cock Alders would get his head down for an afternoon nap, with Bruce for his pillow. 'Hands to make and mend clothes' was usually piped on Saturday and Sunday afternoons, and sometimes on either Wednesday or

Thursday afternoons, if the captain was particularly pleased with the cleanliness he saw on the ship during his rounds. The routine of 'make and mend' goes back to the days before the advent of sewing machines in the navy, when sailors had to cut out and sew their own clothing. In fact, although sewing machines were in vogue in my time in the Service, one of the first things I was taught in the *Impregnable* training ship was to cut a haversack out of coarse duck material and sew it up. Then followed a white flannel shirt and, later, I had to cut out a jumper and a pair of bell-bottomed trousers from six yards of blue serge. We then sewed them up by hand to make a suit of clothes. Though I must admit, this was the only time I carried out this time-consuming task because, when I joined the *Revenge*, the petty officer who ran the sewing firm had a hand-operated sewing machine and would make a suit for five shillings. The customer would buy the six yards of serge from ship's stores in the slop room for ten shillings. In some ships, the captain gave the men who crewed his galley new clothes every six months so that they would always appear very smartly dressed when taking him to the flagship, or ashore, or to visit friendly captains of other ships. (I was a member of the captain of the *Valiant*'s galley crew for only a few months because I had to gain experience in my work as a torpedoman.)

In peace-time, it was the custom for captains, when in warm climates, to stop their ships night and morning and pipe 'hands to bathe', which would happen port or starboard side after ten minutes. The men then packed up their work and went down to their mess deck, where they undressed, put on their Vs, then returned to the upper deck to await the order to 'carry on'. In the meantime, the port or starboard sea boat, a 12-oared cutter, was lowered and pulled to approximately 100 yards on its own side of the ship. The lower boom on that side was swung out to enable those men who didn't wish to dive from the upper deck to enter the water by going out on the boom, climbing down the Jacob's ladders and hopping into the water from the lower rung. This privilege was allowed to encourage men to swim. It was permitted to swim anywhere between the ship and the sea boat until the 'retire' was sounded on the bugle. Then it was time to get out of the water, pronto, either by climbing the Jacob's ladder or swimming to the gangway, which had been lowered for the occasion. When all were out of the water, the lifeboat was hoisted, the boom stowed, the gangway raised and the men piped to breakfast or tea.

On these occasions, Bruce would go onto the upper deck and stand amidships until the bugler sounded the 'carry on'. Then he would rush to the side and leap over the guardrails into the water, the men on either side giving him a clear gangway as he did not respect personal space on such occasions. He loved to swim and the lads would catch hold of his tail and be towed along. It was quite a performance getting him out of the after gangway, where he would be pushed and lifted up onto the lower platform, which was about two feet above the waterline. We thought this quite a feat as our upper deck would have been about 15 to 18 feet above the waterline and he was nearly always first into the water. His love of the sea was also exhibited when going ashore in a boat or our attendant drifter. He would be poised on the gun'le looking eagerly to the landing stage, and then, when he judged it near enough, he would make his leap – and invariably fall in the drink! He would be hauled out by many willing hands, only to show his gratitude by shaking water all over them. I'm sure he thought this a great joke.

Bruce used to love to chew on a penny and Cock got hold of some George IV pennies, which were at least twice as thick as those from Queen Victoria's reign onwards and a little bigger in diameter. We would take his head between our legs and with one hand in the upper jaw and one in the lower, try and force his jaws apart but with no luck. The only way to make him drop the penny was to take one of his forefeet and bend it up alongside the upper part, increasing pressure till he whimpered with pain. Then the penny would drop out of his mouth. But if you let go of his foot before you picked up the penny, he would bend down his head and grab it before you. We would try and trick him by picking up a bight of 4-inch tarred hemp rope, unlaying it with our hands and slipping the penny into the lay of the rope while he was watching us. We would then throw the bight of rope on the deck. Bruce would promptly pick it up in his mouth and start chewing away at it until he could eventually prise the penny free. Then he would lie down to contentedly chew on it.

His favourite food was liver and, when it was on the menu, he would carry his mess dish around the various messes hoping that some of us would place a piece of liver in his dish. When he had done the rounds, he'd return to his mess and devour it with relish. At other times, he had what Cock provided for him.

At the commander's suggestion, the canteen committee voted to give Cock one pound a week for looking after Bruce. I'm sure he more than earned it. He bathed and groomed Bruce regularly and took him for runs ashore at every opportunity. When Cock was 'watch ashore', he would get cleaned up and dress in his shore-going rig, and when 'Liberty men fall in' was piped, he would fall in on the quarterdeck to be inspected by the officer of the watch. Bruce would walk along with the officer of the watch, whining and whimpering to be told he could go ashore. His shipboard collar was an ordinary leather one but his shore-going collar was made by our plumbers out of plates of copper joined with brass links, with 'Bruce' engraved on one side and 'HMS *Valiant*' on the other, all beautifully polished. This collar was kept in Cock's mess, draped over the police light fitting at the head of the mess table. When it was almost time for the liberty men to go down into the boat to go ashore, Cock would say to Bruce, 'All right then, go and get your collar.' Away he'd go, straight down to the mess deck, grab his collar and take it back up to Cock. Bruce would go down one of the steel ladders in the ship in two stretches. He'd reach down from the top of the ladder with his front feet about halfway, followed by his hind feet; the next stretch took him to the bottom. If a sailor was going up or down and Bruce came along, the sailor would have to get over to one side smartly, or take the risk of being knocked down. Bruce was a big dog, he weighed nearly ten stone.

Cock got our sailmaker to make a cloak for him out of white cotton drill and his sister embroidered 'Bruce' on one side and 'HMS *Valiant*' on the other. So when we landed the marines and sailors under arms to march through the various ports we visited, 'showing the flag', Bruce would be out in front of our ship's band leading the contingent, dressed in his cloak and his flash collar and wearing a sailor's cap with HMS *Valiant* on the cap ribbon. On one occasion, a lady's pet Pomeranian dog ran barking to the centre of the road to see what sort of animal this was. Bruce just bent his head down, picked up the Pomeranian, gave him a shake, and dropped him dead! He managed this despite the fact that he was on a leash held by Cock Alders. In the subsequent bubble, the ship's canteen fund paid the dog's owner a considerable sum of money as compensation.

Bruce would not tolerate other dogs or cats, except our own ship's cat, as she was a mature cat before he came aboard. When she had kittens, he would wait until she went away, then he'd pick them up one at a time and deposit them in various places on the mess deck, obviously hiding them from their mother. He'd then lie down and watch for the mother's return, taking great pleasure at her distressed search for them. All we would see of the kitten he was carrying would be its head out at one side of his great mouth but he was most gentle with them and they didn't seem to mind.

Sometimes one of Cock's mates would say, 'I wonder what Bruce would do if someone attacked you?' and Cock would reply, 'I don't know. Grab me and see.' Whereupon the questioner would make a lunge, only to see Bruce immediately rear up and place his forefeet on the attacker's shoulders, growling deeply. If Cock hadn't been released at once, Bruce would have torn the 'assailant' to pieces, I'm sure. When we returned to home ports for refit after our two years in the Mediterranean Fleet and went on foreign service leave, Cock decided to take Bruce home with him to London. On the way, between Plymouth and Bristol, the conductor came into the carriage to check tickets and noticed Bruce under the seat, unfortunately with his head showing.

The conductor said, 'He can't stay here, he'll have to go into the luggage van.'

Cock replied, 'You take him, then.'

As the conductor approached, Bruce let out a deep growl. The fellow thought better of it and said Bruce could stay, so long as he wasn't allowed to roam around the train. On return from his 28 days' leave, Cock told us that he would sit on a bike and have Bruce tow him around Clapham Common. All the kids in the neighbourhood got to know him.

We lost Bruce soon after this. One day, during our refit, he saw a strange cat in the dockyard and chased it into a heap of steel plates and girders. His weight caused the stack to tumble and one of the falling girders broke his leg just above the foot. A vet put his leg in plaster but Bruce chewed the plaster right off. So it was back to the vet but Bruce did the same thing again. We tried putting a muzzle on him but he was distressed by that, and he was losing weight, so it was decided that the kindest thing would be to have him put down. Everyone in the ship's company was very sorry to lose him but poor Cock was heartbroken. We paid off the *Valiant* soon after this and I lost touch with him, so I don't know if he ever became guardian of another ship's mascot.

CHAPTER SEVEN

Leading Torpedoman

THE *VALIANT* TOOK ME BACK TO THE MEDITERRANEAN, where we visited Barcelona with the rest of the squadron of battleships. On the way, we ran into a very fierce gale. Just after dawn, the *Warspite*, our next astern, had two men washed overboard from the quarterdeck. Luckily, they were picked up by one of our attendant destroyer flotilla, so all was well.

A couple of days after our arrival, on a Sunday, the Spaniards put on a special bullfight in our honour. As I was 'watch ashore', I went to the bullring with some of my shipmates and others from the squadron. It looked like a vast gasometer from the outside. Not having much money, we went into the cheapest seats, right up top and on the sunny side. We saw the first bull killed, a cruel, disgusting sight.

The second bull was in the ring, being taunted and worn down. The *banderillero* had just plunged his darts into the beast's shoulders and was racing for one of the escape gaps in the palisade surrounding the arena when one of our men, from the destroyer *Wild Swan*, stood up in his seat, about 40 feet up, and flung an empty wine bottle at the Spaniard, saying, 'Take that, you cruel sod!'

He missed but the gendarmerie, armed police, rushed in and cleared us out, arresting all the men from the *Wild Swan* and putting them in the cooler. We didn't mind too much, as we had seen more than enough of the bullfighting, but the admiral had to go ashore and do some fast talking to get the men released. I don't know if the culprit was ever identified.

Bullfighting is a terribly cruel spectacle, it is so one-sided. Once the bull enters the arena, he is certain to leave it dead. There is no element of chance. Before he dies, he is badgered until he is worn out by men and horses. Finally, frustrated, bewildered and fatigued, he is killed by a matador thrusting a sword through his heart. A team of horses drags the body out of the arena, accompanied by the cheers of the spectators. I believe there were to be six bulls killed that day, as a special treat for the visiting ships' companies, but one was enough for us. I only attended one other bullfight; that was whilst I was serving in HMS *Eagle* – and we were slung out of there too. But that's another story.

Although little understood in northern European states, bullfighting remains a popular spectacle in those nations that hug the Mediterranean. It has been a feature of southern European lifestyle since Classical times. A wall painting dating back to about 2000BC depicting a contest of man against bull was found in Knossos, Crete. In it, the 'bullfighters' rely on acrobatics to avoid the bull, rather than spears.

There were bullfights taking place in ancient Rome, but it was on the Iberian Peninsula that the sport found its greatest foothold. When the Moors invaded, they overlaid the rather brutish displays that took place with ritual and horsemanship. Further refinements were made down the centuries. Today's bullfights resemble those that would have taken place during the eighteenth century. Each week, several thousand Spaniards visit their local bullring and the sport's annual audience is thought to be about a million.

Those who witness a bullfight today will probably see the death of six specially bred four-year-old bulls, killed by three matadors. Each battle lasts 15 minutes and is conducted by a flamboyantly dressed matador flourishing his magenta and yellow cape. Bulls are colour-blind, so it is the swish of the cape rather than its colour that incites the animal to action.

While the movements with the cape are fairly standard, it is the distance at which they are carried out from the bull's horns that inspire excitement in the crowds. Even when the horn tips are tantalisingly close to his body and the bull is snorting with rage, the matador is expected to stay calm and collected if he is to receive plaudits from onlookers.

Then the matador gives way to the picador, riding a horse and armed with a lance. He is usually expected to spear the bull three times before the banderilleros *enter. Their task is to attack the bull with* banderillas, *which are brightly coloured barbed sticks, on foot.*

Before the bull dies, the matador takes over once more, performing intricate and bold moves to please the crowd while preparing to plunge his sword between the shoulder blades of the bull, to rupture its heart. It's a blend of dance and drama. For bullfighting aficionados, this final part of the fight – which requires courage, accuracy and experience – is known as 'the moment of truth'.

Should the matador fail to make the kill with his sword, he has another chance to stab the animal in the neck to ensure a speedy death. The matador is awarded trophies from the dead animal, including its ears, tail or a hoof, by the president of the bullfight. Meanwhile, the audience, waving white handkerchiefs as a sign of appreciation, throw flowers for the bullfighters.

On following days, football teams from the ships went ashore to play the Spaniards, who were just then taking soccer more seriously as a sport. However, our ship's teams would almost always beat them. It was the same in other Mediterranean countries we visited. But we were delighted to see they were all finding soccer a fascinating sport. I suppose our presence encouraged this, as we were always looking for grounds on which to play inter-ship matches. Also, we were always pleased to find a team ashore who wanted to play. Some seeds were sown by the Royal Navy in this regard while we were on our travels. Some of these countries, Spain and Italy for example, now produce players that can beat the best teams Britain can pit against them. It shows how popular the game has become and demonstrates how, with some effort, a country can become proficient enough to win matches against the country recognised as the home of that sport.

Although it has only one World Cup win to its name, Britain is known as the home of football. The sport did not get off to a promising start in England – successive kings took against it and during the rule of King Edward III players were threatened with jail under a royal proclamation stating: 'For as much as there is a great noise in the city caused by hustling over large balls, from which many evils may arise, which God forbid, we command and forbid on behalf of the King, on pain of imprisonment, such game to be used in the city future.'

Kings Richard II, Henry IV and Henry VIII also legislated against football;

Queen Elizabeth I decreed that soccer players should be jailed for a week as well as doing penance in church. One of their biggest problems with football was that it distracted competitors from archery practice. All Scottish monarchs in the fifteenth century opposed football.

The device of a ball being controlled at the feet was noted down the ages in places as diverse as China and Italy. It has led some historians to speculate it emerged out of an early fertility rite. There is even a belief that the ball was, in some cases, the severed head of an enemy. At any rate, with no limit on numbers, time or tactics, the accurate term for the game at this stage in its evolution was 'mob football'.

It wasn't until 1681 that the sport got the green light from government in England. Even then, it took some 200 years for its popularity to spread, generally through schools. Rather more robust than today's game, it wasn't unusual for players to suffer broken bones and bruises during 'footballing' encounters.

By 1863, the need for a basic set of rules became apparent and there was a meeting among London's 11 clubs to hammer out some necessary regulations to govern ball-handling, shin-kicking and tripping. Rugby players realised this was no longer the sport they loved, and departed. The remainder became the Football Association and, six meetings later, came up with a rulebook that would look familiar today.

Within eight years, the Football Association had 50 members and the FA Cup was created to provide structured competition. On 16 March 1872, the Wanderers FC beat the Royal Engineers by one goal to nil at Kennington Oval, in front of 2,000 spectators, and won the inaugural FA Cup match. Players wore long shorts and buttoned shirts.

The first international match was between England and Scotland in the same year. Hosted at the West of Scotland Cricket Club ground in Partick, Glasgow, the clash was marked by exciting play between a bullish England side and their nimble Scottish opponents – and a complete absence of goals. Seventeen years after that, the leagues came into existence, but outside the home nations there was little recognised participation in football.

It wasn't until 1889 that the Netherlands and Denmark formed football associations, followed in 1891 by New Zealand, in 1893 by Argentina and in 1898 by Italy. Germany, Hungary and Finland did not have recognised football associations until the turn of the twentieth century. Participation and skill levels among overseas players fell way below their English counterparts. In 1904, the same year that FIFA (the Fédération Internationale de Football Association) was formed, a visiting French side was defeated 26 goals to one by Woolwich Arsenal. FIFA still had only 21 members by 1912. In 1930, when the first World Cup was held, membership stood at 41. By contrast, at the end of 2007 the membership of FIFA stood at 208.

In the First World War, the continuation of football fixtures was not universally popular, with critics claiming that the distraction of matches helped the enemy. After conscription was introduced, the numbers of players and spectators dwindled but the sport survived, with teams playing in regional contests. Premier teams of the era included Leeds City, Nottingham Forest, Chelsea, West Bromwich Albion and Aston Villa.

The *Valiant* was a very happy ship, but we were all glad to return to our home port to pay off and go on foreign service leave at the end of our two years abroad. I was drafted to HMS *Defiance* after leave was finished, to qualify as a leading torpedoman (LTO), being the youngest seaman torpedoman to be recommended for LTO. I was very pleased to return to the *Defiance*, and after a six-month course, I had qualified.

Whilst in *Defiance* qualifying for seaman torpedoman, I had an experience that demonstrates how sailors are always ready to skylark and play the fool. One of the things we had to learn was how to test the lightning conductor of a ship – a copper strip connected to a metal spike erected above the masthead, which runs down the mast to the keel, where it goes through the hull and is there connected to a copper plate. The conductor ensures that any lightning strike will be carried down the mast and discharged safely into the ocean, instead of doing possibly severe damage to the ship.

To carry out this test, one man had to go aloft with a flexible cable and connect the copper core to the metal spike at the masthead. When he had done this, he sang out to his mates on deck, 'Connected up.' They then joined up the other end of the flexible cable to the bridge megger, an electrical measuring instrument, one terminal of which was connected to a cable payed out to a copper plate immersed in the sea, overboard. When the handle of the bridge megger was heaved around, a current passed through the lightning conductor at

240 volts and the resistance of the conductor was measured by the reading on the instrument.

When we came to our day for the test, our instructor sent me aloft with the cable, which the rest of the class payed out to me. When I was at the masthead connecting up, one of my classmates gave a turn on the handle of the megger, which gave me a shock. I sang out, 'Why can't you so-and-sos leave that megger alone?'

When the instructor, whose attention had been momentarily diverted, saw the culprit let go of the handle he said to him, 'If you ever do anything like that again while you're in my class, you'll be out of this ship so fast, your feet won't touch the deck. And what's more, you'll never be a torpedoman, no matter how long you stay in the Service. You could have killed him if he had fallen.'

Luckily, I had a good hold when he did it, and, when I came down on deck after the test, he apologised and there was no ill feeling.

From *Defiance*, I was drafted to HMS *Victory* at Portsmouth Naval Depot to stand-by the *Eagle*, an aircraft carrier being built in the naval dockyard there. When a naval ship is being built, a certain number of senior men and officers are selected to stand-by her to watch the equipment and armaments being constructed and put in place. They are therefore completely familiar with it when the ship finally does her acceptance trials and is commissioned.

HMS *Eagle* was launched in 1918 as a battleship, completed in 1920, then converted and commissioned as an aircraft carrier in 1924. The island superstructure offset to the starboard side was introduced on her and this was to become characteristic of British and American carriers from then on. Her length was 667.5 feet, maximum speed 22.5 knots, and she had a crew of 950. There were six 23-inch torpedo tubes and 21 aircraft aboard. I served on her from 23 September 1923 till 7 February 1926.

On the day we were due to sail for the Mediterranean to join the fleet there, the senior LTO, a petty officer, was severely injured. He was in charge of all the electrical gear in the hangars and the electrical aircraft crane on the flying deck. One of the bomb lift motors fell on him and he was rushed to hospital. Since there was not time to get a relief for him from Devonport, the torpedo officer sent for me and asked if I thought I could take over his job. Of course I replied in the affirmative and he said: 'The job is yours!'

I held it for the rest of our two years in the Med. My action station was driver on the aircraft crane and, as the Fleet Air Arm was in its formative years, I had some very exciting moments recovering aircraft which had ditched either during flying off or landing. It was strange to see some of our lads in RAF uniforms. We were always trying out new types of aircraft to find those most suitable to operate from carriers and we tried to discover better methods of arresting gear on the flying deck. We once lost the whole of our squadron of aircraft because their critical flying speed was too high.

In the early twentieth century, the Royal Navy saw the potential of flight but focused on balloons and airships, both generally used for reconnaissance. There was funding for a military airship made available as early as 1909 but the age of the airship was soon over. Even prior to the First World War, it became apparent the country was going to need military aircraft if it was going to compete on level terms with other nations.

By 1912, the government had formed the Royal Flying Corps, which would concentrate on the development of aircraft. The British Army's airships were in turn handed to the Royal Navy, along with a dozen aircraft. But the Royal Navy did not abandon the notion of operational aircraft, especially when Eugene B. Ely successfully took off in a plane from a ship in 1910.

The first flight from a moving ship occurred in May 1912; the following year, there came a commission for a specially designed seaplane. Still, for a while the art learned by Royal Navy sailors was how to hoist planes out of the sea using a crane.

At the same time, the navy began building a chain of coastal air stations. Before the advent of the First World War, the Royal Naval Air Service had been established, quickly embracing 217 pilots and 95 aircraft, more than half of which were seaplanes. Indeed, that outnumbered the planes belonging to the Royal Flying Corps. The RNAS saw its role mainly in reconnaissance, looking out for enemy ships and submarines marauding in British waters. There was potential for attacking enemy territory if it was no more than a short hop away. It was also poised to defend the skies above Britain from enemy aircraft.

It was generally understood that aircraft would be best used as look-outs rather than for combat. This policy was partly inspired by the flimsy nature of early planes. To add bombs or guns to them seemed almost foolhardy but with war came swift technological advances, not least the gear that would enable a navigator to fire his machine gun without putting his plane's propellers at risk.

It was the perceived failure by the RNAS to halt the Zeppelin bombing raids using its earliest aircraft that compromised its popularity both inside and outside government. Responsibility for the safety of the skies above London was handed to the Royal Flying Corps, while the RNAS was tasked with attacking Zeppelins on the ground.

Replicating the work of the Royal Flying Corps to some degree, the RNAS also had fighter squadrons on the Western Front flying planes like the Bristol Scout, the Sopwith Pup and the Sopwith Camel. These were sturdier and more reliable than their predecessors. Innovation continued to surge forward. In 1914 the familiar BE2c plane boasted a top speed of 72 mph from its 90 horsepower engine and was airborne for a maximum of three hours. Just three years later, the SE5a flew at 97 mph, had a 200 horsepower engine and could stay in the air for eight hours.

Furthermore, in 1917 a Sopwith Pup piloted by Squadron Commander E.H. Dunning of the Royal Navy landed on the world's first aircraft carrier, HMS Furious, *a converted warship. Future possibilities for the RNAS began to gel.*

By April 1918 the government had decided to merge both arms of the military dealing in aircraft and formed the Royal Air Force, eliminating rivalries and creating a force with which to deliver a hammer blow to Germany.

With perhaps unfortunate timing, it was the same year that HMS Argus *– the navy's first purpose-built aircraft carrier – came into service. Planes could both land and take off from it, laying down the standard for future aircraft carrier design. Had it appeared a little sooner, it might have saved the RNAS from a merger that was unpopular in its ranks, although government was clearly unhappy with two flight departments. With its flight deck atop the ship,* Argus *became known as 'ditty box' for its likeness to the small case handed out among seamen's kit. At the end of hostilities,* Argus *was used primarily for training in open water, honing the skills of RAF pilots in seaplanes.*

As former RNAS servicemen feared, the RAF neglected the potential of the Royal Navy at the end of hostilities. Scarce resources were diverted to land-based ventures.

As early as 1924, the Admiralty argued successfully for the introduction of a

'Naval Air Branch' to distinguish its activities from those of the RAF. It wasn't until 1937, however, that it became the Fleet Air Arm.

Another excitement occurred when the C-in-C Mediterranean, Admiral John de Robeck, was flown aboard to carry out an inspection. Everything went well until he was flown off and his machine was ditched just after take-off. But he was quickly picked up by one of our escorting destroyers with nothing worse than a wet shirt as a result.

It wasn't the first time Claude's path had crossed with that of Admiral John de Robeck (1862–1928), but it was Claude's brothers, Leslie and Doug, who had better reason to remember him.

De Robeck had served in the Royal Navy since 1875 and, by the time the First World War broke out, he had reached the rank of rear admiral. Appointed deputy to Admiral Sackville Carden, de Robeck came to the fore when his boss returned home with mental stress before the planned Dardanelles campaign. It was de Robeck who orchestrated the unsuccessful naval assault on Gallipoli in March 1915, in which six Allied ships were sunk or scuppered by enemy mines.

Stung by criticism, he then refused to attempt another assault from the water until ground troops were in place on the heights commanding the straits. To some, it was de Robeck who consigned the entire campaign to failure. He did, however, earn praise for the manner in which Allied troops were withdrawn without the loss of a single life.

Despite the blemish against his military reputation, de Robeck was promoted to vice admiral during the last years of the war. Between 1919 and 1920, he was high commissioner at Constantinople and between 1922 and 1924 he was commander of the Atlantic Fleet. On both occasions, without either man knowing the other, he was atop Claude's chain of command.

The trouble was that we didn't have catapults to assist take-off and sometimes the planes had not gained sufficient speed when they left the flying deck and so they ditched. If there was a stiff breeze blowing, that was good because the ship always steamed dead into the eye of the wind. That added to our 25 knots, because the apparent wind speed appeared to increase along the flying deck, so helping our planes to take off safely. We were always trying out new ideas to increase the safety of our aircraft but, nevertheless, we lost quite a few during our two-year commission.

One of our chief petty officers had served for some years in the Royal New Zealand Navy on loan. Whilst there he had been a member of a *haka* party – a New Zealand Maori war dance team – so he formed a *haka* party on board to augment the ship's concert party, comprising 20 volunteers, of whom I was one. We made our grass skirts from teased-out manila rope and, for the performance, we blacked our faces and bodies with burnt cork and grease paint. If the ship gave a dance, it would be held in one of our hangars. When the dance was well under way, we would dash out and perform our act. It used to scare the daylights out of the ladies present, to see these wild men invade the dance floor.

On one occasion we put on a special show when our captain left the ship to return to England following his promotion to rear admiral. The passenger liner he was to travel home in was moored at Custom House Steps. He was taken there from the *Eagle* in his galley, manned not by its usual crew but by the senior officers of the ship, as a mark of the great regard in which we held him. We followed, all done up in our war paint, paddling one of our whalers, a 27-foot double-ended boat rigged up to look like a native canoe by our shipwrights. As soon as the captain reached the saloon deck, we went alongside, rushed up the gangway and performed our *haka* dance, much to his delight and the surprise and alarm of the liner's passengers.

Thanks to the travels of the New Zealand rugby team across the globe, the haka, *a tribal dance performed by the team before every match, is well known and oft imitated. It is probably the Maoris' best-loved export. In fact, there's a lot more to the* haka *than most people realise.*

The haka *performed by rugby players is said to have been the dance of Te Rauparaha (1768–1849), chief of the Ngati Toa tribe of North Island and perhaps New Zealand's last great warrior chief. Te Rauparaha and his men battled their way south, where they killed both European settlers and southern Maori.*

His haka *is thought to have been created when, being chased by his enemies, he hid in a sweet-potato field one night, slept there and experienced vivid dreams. In the morning he awoke to be told by a chief that his enemies had gone. He then performed his victorious* haka.

The following are the words of Te Rauparaha's haka *(1810), used by the All Blacks:*

> Ka mate, ka mate
>
> Ka ora, ka ora
>
> Tenei te tangata puhuruhuru
>
> Nana i tiki mai whakawhiti te ra
>
> Upane, upane
>
> Upane kaupane
>
> Whiti te ra.

These words translate as:

> *It is death, it is death*
>
> *It is life, it is life*
>
> *This is the hairy man*
>
> *Who caused the sun to shine again for me*
>
> *Up the ladder, up the ladder*
>
> *Up to the top*
>
> *The sun shines.*

But this is not the only haka, *nor are they always performed by men. Traditionally, there were* hakas *for all of life's great occasions, from the joy of birth through to death and mourning.*

Hakas are expressed through specific postures and facial expressions, all of which have a significance familiar among Maoris. From his description, it is clear that Claude and his party were mimicking a war haka, *in the same way as the All Blacks do today. It is not known how accurate it was.*

An exciting episode occurred in this commission in 1925, after Sir Lee Stack, the Sirdar (Commander) of Egypt, was murdered. At the time, we were exercising Flying Operations and were ordered to fly off all aircraft and return to Malta with speed. Our aircraft flew to Hal Far aerodrome in Malta and we secured alongside in the dockyard when all the shipwrights from the dockyard came aboard with the necessary timber and other materials to build mess tables and stools or forms sufficient to accommodate the First Battalion of the Gordon Highlanders, a total of 1,000 men. They were assisted by our own shipwrights while the ship's company was busy taking on stores and ammunition for the Scotties. We worked round the clock and, as soon as we were ready, the battalion marched down to the ship led by their pipe band of 40 pipers and came aboard. Their officer's chargers were brought down in horseboxes and I hoisted them onto the flying deck with our aircraft crane. Here they were secured against any movement of the ship in a seaway.

As soon as they were all aboard, away we went at full speed for Port Said, some 1,000 miles away. The weather was kind to us all the way and each dinnertime, noon to 1 p.m., the band went onto the flying deck and played for us all and we danced to their wonderful music. We were amazed at their perfection. The pipe major was stationed on the foc'sle, and each piper in turn presented himself with his pipes before him and tuned his drones, and when the pipe major was satisfied, the piper went up the ladders onto the flying deck. When all were assembled, the pipe major joined them and they commenced playing.

Some of our lads took a handful of dried peas up to the flying deck to feed the officers' chargers. One wag, trying to show off, after giving one of the horses his peas, put his arm round the horse's neck, which promptly bit the end off his nose! That effectively put an end to dried peas for horses. The surgeon sewed the man's nose back on again.

It was evening when we arrived at Port Said. We went alongside and discharged all the stores and ammunition for the Gordons and they formed up alongside the ship. Then they marched off into the desert on that beautiful starry night, accompanied by their pipes. We could hear them for what seemed a very long time before the music faded into the distance. It was most impressive.

Incidentally, the Scotties slept in hammocks provided by the navy while aboard *Eagle*. We looked after them well and they deserved it. The next morning, having seen all their gear loaded into British Army trucks, we slipped anchor and proceeded back to Malta to recover our aircraft and their crews, to continue with our duties with the Mediterranean Fleet.

The assassination of Major General Sir 'Lee' Stack on 19 November 1924 was a flashpoint in Egyptian history.

Most schoolchildren can tell you about Egypt's glorious era under Pharaoh rule, after which period the region's fortunes were chequered. By 31BC Egypt was under Roman rule, following the defeat of Cleopatra's forces. Ultimately, the Roman Empire went into decline and, by the middle of the first millennium, Egypt had fallen under Arab influence. From 1250 Egypt was ruled by the Mamelukes, slave soldiers from the Arab tradition who established themselves on the back of an astonishing victory against the Mongol forces led by Genghis Khan's grandson. A particularly ruthless Mameluke leader secured the religiously significant sites of Mecca and Medina as well as driving the Christians back in the Holy Land.

However, by 1517 the Mamelukes found themselves unable to resist Ottoman pressure. Egypt became part of the Ottoman Empire, which, with British assistance, fended off the attentions of Napoleon Bonaparte in 1798. Now the threat to Egypt came from the apparently friendly overtures of the British Empire.

Sensing frailty in the Ottoman rule, British troops took control of Egypt in 1882 and, by the beginning of the First World War, it was a British protectorate. At the end of the conflict, an Egyptian delegation at the peace talks – bolstered by scenes of near revolution on the streets of Cairo – demanded independence. The request was denied.

However, further civil unrest led to the declaration of Egyptian independence in 1922 and a monarchy was created along with a democratic government. But Britain, in control of neighbouring Sudan, could not resist meddling with internal Egyptian affairs and maintained control of the Suez Canal and of Egypt's external defence.

There was a growing resentment of British imperialism among Egyptians and recruits flocked to the newly formed Islamic fundamentalist groups. It was just such an organisation that engineered Stack's murder.

His untimely death was followed by a sharp backlash from furious Britons, whose wildly inflated demands for recompense for Stack's murder brought down the infant Egyptian government. Although he was a prominent nationalist, Prime Minister Saad Zaghlul quickly observed that the assassins were no friends of independent Egypt. 'I feel the profoundest distress at this atrocious crime,' he stated. 'I do not know what purpose the perpetrators sought to accomplish, nor to which segment of the nation they belong or to which political organisation or party they are affiliated. However, I believe that those who committed this appalling evil aimed only to disrupt the peace and security of this country.'

Claude's ship was sent to enforce British 'strong-arm' tactics. It seemed the shine of the British Empire's reputation was rated more highly than the welfare of a newly independent state. From its position of control in the Sudan, Britain could effectively place a noose around Egypt and swiftly did so. But the reality was that Egypt was independent and was not about to surrender that prize to the English. There followed a political impasse from which Britain ultimately had to withdraw.

In Egypt itself, eight men were sentenced to death for their part in the assassination; another received a two-year sentence of imprisonment with hard labour. As for the British, the man behind the tough British stance, Field Marshal Edmund Allenby (1861–1936), effectively lost his exalted position when it became clear that Britain had gained little from the episode.

When our ship was stopped for 'hands to bathe', 'Snowy' Mitchell, a fellow leading torpedoman, and I used to dive off the flying deck of the ship, which stood about 40–45 feet high. We would then swim up and down the length of the ship together until the 'retire' was sounded on the bugle. Snowy was a good mate of mine and we were the only two out of our ship's company who dived in from the flying deck. I preferred to run and dive if I could get Snowy or someone else to tell me if it was all clear below. It wouldn't have been much fun landing on the back of a shipmate! Snowy came out to Australia with me in the SS *Diogenes* early in 1926, when we were on loan to the Royal Australian Navy as instructors for two years.

On one occasion, after a run ashore in Malta, while our ship was lying alongside in the dockyard at Grand Harbour, somebody made a bet with Snowy and me that we were not game to swim across Grand Harbour from Custom House Steps to rejoin our ship.

We took on the bet, stripped off and put our clothes in a *dghajsa*, a Maltese boat. We told the boatman to take our gear and our shipmates alongside *Eagle*, then off we went. When we arrived on board, stark naked, the officer of the watch said he would run us in for coming aboard improperly dressed. But, on being told of the bet, he let us off with a caution.

I was lucky he did not take us before the commander for, had he done so, I most probably would not have received an 'exceptional' for ability that year, 1925. I considered it an honour, as only one or two men were given the award each year by their captains. It ranked highest of all, above 'superior', and I think it had an influence on my being selected as an instructor for two years in the RAN.

On our last visit to Gibraltar, there was a bullfight arranged in the Spanish town of Algeciras across the Bay of Gibraltar. Some of my messmates prevailed on me to go along with them to see it, though I told them they would be disgusted, and I was right.

However, there was an amusing incident before we had to leave. The ceremony had got to the point at which the *banderillero* came into the arena to plunge the tasselled darts into the bull's shoulders. He does this as the bull charges towards him and then he must make a dash for one of the escape breaks around the arena palisade. On this occasion, he was not quick enough and the bull caught him just before he reached safety. The bull's head met him fair behind the knees and he literally sat back between the horns. When the bull pulled up its head it flung him into the air right over the palisade, to land among the toffs in the ringside seats. We cheered instead of groaning like the Spaniards and, rather than wait for the gendarmerie to throw us out, we walked away, glad to be gone from so cruel a spectacle.

It is dreadful to see a bull charge a poor horse, which is blindfolded on the side nearest to the bull but is trembling with fear, sensing the danger. As the bull charges, the rider of the horse plunges a lance into the shoulder of the poor animal and then slips off and over the palisade while the bull proceeds to disembowel the terrified beast. This is all done so that the strength of the bull is so worn down, the matador can kill him.

Quite often, when the *Eagle* was at Malta, we anchored in Calafrana Bay, as it was difficult for us to enter Grand Harbour if it was blowing hard, as we had so much top hamper and the space was limited. On one occasion there one of our fighter pilots, doing a spell in the aerodrome ashore, came out to have a look at the ship. He made a dummy run past the flying deck, which they often did when the ship was at sea, prior to landing. He circled round, and coming up from astern, landed his aircraft on the flying deck and ran the full length of the ship. Fortunately, he pulled up just before he reached the stern, being helped by some of the sailors, who grabbed his wings to act as breaks, as they always did during flying exercises. Luckily for the pilot, there was about a 15-knot wind blowing at the time, which assisted him in pulling up. He had to go before the wing commander, the senior air officer aboard, and then the captain for a 'please explain'. He remained with his squadron, so we thought he must have been warned of dire consequences if he tried that trick again.

One very amusing incident occurred at one of our ship's concerts in Grand Harbour. It was rumoured aboard ship that one of our torpedomen, a West Countryman called Jan, was a hypnotist. Assisted by the concert officer, we persuaded him to give a turn. To assist his performance, he called for volunteers as subjects. Four of the tough boys were persuaded to go on stage, to yells of, 'Go on, I bet he can't put you under!' from the audience.

Jan sat the volunteers down on chairs, then proceeded to put each one in turn into a trance. When he had them all hypnotised, he said to the first one: 'You are filthy! Look at you, you are covered in fleas!' The subject duly started to scratch himself violently. Then Jan led him over to a small table, on which lay one of the chief cook's large dishes filled with flour. Now Jan told him: 'Strip off and have a jolly good wash in this nice warm water!' So the lad promptly did as he was told, throwing flour all over the place.

Jan then went to his second subject and said, 'You like apples don't you?' On receiving a reply in the affirmative, Jan said, 'Well, here's a lovely one for you.' But instead of an apple he gave the man a big Spanish onion, already peeled. The lad started to eat it just as if it were a juicy apple.

Our hypnotist then went to his third subject and said to him, 'You like fishing, don't you?' Given an answer in the affirmative, he took the man to a seat at the edge of the stage and handed him a broom handle with a length of heavy spun yarn attached to the end. This he threw down among the marine bandsmen, our orchestra, asking, 'You like to smoke a cigar, don't you?' He then handed the fisherman a wax candle trimmed off at the butt end so that he could put it in his mouth, saying, 'I'll light it for you.' This he did and the lad went through the motions of smoking a cigar with much relish, scattering melted wax freely around.

Jan then went to the fourth subject and said, 'You have a lovely sweetheart to whom you write regularly, haven't you?' On being assured that this was correct, he continued, 'You'd like to see her now, wouldn't you?' The lad replied, 'My word, I would.' Then, pointing to the flying deck, Jan said, 'You see that big building opposite? There she is on the fourth floor, looking out of the window. Call to her!' And the lad sang out, 'Yoohoo, Maggie!' and waved his hand. Jan said, 'You'd like her to come down, wouldn't you, so I'll call her for you.' 'Oh, yes please!' the lad responded. At this point, Jan brought a new volunteer on stage, led him to his subject and announced, 'Well, here's Maggie. Now take her on your knee. The two of you are all alone.' The subject went through the motions of giving Maggie a very warm welcome indeed.

Jan then went back to the lad who was fishing and took the candle from him, commenting that he had smoked it down enough, adding: 'Look, there's a man over the other side of the river throwing stones at your float. Tell him to shove off. No wonder you can't catch fish!' So the lad proceeded to tell the imaginary stone-thrower, in rich nautical terms, what would happen to him if he didn't desist immediately.

Finally, Jan woke his subjects up and they were all amazed to realise what they had been doing. He was the only hypnotist I was ever shipmates with, and he was a good one at that.

Not long before I left England, I think in late 1925, during the period of unrest that led up to the General Strike of May 1926, I was part of a navy battalion sent on a special train from Plymouth to Cardiff to guard merchant shipping anchored there. Nothing was to be moved or damaged. We were housed in a very large factory building and played soccer every day against local teams, which was great fun as well as being part of a strategy to keep them from getting involved in the unrest. During the General Strike, the navy helped wherever it could, even manning essential trains – one petty officer and four sailors to each one – to keep them running; it was seen as part of the navy's job to defend the country against unrest, riots and losses in personnel and belongings. By the time the General Strike came, however, I was in faraway Australia – fighting bushfires.

CHAPTER EIGHT

With the Royal Australian Navy

JUST BEFORE WE WERE DUE TO GO BACK HOME AT THE end of our commission, a notice was pinned on the ship's company noticeboard stating that a dozen volunteers were required among petty officers, or leading seamen passed for petty officer, to serve for two years on loan to the Royal Australian Navy (RAN) as instructors.

As I had the necessary torpedo rating, and having passed professionally for PO, I told Snowy Mitchell that I was going to volunteer. This would give me a chance to visit my brother Leslie and my sister Phyllis, both of whom lived in Western Australia. Snowy said he'd have a go too, as Australia looked a better prospect for his next commission than other British naval stations such as the Persian Gulf, China Sea or the West Indies. We both submitted our names to the captain, who duly forwarded our Service Certificates to the Admiralty, with his recommendation. We heard no more until we had paid off the *Eagle*. Then we were called into the Captain's Office of Portsmouth Naval Depot, HMS *Victory*. Along with the ten other volunteers, one of whom was a chief petty officer, we were given a talk by a commander, RAN, telling us what to expect to find on service in Australia.

The Flinders Naval Depot, where we were to be employed as instructors, was about 40 miles from Melbourne. Whereas naval depots in England were only a few acres, Flinders was over 6,000 acres in extent. The officer of the watch did the rounds on horseback because the depot was so large. Also, there was no rum issue in the RAN, which didn't worry Snowy or me, as we didn't draw our rum anyway.

After the commander's briefing, he sent us on pre-embarkation leave, with orders to report to HM Australian Naval Office in London. From there we embarked on the passenger ship SS *Diogenes* at the end of February 1926, sailing from Tilbury Docks. She was one of the Aberdeen White Star Line ships running a regular service to Australia, and comfortable too, though not fast. We took six weeks from London to Melbourne, with calls at Tenerife in the Canary Islands, Cape Town, Albany (Western Australia) and Adelaide.

Initially, the colony of Australia was patrolled by the Royal Navy, despite the fact that its main naval bases were hundreds of miles away. In 1859, Australia became a separate British Naval Station equivalent to, say, Hong Kong or Malta. This meant a squadron of ships was always on hand in Australian waters.

In response to a change in Australian status, an Imperial Conference held in 1909 agreed to the creation of an Australian Fleet Unit. By the time King George V granted the title of 'Royal Australian Navy' to the new force in 1911, the destroyers Yarra *and* Parramatta *were already in Australian waters. More ships followed and, in October 1913, British input into the Australian navy came to an end.*

When the First World War broke out, the Australian Fleet had a battlecruiser, six light cruisers, six destroyers, two submarines and assorted support vessels to its name. Thanks to fraternal relations with the Royal Navy, Australian ships could make use of British bases across the globe. At the start of the war the RAN had 5,263 men in its ranks.

Among the first targets of the war for the RAN were German colonies in the Pacific. Its success was marred by the loss of a submarine, AE1, and all crew off New Britain on 14 September.

At the end of 1914, HMAS Sydney *got the better of the German light cruiser* Emden, *which had been leaving a trail of havoc around the southern seas, acting in the manner of an old-fashioned privateer.* Emden *had sunk a cruiser, a destroyer and 16 merchant ships, and its raids had become a thorn in the side of the British trying to maintain trade and communication with its empire outposts.*

The RAN also had a supporting role during the Gallipoli campaign, where a submarine, AE2, was scuttled by her crew in the Sea of Marmora on 30 April 1915.

At the end of the war, the Australian navy had been distinguished by the conduct of its newly trained sailors and the durability of its ships. Almost immediately, however, it faced a blow. The Washington Treaty of 1922, aiming to cut the competitive accumulation of weapons that had led to the conflict, imposed limits on the fleets of its signatories. Although only commissioned nine years previously, the battlecruiser Australia *was scuttled off Sydney Heads in 1924. It was size rather than number that interested those drawing up the Washington Treaty. As a result, the RAN soon received numerous additions from the Royal Navy, including six submarines, five destroyers and a number of sloops. Further purchases were also in the pipeline.*

On our first day aboard, as we steamed down the English Channel, we made ourselves known to the rest of the passengers and I met the young lady who was to become my wife, Ethel Wildgoose. She was one of a group of twelve lasses going to Australia under the auspices of the Victoria League, to work in various occupations. Ethel had been trained as a children's nurse in St Anne's College, Cheltenham, and was going to Melbourne to look after two small boys, the children of a local dentist. After I first met her in company with some of the other girls, she thought that I was interested not in her, but in Agatha Taylor, a petite brunette. But I soon convinced her that she was wrong! When I told her my name she was very surprised, saying she had never known a Claude before and how much she admired the name. She was a tall brunette with dark brown eyes, a real stunner. It was love at first sight, certainly on my part.

We Royal Navy men got along famously with the Victoria League girls. Together, we organised deck games for the passengers and, morning and evening, I took the VL girls for physical training exercises on the poop deck. There were a few days on which these activities were cancelled owing to bad weather, but mostly the sun shone down on us.

When Ethel was part of the Victoria League, the organisation had just

115

celebrated its 25th anniversary. A group that extolled the virtues of friendship and co-operation, it was founded during the Boer War when a Mrs Mary Davis, travelling by train in South Africa, was struck by the tragedy of its turmoil. This public-minded woman turned to her companion, declaring: 'I am so weary of the bitterness of this war. Why can't we have a Society of Friendship?'

The idea was carried forward to 10 Downing Street by the Guild of Loyal Women in Cape Town and other dignitaries impressed by the simplicity and sincerity of the message. A meeting held in 1901 laid plans for an independent, non-political organisation to promote 'a closer union between the different parts of what was then the British Empire by the interchange of information and hospitality and by co-operation in any practical scheme tending to foster friendly understanding and good fellowship with the Empire'.

It was named for the late Queen, and its first president, Margaret, Countess of Jersey, was still at the helm when Ethel made her visit to Australia under its auspices. Initially dominated by women, men were soon admitted to its ranks. The League attracted the immediate support of many public figures and it was dubbed 'the organisation of sympathy' by the author Rudyard Kipling.

The first tasks undertaken by the Victoria League were in South Africa. Funds were raised to tend war graves, help British refugees and provide for Boer women and children penned in British concentration camps. Soon papers, books and magazines were being distributed worldwide to assist in education projects.

In 1906, the Princess of Wales, the future Queen Mary, became patron, signalling rapid expansion. During the First World War the Victoria League provided hospitality, in the form of new clubs and hostels, to Commonwealth servicemen. It also acted as a focus for gift distribution and provided food parcels for soldiers overseas and their families at home. The Victoria League, underpinned by similar principles to those that governed its inception, still survives today, working largely with students.

As we approached Melbourne, it looked as though we were running into dense fog but one of the ship's officers informed us that it was smoke from bush fires. After arriving at Flinders Naval Depot, instead of going to instructions as usual, all hands were sent out into the surrounding bush to fight the fires, day and night. The fires were burning in all directions and scared the daylights out of me – I had never before seen a forest fire. Several people lost their lives in the inferno but naval base personnel sustained no casualties.

Snowy and I were both promoted to acting petty officer on being accepted to serve in the RAN – earlier promotion than we could have hoped for had we stayed in the RN, though when we volunteered we had no idea it would happen. At the end of the 12-month trial period, we were both confirmed as POs and were given new uniforms: gone were the bell bottoms and three rows of tape on the collar; we were now kitted out in square rig with gold buttons and a double-breasted coat. Unlike me, Snowy returned to the RN on completion of his two years.

After a couple of months, the officer in charge of the Torpedo School, Lieutenant Commander Welman, sent for me to ask if I would like to change over to the RAN permanently. When I said yes, he said application would be made to the RN for my transfer, which was approved in July 1926. After completing a three-month preliminary course, I was sent with four other RAN petty officers to HMS *Vernon* in Portsmouth, England, to qualify as torpedo gunner's mate, commonly called TI, torpedo instructor.

Claude was exactly the kind of man that Australia welcomed. He was young, skilled and, crucially, white – at the time the young nation observed a 'White Australia' policy, which lasted more than 70 years before it was entirely dismantled.

The roots of the policy lay back in the 1850s, when miners were hoping to get rich quick on the back of rich natural mineral deposits. Chinese diggers were working at the same sites, with similar aims. Ultimately, both sides clashed. As a result, restrictions were imposed on Chinese immigration.

There was also resentment of the Pacific Islanders, known as kanakas, who often worked in tropical conditions on Queensland's sugar plantations. When the Australian states federated in 1901, the Immigration Restriction Act was passed, ending employment opportunities for Pacific Islanders and throwing up hurdles to prevent other races from entering the country. The Act also barred anyone who was insane, ill, dangerous or lacking in means from entering Australia. Those enterprising enough to circumvent those rules faced a written test in a language nominated by an immigration officer – not necessarily English. Nor was the content of the test always easy to comprehend, as the following example of one of the dictation tests shows: 'Very many considerations lead to the conclusion that life began on sea, first as single cells, then as groups of cells held together by a secretion of mucilage, then as filaments and tissues. For a very long time low-grade marine organisms are simply hollow cylinders, through which salt water streams.'

Egon Kisch, a prominent Czech anti-fascist writer, fell foul of the rules in 1934 when he failed a dictation test given in Gaelic.

These exclusions were underpinned by the 1903 Naturalisation Act, which laid down that applicants for naturalisation could not be natives of Asia, Africa or the Pacific Islands, other than New Zealand.

Although it was clearly flawed, the White Australia policy was popular among Australians, not least because it was seen as a way of protecting jobs. Alfred Deakin, the Australian minister responsible for promoting the White Australia ethic, said: 'It is not the bad qualities, but the good qualities of these alien races that make them so dangerous to us. It is their inexhaustible energy, their power of applying themselves to new tasks, their endurance and low standard of living that make them such competitors.'

The policy was unpopular with many other nations. The Japanese were so incensed by what they perceived to be racism among white nations worldwide, they tried to force the inclusion of an equality clause into the peace treaty that ended the First World War. Their attempt was unsuccessful.

The outbreak of the Second World War and the subsequent involvement of Japan did much to confirm the prejudices of Australians. In 1941, Prime Minister John Curtin affirmed: 'This country shall remain forever the home of the descendants of those people who came here in peace in order to establish in the South Seas an outpost of the British race.'

However, the war effort meant that Australia was compelled to welcome foreign workers. After the hostilities ended, the injustice towards non-white immigrants became headline news.

One man, Samsudin bin Katib, put the issue into sharp focus. Born in Sumatra, Samsudin was 18 when he arrived in Australia in 1937 to work as a pearl diver. After the Japanese attacks on Australia, he joined the Australian militia in Perth and was eventually seized upon by the top brass of the elite commando force known as Z Special Unit. Samsudin qualified as a parachutist, worked behind enemy lines in Borneo intelligence-gathering and was made a corporal before he was discharged from the Service in Melbourne in May 1946.

For a while, he found assorted jobs and decided to apply for naturalisation, hoping that his courageous war service would speak volumes for his character. Unfortunately, his application failed. The rules governing immigrants at the time meant he had to work as a pearl diver or leave Australia altogether. Australia's pearl diving companies had banked plentiful supplies during the war, when they were unable to sell their wares. Foreign workers like Samsudin were now diminishing the profits made by the bosses. In 1948, when the employers proposed a 10 per cent cut in wages, Samsudin helped to lead the revolt that followed among Malay and Indonesian workers. He was ultimately banned from working as a pearl diver and, as such, could only stay in Australia illegally.

Efforts to prevent his deportation were widespread. Samsudin wrote to Arthur Calwell, the Minister for Immigration, saying: 'It would indeed be a tragedy if those of us who offered our lives in service for freedom and the right to work and earn at reasonable wages and conditions were to become the subject of persecution only for the reason that we desire to put those ideals in practice.'

If Calwell hoped for compromise when a pearl sheller agreed to reinstate Samsudin rather than see him deported, then he was mistaken. The powerful employers in the pearl industry launched strong and loud protests. The post was ultimately withdrawn and Calwell had to deport Samsudin, or see the White Australia policy crumble before him. Now the Seamen's Union weighed in on behalf of Samsudin, alongside other groups opposed to the racial laws, all to no avail. Samsudin was dispatched for Singapore with hastily assembled paperwork, including a certificate that stated his exclusion from Australia was permanent. It was endorsed by Stanley Davis, the manager of the largest of the pearl fishing companies.

A later report into the scandal confirmed that Samsudin had been victimised because of his opposition to management. It stated: 'There seems little doubt that they have chosen to settle the recurring disputes in their own favour by direct action within the law, to remove any workers who might succeed in organising their fellow workers.'

Although it must have been of little comfort to Samsudin, his case and others linked to the war caused hairline fractures in the White Australia policy which would ultimately bring about its demise. In 1949, the immigration authorities allowed 800 non-white European refugees to stay in Australia and agreed the admission of Japanese war brides.

By 1957, non-Europeans who could prove 15 years' residency in Australia *were permitted to become citizens. A Migration Act in 1958 substantially relaxed conditions necessary for immigration and, by the mid-1960s, the emphasis was moved to qualifications and suitability rather than skin colour, and rules for non-whites were brought into line with those applied to whites. In the 1970s, more rule changes saw the end of anything that could be construed as a White Australia policy.*

For his part, Claude appears from his writing to have been singularly unprejudiced in his approach, making friends as easily with Aborigines, Filipinos, Britons and Australians.

On 3 December 1926, at the start of my 28 days' annual leave, Ethel and I were married in the Scotch Church in Caulfield, Melbourne. The following morning we caught the train to Perth, Western Australia. The journey took five or six days and was most interesting. Crossing the Nullarbor, a vast, treeless plain, we saw our first Aboriginals, who came on board selling boomerangs and such like.

We spent my leave visiting my brother Leslie and sister Phyllis and their families. Phyl and her husband, Stan Maidment, had a farm at Mylor, half-way between Balingup and Nannup in the south-west of the state. So we took the train from Perth to Balingup, where Stan met us and drove us to Mylor. It was a pleasant, leisurely trip in the train, with several stops on the way. We had excellent views of the bush, especially from Brunswick Junction southwards. During our visit, he asked me to help him drive a flock of sheep to Balingup. I wondered if we'd be walking and he said, 'No, we'll be on horseback.'

I told him I couldn't ride.

'Oh, you'll be all right,' he assured me. 'The old mare is very quiet and comfortable.'

Well, we set off in the early morning and, after riding all day, arrived at Balingup station where we put the sheep in the railway yards. 'You'd better go home now,' Stan told me. He himself planned to stay there overnight to load the sheep on the train in the morning.

I was so tired, I didn't fancy riding all the way back at night but he insisted I'd better go, saying our wives would be worried. He told me not to worry about getting lost, the old mare knew the way. Sure enough, as soon as her head was turned for home, off she went full speed. I reckon we did that 15 miles in record time and I had my work cut out staying on. We didn't encounter a single soul. I ended up saddle-sore and walked bandy-legged for some while afterwards.

I have never ridden a horse since.

CHAPTER NINE

Delivering HMAS *Canberra*

OUR PASSAGE BACK TO ENGLAND, WHERE I WAS TO qualify as a torpedo gunner's mate, was booked on the SS *Jervis Bay*, one of the 'Bay' ships of the Commonwealth Line, which ran a regular service between Australia and the UK via the Suez Canal. We joined the ship in Fremantle and had a very comfortable, two-berth cabin.

Among the passengers was a Mrs Petrie, an artist who was looking after her nephew, a small boy named Donald aged about 15 months. When we got out to sea, Mrs Petrie became very seasick and could not attend to the little boy and so we took over the job of looking after him. She was very grateful and we were very happy to have him. Being a naval man, I was able to scrounge a deckchair from the bos'n, which I modified to make a cot for Donald. This was placed alongside the lower berth in which Ethel slept. I also arranged with the chief steward for Donald to have a place set for him between Ethel and me in the dining saloon so that he could have his meals with us instead of him having to go to the children's dining room. The other passengers used to ask how our son was getting on and at first this was a bit embarrassing, with us being newly-weds, but they soon learned the true set-up.

An amazing thing happened at Fremantle. Just as Mrs Petrie was about to step off the gangway and step ashore, the ship gave a slight lurch. It seemed as if she would fall between the ship and the wharf, to be injured or even killed. However, it was almost as if an unseen hand pulled her back and she regained hold of the manropes. Ethel and I both saw this happen and remarked to her how fortunate she was not to have been seriously injured. In a conversation a few days later, she explained to us that she was a Rosicrucian. According to her, some Rosicrucians had knowledge of the transmutation of metals and could project thoughts and physical powers over great distances. She made the extraordinary claim that she had been saved from falling by a Mr Davidson, a member of her order based in Ceylon. When we reached Colombo, Mrs Petrie invited us to go ashore with her to meet Mr Davidson. After greeting us, the first thing he said to her was: 'That was a near squeak you had on the gangway at Fremantle!' And without hesitation, she replied: 'Yes, thank you for helping me.' This was extraordinary. There was no way she could have informed him about what happened before our arrival – we were ashore well before the mail was landed, much less sorted and delivered.

Rosicrucianism began in the Middle Ages and enjoyed a resurgence at the end of the nineteenth century when mysticism became popular across all classes of society. The popularity of 'otherworldly' movements was heightened during the First World War, as many families struggled to come to terms with the grief of losing a loved one in a distant battle.

Rosicrucianism centres on the power of higher thinking and esoteric wisdom. Most of its branches use the symbol of the rose, or rosy cross, as their emblem.

Later on, when I was stationed in Glasgow at John Brown's Shipyard, standing by HMAS *Australia* and *Canberra*, we went to visit Mrs Petrie, who lived nearby. In the room where she entertained us were a number of budgerigars, flying around freely and every so often settling on one's head or shoulders. It was most disconcerting and demonstrated once again how eccentric she was, though she was very kind. We did not see Donald again, however. By this time, we had a baby of our own, Daphne Joan.

Daphne was our pride and joy. Born on 13 December 1927 in the Naval Maternity Hospital, Southsea, Portsmouth, she arrived when the ground was covered with snow. At this time we had two older ladies, Miss Carpenter and Miss Messenger, as neighbours in Elm Cottage, Southsea. They made quite a fuss of Daphne. I was allowed to spend most nights and weekends ashore when I was at *Vernon*, which was considerate of the navy hierarchy. Poor Daphne, coming into this world on the day of a blizzard. Being the daughter of a sailor, she had to get used to moving about from an early age. The first stop after her birth was Scotland.

Our Clydebank flat was just outside the shipyard gates, in Dalmuir. One day, after Ethel had gone out to do a little shopping, she discovered she had locked her door key inside. So she went to the nearest police station where the sergeant said to her, 'Don't worry, Madam, I'll open it for you.'

'How?' she asked.

'With this key, I can open any door from here to Glasgow!' He went along with her and, sure enough, promptly opened it with his magic key. The Glasgow police stocks went up a few points in our household, as Ethel had been having visions of pushing the pram into the shipyard to find me if they hadn't been able to help.

The *Australia* and the *Canberra* were built by the same firm and on adjacent sets of stocks, so that we could walk from one ship to the other, a distance of about 20 yards. We had plenty to do. One of our duties was to weigh every piece of equipment coming into the ship in order to conform to the Washington Treaty, which demanded a 10,000-ton limit for cruisers. We also had to see that each item was properly installed. When naval ships are built by private firms rather than in naval dockyards, a certain number of personnel, both officers and men, are detailed to 'stand-by' to supervise their construction. When such a ship is completed, she is taken to sea for trials; her gear is tested, first by the dockyard personnel and then by the naval men.

The *Australia* was completed first, so she did her trials three months before the *Canberra*. These went well for *Australia* but the same could not be said for the *Canberra*. During rudder trials, the captain had the ship going full speed ahead at 32 knots and ordered 'full speed astern both engines'. When this was accomplished, he ordered 'hard a'port'. And when this had taken maximum effect, he ordered 'hard a'starboard'. His aim was to turn the ship this way and that, to see how it responded. The effect of this manoeuvre was that the whole rudder lifted approximately 12 inches, causing very severe damage to the steering engine and structural work aft, necessitating going back into dry dock for over a week to get the defect rectified. After that, the trials were successful.

The final tests were carried out on the ship's gunnery and torpedo equipment. Specially trained crews from Portsmouth Naval Depot were sent up for the trials of the new armaments, which went off well. On completion of all the testing scheduled for us, we commissioned in July 1928 and joined up with the British Atlantic Fleet for shakedown exercises.

During this time, we spent a period at Invergordon, and Ethel, who had been staying with her mother at Elgin, in Morayshire, came up with Daphne to visit me. Since we were to be operating from there for a few weeks, I obtained our commander's permission to go ashore each afternoon with the postman who collected our mail, and to return with him after his morning trip. All my messmates said I was extremely lucky to be granted native leave in this manner, and I thought so too.

Claude seems happy with his treatment in the Royal Navy. There's no indication that he believed he was underpaid, or that pay or working conditions were the motivation for his move to Australia.

However, there was an undercurrent in the Royal Navy among men who were sore at the treatment they received from the government. That included men on HMS *Valiant, one of the ships on which Claude had served.*

At the end of the war, stokers and able seamen discovered they were paid considerably less than their counterparts in the American navy. More than that, their pay packets seemed slim as compared with those of munitions workers in civvy street.

A new pay structure introduced in 1919 elevated able seamen's daily pay from one shilling eight pence to four shillings. 'An old scandal, which lay heavily on the nation, has at last been removed,' declared the Daily Telegraph.

But spending among seamen soon caused concern. The head of the Naval Personnel Committee wrote: 'Undoubtedly the lower decks are very well off. Some of the higher ratings keep motor bicycles and can afford to take the more expensive seats at local entertainments and their meals at places which officers patronise. In some cases, they are able to buy their houses . . .'

He was probably also mindful of the fact that many of the revolutions that swept through Europe after the First World War had been fomented by disconsolate sailors. It wouldn't do to permit them airs and graces.

In 1925, navy pay was dramatically cut. While existing personnel stuck to the raised rates, new recruits were to earn even less than the crews that came home from war back in 1919. It meant that men working side by side on the same job received different pay. However, Claude's pay packet would not have been affected. After he transferred to the RAN, there was worse to come for his erstwhile colleagues.

During an economic crisis which crippled Britain in 1931, those whose wages had thus far been protected were exposed to pay cuts of about 10 per cent. This was an economy too far, according to many sailors serving at Invergordon.

On 11 September 1931, ten warships of the Atlantic Fleet berthed in the Cromarty Firth. They were flagship HMS Hood, HMS Adventure, HMS Dorsetshire, HMS Malaya, HMS Norfolk, HMS Repulse, HMS Rodney, HMS Valiant, HMS Warspite and HMS York.

After a spell at sea, the men aboard had access to newspapers in which talk of pay cuts was rife. A letter from the Admiralty read out to some crews soon afterwards explained the reasons why their wage packets were going to become leaner. But not all ships received the letter and many sailors got wind of what was happening through gossip, without the accompanying explanation. Hearing rumours of an imminent pay cut, disgruntled sailors gathered on a local football pitch to protest. Officers felt a chill when they heard men leaving the gathering singing 'The Red Flag'. There was another protest meeting in the canteen at the base. Within four days, a number of the battleships found themselves unable to put to sea after sailors refused to obey instructions.

Men gathered on the forecastles of ships to catcall at officers, who vainly tried to regain the initiative. On HMS Rodney, a piano was wheeled out and the sailors sang lustily with tuneful accompaniment.

It was time for officers of quality to step to the fore to pour oil on troubled waters. Alas, some added fuel to the fire with their absurd comments. One pointed out to sailors below deck that he too was suffering in the Depression – indeed, he had written to his wife telling her to sack one of the maids. Another told hard-

up sailors they should send their wives out to work in order to raise household income. There was an alarming lack of officers who could muster the common touch when necessary. Most were convinced that the agitation was orchestrated by communists and should be harshly suppressed. For the most part, officers inhabited a different world from the men in a class-ridden service that showed no sign of changing.

For all their protests, the sailors never resorted to violence. This counted in their favour when the episode came to an end. The sailors themselves refrained from using the term 'mutiny'. For them, it was merely a bellow against injustice.

Eventually, the government accepted a naval recommendation that softened the effect of the pay cut for the worst-paid. With this sop came the warning that further action by the men would be brutally put down. Admiral John Kelly was appointed to restore order among crews of the Atlantic Fleet (later known as the Home Fleet).

Not everyone got away scot-free. Organisers of the protest were jailed and 200 men of the fleet were purged from the Service. Several hundred others from elsewhere in the navy, who were considered a security risk, were also discharged.

As for the officers, many found their careers effectively at an end, with top brass finally realising that calibre in the higher ranks had been questionable.

From Invergordon, we were sent to Plymouth to carry out experimental torpedo running for the RN. This was necessary, as the torpedo tubes in this class of ship were much higher above the water-line than in previous cruisers and our torpedoes were sometimes damaged due to the height they had to fall before reaching the water. We eventually obviated this with several modifications, for which we were complimented. The Royal Navy finally had a dozen or so of this class of ship, and very fine ships they were.

From Plymouth we sailed for Australia via West Africa, where we spent some time off Nigeria doing speed trials under tropical conditions. During one of these, the electric fan for No. 1 boiler room failed and the heat down there was so excessive that the men repairing it were only allowed to stay for 20 minutes at a time. However, we got it going again and all was well, though it is not much fun doing speed trials at or near the equator.

On one occasion, at anchor off Sekondi on the Gold Coast

Wyre Piddle, 2005.

Madeline Winn and Harry Choules,
mother and father of Claude.

Les Choules (left) and
Douglas Choules (right).

TS *Mercury*, Hamble River,
Southampton Water, 1915.

Claude Stanley Choules aged 14.

Claude aged 14 after he joined
TS *Mercury*.

Claude aged 16, 1917.

Claude, 1918, during his time
on HMS *Revenge*.

HMS *Revenge*. (Royal Navy Archives)

HMS *Revenge* landing party, Black Sea, 1919.

HMS *Eagle*. (Royal Navy Archives)

Landing Seaman Claude Choules of
HMS *Eagle*, 1923.

Claude and his future wife – Ethel Wildgoose
– on board SS *Diogenes*.

Claude in Scotland, July 1927.

Claude on board HMAS *Canberra*, 1929.

Claude, Chief Petty Officer in the
Royal Australian Navy, 1936.

Claude and Les Choules
in England, 1941.

Claude and Ethel at home,
April 1945.

The family
at Anne's wedding,
St John's, Fremantle,
17 December 1949.

Garden Island:
John Edinger and
Claude Choules
craypot setting while
the children watch.

(Ghana), I asked the commander for permission to take away two cutters and go inshore with the seine net to a likely stretch of beach, to see if we could catch some fish for the ship's company. About two miles distant from this seemingly deserted beach, out went the net. It was being hauled in by the lads – about 30 of them, singing out as sailors do when hauling on ropes – when we noticed, peering at us out of the dense forest that fringed the beach, a large number of men wearing loin cloths. As the bag of the net neared the shore, the locals gained confidence and came out onto the beach. Then, at our invitation, they clapped onto the ropes and helped us, hauling and singing with the best of us. We had very good luck and in two hauls had enough fish to feed the ship's company of over 700 men. We offered the locals some of the catch but they declined everything apart from a couple of large stingrays, which they proceeded to squabble over. On being asked what they required them for, they said, 'the stings', which they apparently used as needles for sewing animal skins.

In several places we anchored off the West African coast, we saw fishermen in small dugout canoes, sometimes several miles out to sea, using their cast nets. The fisherman would stand in his canoe gazing around, and, on sighting the ripple of a fish, he would paddle rapidly towards it. At the right moment he'd cast his net out to encircle the fish. This was a most ingenious method of fishing, carried out by very good sailors. They did not seem to resent us taking their fish in our seine net, which we did on more than one occasion and on more than one stretch of beach, though we always gave the stingrays to the locals. I think they liked to help us haul the net mainly so that they could take part in the singing.

I went ashore at Lagos, in the Bight of Benin, Nigeria, with some messmates, to go into a hotel for a refreshment. There, a diminutive Scotsman came up to us, introduced himself and bought us a drink. In the course of the evening, we returned the favour, noticing that the barman handed him the whisky bottle for him to pour his own drink. He said he always had his own bottle with his name on it. When one was finished, his name was placed on a new one. He was dressed, as we were, in tropical rig, the climate being very oppressive.

His profession was construction engineer and he invited us to go out with him to pay one of his road-making gangs. His big car had been left outside the hotel in the charge of his African driver. When we went out, the man was nowhere to be seen but in a few seconds he appeared. The driver's boss immediately gave him a smack on the jaw, saying, 'I told you not to leave the car.' The driver showed no resentment at this treatment, though he would have made three of his boss and in a fight could have defeated him with one hand tied behind his back. Fortunately, the money was intact and we had a very interesting trip. The engineer told us he had another big gang to pay the next day. Lagos was a very progressive and expanding port at that time.

From West Africa, we proceeded to Cape Town and to Simon's Town, South Africa's Naval Base. At Cape Town, we climbed to the top of Table Mountain and enjoyed a marvellous view of the surrounding countryside and the ocean. Then we went to Durban on the east coast, where we stayed for a couple of weeks. Here, I learned to ride a board in magnificent surf rolling in across the Indian Ocean. I went ashore every day that I was allowed, six out of seven, and spent the day surfing. The board was simply a piece of marine plywood, about 4 foot 6 inches long and 18 inches wide, rounded at the leading end and slightly curved up. After being dumped several times and getting severely bruised, we watched the locals carefully to see how they managed. There was an old wooden jetty adjacent to the surfing beach, and the trick was to walk out along this to a point beyond where the waves were breaking. Then the challenge was to throw the board in, dive after it, grab it and hold it in one hand whilst looking over the shoulder watching for the right wave to come along. We soon got the hang of it and found it most exhilarating. We hired the boards for threepence a day. The black Africans had to use a separate beach from us, which we thought strange and unnecessary.

Today it is a multi-million-pound industry but surfing existed at least as long ago as the eighteenth century, although without the bells and whistles that accompany board and wetsuit design now.

In records that came back after Captain James Cook's final voyage in 1779, there's a description of islanders surfing off Hawaii:

> *The men, sometimes 20 or 30, go without the swell of the surf and lay themselves flat upon an oval piece of plank about their size and breadth. They keep their legs close on top of it and their arms are used to guide the plank. They wait the time of the greatest swell that sets on shore and altogether push forward with their arms to keep on its top. It sends them in with a most astonishing velocity and the great art is to guide the plank so as always to keep it in a proper direction on the top of the swell and as it alters its direct . . . The greatest number are generally overtaken by the break of the swell, the force of which they avoid, diving and swimming under the water out of its impulse. By such like exercises, there men may be said to be almost amphibious . . . The above diversion is only intended as an amusement, not a trial of skill and in a gentle swell that sets on must I conceive be very pleasant, at least they seem to feel a great pleasure in the motion which this exercise gives.*

The presumption is that surfing arrived with or evolved from the Polynesian colonisers of the Hawaiian islands. Men would generally surf on boards as long as 12 feet while their chiefs rode waves on different, designated beaches on boards perhaps twice that size.

Westerners were slow to embrace the sport, however. Missionaries who visited Hawaii in the nineteenth century discouraged surfing – one of many ritualistic and sporting pastimes of which they disapproved. The sport of surfing survived in a contracted form.

Writer Mark Twain visited Hawaii in 1866 and unsuccessfully tried surfing. 'I got the board placed right and at the right moment, too; but missed the connection myself. The board struck the shore in three-quarters of a second without any cargo and I struck the bottom about the same time, with a couple of barrels of water in me.'

Another writer, Jack London, helped to reverse the failing fortunes of the sport in 1907 when he published A Royal Sport: Surfing in Waikiki. *His observations about one of the wave riders he witnessed were so powerful that a business magnate invited London to display his surfing skills on the Californian cost, and surfing took off as a sport in the USA. In the years since then, particularly since the 1960s, surfing has become popular around the globe.*

The mode of travel in Durban was not by taxi, but by rickshaw. The rickshaw men were all decked out in ornamented white tunics, white shorts and stockings, and elaborate head-dresses with wide-spreading bullock horns. We used to offer them extra pay if they won the race back to the ship against their mates and they would tear away as if their life depended on it.

After about 14 days in Durban, we were pretty proficient at surfing and sorry to leave those wonderful beaches. We sailed from Durban to Fremantle, then on to Adelaide, Melbourne and Sydney, where we received very warm welcomes. Our sister ship, *Australia*, had travelled via America and the Panama Canal and their ship's company reported a very happy trip.

CHAPTER TEN

Exploits Aboard the *Canberra*

AFTER CARRYING OUT SQUADRON EXERCISES, *CANBERRA* left Sydney to travel north about to Fremantle, where she represented the RAN in Western Australia's 1929 Centenary celebrations. We made several stops in the Great Barrier Reef, then sailed to Thursday Island, north of Cape York in the Torres Strait, where we spent a couple of most interesting days.

Our programme, as shown on the ship's company notice board, reported that we were due to leave Thursday Island at 2200 hours on 13 September 1929 – a Friday the 13th. The sailors all said that this would bring bad luck, a common nautical superstition. There was so much talk of it since leaving Sydney, that word eventually reached the commander, who was second-in-command. A request was then made to the captain, asking that we delay our departure by two hours and one minute, so leaving Thursday Island on Saturday, the 14th. The captain pooh-poohed the idea with the words, 'Our programme shows we leave on Friday the 13th and that's what we shall do.' Accordingly, we sailed as per programme, to our next port of call, Darwin, where we stayed a few days before proceeding to Broome, in Western Australia.

My special duty, prior to the ship getting under way, was to test all sea communications and to see that all special sea communication men were at their stations. Once this was done, I could relax. On the morning we left Broome, we had been under way for about 20 minutes with engines doing revolutions for 12 knots, and I was alone in the petty officer's bathroom having a shower when I heard a tremendous clatter along the ship's hull. It sounded like machine-gun fire, but louder. My first thought was that the port bower anchor had been slipped and that I was hearing the cable rushing along the hull as it tore out of the cable locker.

The next second I heard the order piped, 'Clear lower deck.'

As I rushed out of the bathroom, I hailed a leading seaman dashing past.

'What's wrong?' I asked.

'We're aground!' he replied.

I slipped into an overall suit and dashed on deck, where the order was given: 'Everybody aft!'

With the band playing, we jumped ship – literally. Everybody jumped in unison as the engines were run full astern in an effort to shift the ship. She failed to come off, so we were all ordered to go for'd and repeat the performance. This failed also, so we went aft again and this time, with more prolonged jumping, she came off.

We returned slowly to Broome, where a thorough examination of the damage was made. It was found that, when the ship grounded, luckily on a sandbank, the outer shell plates of the hull for'd were forced up towards the inner plating of the double bottoms. So the noise I'd heard was the rivets being sheared on the frames between the inner and outer plating. Some of the inner plating was distorted, causing considerable leaking. To allay this, we shipped all the bagged cement available in the town, which stopped the leaks sufficiently for our pumps to control the situation.

We carried on round to Fremantle, where we were joined by the engineer rear admiral from the RAN dockyard, Sydney. He ordered more cement to be placed in the damaged area. After our re-enactment of the landing of Captain Fremantle on Fremantle Esplanade, we carried on to Sydney, where we went into dry dock. Here, repairs to our hull were made at a cost of £30,000. The captain and navigating officer were reprimanded over the incident and the lads all said: 'We told him something unlucky would happen to the ship if we sailed on the 13th.'

Not long after this incident, we had a bit of strife in my mess over its president, who was always the senior petty officer. In our case the senior PO had recently joined the RAN from the RN for two years on loan, as I and many others had done previously. He was a West Countryman from Plymouth, and nearly due to retire on pension. Thus, he was very senior to any of my 44 messmates. But he was also very heavy-handed and became unpopular, so much so that, at a mess meeting, the other men asked me if I would take over his job as president.

I pointed out that, like him, I was a Pom and was not even the next senior PO. They replied that those things didn't matter, they wanted me to take it on. So, after thinking it over, I said I would, providing they explained the position to the commander and he agreed to the arrangement. I also told them that if they didn't like the way I ran the mess, they'd be landed back with the previous arrangement. The commander sent for me and had a yarn about the affair, saying he hoped I'd have a happy term as president. Well, things settled down and I held the job for the next two years. My predecessor did not attend our mess meetings, which was understandable, and I did not fall out with him; he was a gunnery man and I was a torpedo instructor, so our paths did not often cross. As soon as his two years on loan were up, he high-tailed it back to the RN, 'back to dear old Guzz', as we used to call Devonport and its Naval Depot, HMS *Vivid*.

Shortly after I became president of the mess, the squadron went up to Hervey Bay, in Queensland, near Bundaberg and Fraser Island, to carry out exercises. One evening after supper, my messmates and I were playing 'weak horses', a game for teams of up to ten men a side. Basically, one side has to bend over in a scrum and sustain the weight of the other team jumping on their backs. The aim of the game for the second team is to collapse the formation of the first. It's a bit rough but great fun.

On this occasion, we were having such a good time that we didn't hear the bugler's call alerting us that the commander was doing his nine-o'clock rounds. Both teams were in a heap on the deck amid roars of laughter, so the commander drew aside the heavy curtain at the door of the mess and said, 'This is not very elevating for my petty officers.'

'Sorry, Sir,' I replied. I should have been standing at the door to report, as usual: 'All correct, Sir.'

The commander carried on with his rounds and I heard no more about it, but I made sure it didn't happen again.

Hervey Bay was remote, the nearest person living in the area being the lighthouse keeper at Sandy Cape on Fraser Island, many miles away. It was at Hervey Bay that I made my first acquaintance with dingoes in the wild. We often saw their tracks on the beach where they had been scavenging for dead fish, sea birds and whatever else they could find, but we never saw them in the daytime.

One day I took a party of torpedo men ashore for instruction in underwater demolitions, having, as usual, drawn the demolition drill handbook from the sentry in charge of the 'Official Use' (OU) books before leaving the ship. I had put it in the inside pocket of my uniform jacket, which I draped over the limb of a tree, alongside the channel leading into the lagoon, where I conducted the class. I exploded the charges in the channel, which was full of fish, many of which were picked up by the lads as they came to the surface. After the drill, we planned to take our 'catch' back to the ship, where it would provide an excellent meal for the whole company. On our way back, we passed the *Australia*'s motorboat taking several of her senior officers ashore to stretch their legs around the lagoon. It was only when I got back aboard that I realised I had lost the OU book.

I was very concerned. I thought that one of the *Australia*'s officers might have found it, which might have meant trouble, so I got our chief yeoman of signals – a pal of mine – to make a private signal to his opposite number in the *Australia*, asking him to make discreet enquiries as to whether this had happened. In due course, back came his reply, in the negative.

My next problem was to get ashore and search the area where I had conducted the demolition class. I felt sure it must have fallen out of my pocket while my jacket was hanging on the tree, as I had not needed to refer to the book during the instruction. I managed to get a lift to the lagoon next morning with a racing cutter's crew doing training before dawn. They dropped me at the entrance to the lagoon and were to pick me up in half an hour. I walked up the sandy beach to the edge of the scrub and suddenly saw two big dingoes standing facing me. I pulled up smartly, wondering if they were going to have a go at me or, if I stood my ground, would they shove off? After a couple of seconds they lowered their gaze and trotted off up the beach, much to my relief. I carried on to the tree where I had hung my coat and there was the book, ready to be safely returned to the ship.

The banks of the lagoon were covered with beautiful white sand, home to thousands of soldier crabs. These could be observed marching en masse, forward, rather than sideways, just like soldiers. But if one made a sudden move, they would all change course together and suddenly disappear under the sand. It was great fun watching these fascinating creatures.

On one of our visits to Hervey Bay we watched a school of sharks attack a very large whale. The poor whale would dive first under one cruiser then swim to the other and dive under it in an attempt to stave off the attack. Both ships were at anchor and the whale stayed with us most of the afternoon, during which time the ship's company were allowed to watch the battle. Eventually, the whale swam away out of the bay and into the open sea, still pursued by these voracious creatures. We were told that the sharks would eventually kill the whale, which was very sad.

About this time, we observed a large grey nurse shark hanging around the ship, so we baited up our shark line's huge hook with the liver of a smaller shark caught previously. After much trouble, we eventually hauled it on board and big Jim Mackie killed it, thanks to a couple of hefty clouts on the head delivered with his heavy blacksmith's maul. When we opened it up we found several Ideal Milk tins, two empty 4-gallon drums that had been thrown overboard, together with a whole heap of chop bones – we had had mutton chops for dinner at noon that day. We boiled the head in a big tub so that we could extract the teeth to distribute among the ship's company. I got one as a souvenir. This shark measured 13 feet and was the largest grey nurse I have ever seen. Needless to say, there was no 'hands to bathe' while we were up there. If we wanted a swim, we went ashore and swam in the lagoon, which was mainly shallow and rather warm.

Once, we found a number of small sharks in waist-deep water and some of the Aussie old hands suggested that we try and run them ashore, as they had done in the past. So we all armed ourselves with stout waddies (Aboriginal clubs) from the bush and formed a semi-circle around the group. We beat the water with our clubs as we advanced towards the shore, managing to force three of the sharks onto the beach, where they were promptly dispatched.

On one occasion, we were given a very tough assignment at a small place called Bargara. We carried rifles, wore full marching equipment and skirmished our way through the bush until we reached Bundaberg, about 15 miles away, in the late afternoon. We slept that night in the local show-grounds, in the animal stalls. It was not very comfortable, rolled up in a blanket. The next morning, after a breakfast of field rations, we were marched out of town preceded by our ship's band, which left us on the outskirts. Our orders were to march to the coast at Bargara, where our ship's boats would meet us to return us aboard.

The object of the exercise was to see which platoon would arrive at the coast with the greatest number of men in the shortest time. We had to keep as many men as possible together in each platoon. The heads of departments were in charge of platoons and our torpedo officer, Lieutenant Commander Calder, was our leader. He had selected me as second-in-command, as he thought I was in better nick than our other torpedo instructor, Cock Russell, who stayed aboard.

The torpedo officer marched ahead while I kept up the rear. He urged me to use every endeavour to stop men from straggling, by dropping back with them and trying to spur them on to catch up. Before leaving Bundaberg, we were all told that if we couldn't carry on, we could drop out at the roadside and volunteer vehicles from the town would pick us up later and deliver us to the coast. The march was along a tarred road, in tropical conditions, on a stinking hot day – and we were dressed in blue serge. The torpedo officer only carried a service revolver, without the backpack, entrenching tool, rifle and ammunition carried by all the men. Well, we did not win the competition but we ended up with the greatest percentage of men crossing the finish line. Some members of our platoon were so keen to get aboard, they walked into the sea to meet the pick-up boats. Supper was put on early and we were all excused duty till 9 a.m. the next day. Next morning, I was among dozens of men who attended sick bay with blisters on their feet. To my mind, it was a stupid exercise to put the men through, in that heat and in heavy serge clothing.

Our squadron often went to Jervis Bay for exercises and, while I was there, I sometimes took one of our 30-foot cutters away with a fishing party at weekends. The flathead were plentiful in those days and we would sometimes return with enough fish for all hands. It was great fun. I remember on one occasion leaving Jervis Bay in the evening to return to Sydney. The men off watch were catching big skipjack as fast as they could get the line in, and the fish were following the ship after she got under way. We were still catching them until we had almost reached the heads at Point Perpendicular. We caught so much that we could take some home to our families in Sydney.

I found the *Canberra* a very happy and comfortable ship. There was always great rivalry between us and our sister ship, HMAS *Australia*: we competed in both gunnery and torpedo, and in all forms of sport, especially boat-pulling. Our squadron regatta was usually held in Hobart, Tasmania. These were red-letter days. I pulled stroke oar in our petty officers' cutter's crew of 12 men and a coxswain. We usually won but, if we did, it was just reward because we had to train for months prior to the annual race.

Chapter Eleven

Homecraft and Bushcraft

AFTER OUR TIME BACK IN GREAT BRITAIN, ETHEL ARRIVED in Sydney with our Daphne, then about one year old. They came via the Suez Canal in a P&O liner, and docked soon after the *Canberra* and the *Australia* arrived. We made our home in a flat at Bondi Beach, which was very nice but a bit far away from Man-O-War Steps, where I had to go to get the liberty boat back aboard. After a while, we moved to a flat in North Sydney at McMahon's Point on the harbour just west of the new bridge, then still under construction. This was much closer for me. The Australian Squadron spent most of its time in Sydney, where the RAN Dockyards at Cockatoo Island and Garden Island were situated. So I had generous shore leave when the ships were in port, being only required to spend one night in seven as 'duty on board'.

When I was at liberty on Friday nights I used to go to Rushcutters Bay Stadium to watch the heavyweight wrestling. But after a while Ethel told me I should either pack up going or that we would get separate beds, because I used to dream about wrestling and try to put a head-lock or arm scissors on her during the night. So I packed up going.

When the ships were away, Ethel was pretty lonely, as she did not know many people in that big city. It was much easier for me as I had my shipmates for company. Our flat in North Sydney was quite close to Lavender Bay and we frequently used to take Daphne there for a swim, which she loved. She could quite easily have drowned on numerous occasions, as she would always walk out from the shallow beach into the deeper water until she was on her tiptoes. And she would have kept on going, unless one of us grabbed her and pulled her to safety. We loved to picnic on the beach there.

The noise of construction of the harbour bridge was a bit worrying at first, as they worked around the clock, but we soon got used to it. They built out the arch from the pylons on either side of the harbour, with a crane perched on top of each half until they had completed exactly half, when there was a small gap left. Then they eased away the suspension wires, which supported the weight of each half. There were a great number of these wire cables going down through a tunnel in the earth from the top of each pylon and engineers were constantly employed sounding them with hammers to check the tension. It was possible to get permission to go down through the tunnel and witness this. I did, on one occasion. To support these gigantic loads of hundreds of tons of steel was a colossal job; and then, at the crucial moment, to ease away on the cables so as to join the two halves on a giant steel pin was extraordinarily skilful. The engineers had to allow for expansion and contraction due to temperature changes. Finally, the workers had to retrieve the two cranes perched on top of the arch. Then they had to build the roadway beneath, which was fantastic. Considering it was such a vast undertaking, there were very few accidents on the job. In building the roadway, the cranes were gradually walked back down to the pylons on each side.

The Sydney Harbour Bridge is the fourth-longest single-span steel arch bridge in the world, behind present record-holder the Lupu Bridge in Shanghai, the New River Gorge Bridge in West Virginia and Bayonne Bridge in New York. It took more than eight years to complete after work began in July 1923 and cost more than £9,500,000.

As Claude witnessed, the approach spans were the first to go up, before work began on the main arch which stands at 134 metres (440 feet) at its highest point and weighs 39,000 tonnes. The pylons are 89 metres (292 feet) high. The longest span of the bridge is 503 metres (1,650 feet) in length while in total it measures 1,149m (3,770 feet).

Barges were used to ferry some of the heavy girders to a point in the river where they could be hoisted up by 'creeper' cranes. The two halves of the arch met on 19 August 1930, with the road deck being finished some nine months later. Four-fifths of the steel needed for the project was imported from England. It is also estimated to contain 6 million rivets, 52,800 tonnes of steelwork and 17,000 cubic metres of granite. Until 1967, the bridge was the highest point in Sydney.

Our second child, Anne, was born at the North Shore Women's Hospital on 17 July 1929. Soon after this, I was away at sea for about six months and on my return she cried when handed to me, as she had not seen men around much. However, she soon got used to me and would welcome me just as Daphne did.

On one occasion, when Ethel was shopping in North Sydney, she had Anne in the pram and Daphne, a toddler, holding on the outside, when she stopped to look in a shop window. At the same time, another woman with an identical pram, stopped to look also, only she was going in the opposite direction, and Daphne took hold of the wrong pram. When Ethel started to move on, she realised that Daphne was missing!

She promptly went to a police station close by. The sergeant told her not to worry, as the child would soon be brought in. But Ethel was frantic and wanted to call out the army, navy and air force in a general search. A couple of minutes later, she saw the other woman approaching, with Daphne toddling along as usual, holding her pram. When they met, Ethel played it cool and Daphne never realised she had been lost.

Whilst we were in Sydney, Ethel would often bring the two girls aboard to visit me on my duty weekends. After looking around the ship, we would go down to my mess for afternoon tea and big Jim Mackey, our ship's blacksmith, would pick Daphne up and say: 'What would you like for tea, Daphne?'

Much to the amusement of Jim and my messmates she would reply: 'A boiling negg, please.' Despite their gentle teasing, she would always get her boiled egg.

On these visits, Ethel would bring a homemade cake aboard for afternoon tea but it was always spirited away and we ate cakes baked on board, her cake being consumed at a subsequent party. Jim Mackey would ask Daphne if she would sing a song and she'd reply, 'Yes, thing a thong of thixpence!' As a toddler, she had a lisp and this caused everyone immense delight. She was a great favourite, especially of Jim Mackey's, who was also popular among his messmates and shipmates.

My first engagement in the navy, 12 years from the age of 18, was due to expire on 3 March 1931, my thirtieth birthday. Ethel and I had a discussion about whether I should re-engage for a further five years and decided that I should leave the Service and spend much more time with my family. So I paid off in HMAS *Penguin*, Sydney, on that date.

It was a brave decision. The worldwide recession meant jobs were hard to come by. Perth was hard hit, its wealth being so dependent on primary products like wheat. The value of Australia's exports as a whole fell by a half. Those in work were having to suffer cuts in wages. At the height of the Depression nearly one Australian worker in three was without a job. There were hundreds of unemployed people camping out on the Perth Esplanade. It wasn't until 1935 that the city regained its buzz.

Still, we sold up all our furniture and sailed for Western Australia on the *Karoola*. She was a McIlwraith McEacharn Ltd Lines interstate ship, a beautiful little vessel of just over 7,000 tons, and the most popular on the interstate run. On our way round, we called at Melbourne and Adelaide, then on to Esperance, Albany, Busselton and Bunbury and so to Fremantle. It was a most enjoyable trip.

Built in 1909 by Harland and Wolff in Belfast, the Karoola *worked as a coastal liner around the shores of Australia, one of 164 steamships offering a total capacity of 16,000 passengers. In May 1915, its role dramatically changed after it was requisitioned by the British government. Its first task was to take Australian reinforcements destined to fight at Gallipoli to Egypt for training in June that year. It's possible that Claude's brother Les was aboard the* Karoola *when it left Fremantle. However, Doug was almost certainly already in action. From Egypt the ship headed for Southampton, where it was converted into a hospital ship for the remainder of the war. Painted white and bearing large red crosses to alert roaming enemy submarines that the ship was unarmed, the* Karoola *had room for four hundred and sixty-three patients and spent three years as a berth for casualties. After the war, the* Karoola *returned to its pre-war beat of cruising the coast of Australia.*

I went to work helping my brother Les in his fruit and vegetable business in Subiaco. Because of the economic climate, this did not prove as successful as we had hoped, so I applied for and obtained a job as a prison officer in Fremantle Gaol. This job lasted for about a year, during which time we lived in a small grocer's shop on Canning Highway, East Fremantle.

Towards the end of 1932, I heard there was a vacancy for a chief petty officer instructor in the Naval Training Depot, Fremantle. This was right up my street. After two or three interviews, I was accepted.

Not long after this stroke of luck, we bought a lovely old brick house on a third of an acre in Holland Street, Fremantle East, opposite the entrance to the golf links. Included in the deal was the vacant block (also a third of an acre) adjacent to our house. The house had been built for a Merchant Navy sea captain before 1920. As he had recently died, it had been put up for auction, and we later found out it had not received a bid. Money was generally very scarce. We had to get some of the purchase price from the UK, which meant a delay of about three months, but we did not have to pay any extra. Each block had a frontage of 84 feet and we bought it for £600. For an additional five pounds we bought the Jarrah dining room suite with its six chairs and 8.5 foot extension table.

On the opposite side of Holland Street, Wilson and Johns had a nursery of three acres, so we were nice and private. In those days, the postman delivered the mail on horseback each day from the East Fremantle Post Office with a mailbag slung on each side of the horse. At that time the tram ran from Fremantle up High Street as far as the cemetery entrance at Carrington Street. Beyond that to the east, there were practically no houses, just bush.

My first annual leave in Fremantle fell due at the end of 1933, so Ethel and I had a yarn about what we should do for a holiday.

We thought a trip up the coast would be a good idea so we booked our passage on the *Kybra*, a small, motor-driven, Western Australian State ship on a 14-day return trip to Fortescue Island, a small island off the Pilbara coast, about ten miles out from the mouth of the Fortescue River. The *Kybra* was under 1,000 tons and only carried a few passengers, who dined with the officers. We called at ports on the way up and back and had a lovely holiday, our two girls being great favourites with all aboard.

At Fortescue Island, the ship loaded bales of wool brought off from Mardi Station in the auxiliary schooner *King Bay*. The chief officer took most of the passengers ashore to a beach for a swim, and whilst we were all enjoying ourselves Ethel said: 'Oh! Look at that thing like an eel.'

'That's a sea snake,' said the chief officer. 'Everybody out at once.'

On the way back to the ship he told us all sea snakes were poisonous.

When we were nearly back to Fremantle, Ethel looked for her key to our front door but couldn't find it. I told her not to worry as there was bound to be a window I could force. But when we did get home we found we had left the door from the side verandah into the dining room not only unlocked but open. Nothing had been touched in the house.

Once we were settled in at Holland Street, we decided to try for a third child, who turned out to be our son Adrian. The addition of a son, we thought, made us an ideal family unit, which it certainly proved to be. Adrian was born at St Helen's Maternity Hospital, East Fremantle, on the morning of 4 October 1934. This was at the same time as HMS *Sussex* entered Fremantle Harbour carrying the Duke of Gloucester, the third son of King George V.

I went to the commander of the *Sussex* with a request that Adrian be christened aboard. He and the chaplain happily agreed, so, the next day, the matron of St Helen's and I took him down to Fremantle and he was christened in the ship's chapel, the first christening aboard her. The chaplain gave me a special christening card, a very great honour.

When Ethel brought Adrian home, she tried to introduce him to Bruce, our dog, but all Bruce did was growl and walk away. This was very surprising, considering how attached he was to the girls. However, one day this all changed when the baker came to call. He had come to the back door with our bread and Ethel, who had been feeding Adrian, put the baby down on a bed on the back verandah while she went to get the bread money. Adrian, upset because his feed had been interrupted, gave voice. The baker, whose wife had had twin girls about the same time as Adrian was born, went over to try to pacify him. Whereupon Bruce, who had been lying nearby, hopped up and placed himself between the baby and the baker – growling. After that, the two were inseparable.

We had come by Bruce in a peculiar manner. One day, when we were living in Canning Highway, the girls saw a puppy literally fall off the back of a truck. They could not attract the attention of the driver, so we decided to keep Bruce. He was a cross between a Border Collie and a Kelpie.

He was an excellent watchdog. Soon after my appointment to the Naval Depot I bought a new bicycle, probably the first Malvern Star bike sold in Western Australia. One day, coming home from work, I stopped at the fruit shop to buy Ethel some new-season passion fruit. I propped the bike against the kerb but came out of the shop to discover my bike had been stolen. I reported the theft to the police, but it was never recovered. I then bought a second-hand bike and trained Bruce to look after it – which he did most efficiently.

A couple of years after we went to live in Holland Street, a young couple named Kath and Peter Luff built a house on the vacant block to the west of us. Peter worked for Fremantle City Council as a gardener. Not long after they arrived, Peter took a party of young men kangaroo-shooting in the bush of the Darling Ranges behind Perth. Among them was an inexperienced teenager, not old enough to have a gun licence. During the shoot, in pretty thick scrub at Serpentine, Peter saw a kangaroo running across in front of him. He fired and brought it down, then ran forward to secure it. When this young fellow saw Peter run he mistook him for a roo, fired his borrowed gun and hit Peter in the stomach with the charge. The rest of the party gathered around and, as they examined Peter, they took his belt off and dropped his fob watch, which was in a leather pouch on the belt. They carried him down to the truck and rushed him to Fremantle Hospital where he was on the danger list for a week.

When we heard about this, we offered to lend Kath some money if she needed it and, as a result, our families became very friendly. Luckily, Peter made a full recovery. About six months after the accident, he mentioned losing his watch and said he was going back to retrieve it. I told him he'd never find it but he reckoned he could and asked me if I'd like to go with him. The following Sunday, we travelled by truck to Serpentine and went on a track to the east up into the hills. Soon Peter said we were getting close. He looked around at the trees and said, 'Yes, this is it. The roo ran from my left here; I fired and ran forward a couple of paces and the young fellow shot me and down I went!'

He walked forward a couple of paces and there was his pouch with the watch inside. As he picked it up, the pouch fell apart – the stitching had rotted after being left open to the elements. But he wound the watch and it started as usual. No one could believe that he had found the watch, especially the people who had been with him when he was shot. He was a really skilled bushman.

Peter's father had been a drover, bringing cattle down the Canning Stock Route from the Northern Territory to Wiluna. He had taught Peter his bushcraft very thoroughly. They later had a farm at Popanyinning and Peter took me down there a couple of times prior to the Second World War. We pitched a tent in the bush and cooked our meals in a camp oven. After breakfast, we prepared our lunch in the camp oven with a rabbit or wild duck plus bacon and any of the vegetables we'd brought with us. We raked out the centre of the fire, placed the oven in it and covered it with coals to cook slowly all day while we went shooting.

If we shot a kangaroo, we would gut it on the spot, discard the forequarters, then carry the hindquarters and loins back to camp to hang in a tree inside a chaff bag, to keep the flies away. This would provide our meat for the whole stay. We never shot more game than we could use for meat. Peter showed me how to carve it and also how to make damper in the camp oven. He taught me so much about bushcraft.

Another wonderful bushman was a fellow called Hurtle Nancarrow. We used to go down to Poverty Point on the Harvey Estuary for weekends. Most of the men rode horses to go hunting but Hurtle and I did not ride, so we went on foot – Hurtle in his bare feet! It was Hurtle who taught me how to spot a kangaroo sitting in the bush. I found it very difficult at first to pick out a roo that was stationary, their colouring blends in so well with the surrounding countryside. But by watching carefully, one can see them turn their ears as they listen for sounds around them.

Hurtle usually took his dog, which would sometimes catch a wild pig, hanging onto it by the ear. Hurtle would dash up and lash the pig's legs together with cord, then carry it back to his farm and put it in the sty, fatten it up and sell it to Watson's bacon factory. If it was a sow with piglets, then so much the better. Piglets would follow their mother and in their turn be fattened up for market. The mother pigs were very wild when they had young.

There was a fisherman named Brown who camped at the Point and, if he knew we were coming, he would have a feed of fish ready for us when we arrived. It was there that we first tasted river cobbler – a white fish that's becoming popular again – and they were delicious. There was plenty of fish in the estuary in those days. I recall going out with him one day when we cast the net and hauled in eleven boxes of King George whiting in one haul. Another time it would be herring, cobbler or skipjack; quite fantastic. Sometimes he would lend us his dinghy and we would go across the estuary to the south side, land there and then walk across to Lake Clifton. In those days, the Fremantle to Bunbury road was just a track along the western shore of the estuary and there used to be masses of kangaroos in the bush between the estuary and the ocean.

Some of the other men in the party were married with children and would take their families with them, as we often did. Ethel would make a big pot of soup, which we took in a large thermos that held about half a gallon. As soon as we arrived at the campsite, she would give each child a cup of soup, to warm them up while the adults pitched camp. Sometimes, we went to Dwellingup and hunted in very dense bush. Once, on returning to camp, we stopped at an old, abandoned sawmill where there was a peach tree with fruit, which we picked and ate. I stayed on a while and the rest carried on back to camp, which was only about a quarter of a mile away. A few minutes after they'd gone, I decided to follow and found I didn't know the way! After trying in several directions, I did what Peter had always told us to do if lost, fire two shots in rapid succession, and stay put. When I did this, the party was just settling down for lunch.

Not consciously hearing it, Ethel said, 'Where's Claude?'

'Oh, he'll be here in a few minutes,' said Peter.

Whereupon she announced, 'If you aren't going to look for him, I will!'

At that, Peter said, 'I'll get him for you. If you go I'll have to look for you both!'

He found me and returned with a very shamefaced shooter, to find all the others sitting down to lunch.

When Adrian was at school, he was given a goat as a present. She was a lovely white animal and a most entertaining pet. She loved the hibiscus flowers that grew along our front fence and, when she got free, she would go into the Luffs' front garden and eat Peter's best roses. Adrian and I would play with her and let her butt our hands, and sometimes she would come up behind and butt us. But when she tried this with Ethel, she would say in a stern voice, 'Gypsy!' The goat clearly knew who was boss because she would never actually butt Ethel. After a while, she mated and produced two lovely little nanny goats, which Adrian gave away. Ethel used to milk her and while doing so Gypsy was given some wheat in an aluminium bowl. Sometimes, if she had roamed out of sight, to call her home all Ethel had to do was rattle some wheat in her bowl and she'd come bounding up to her and pull up standing with her nose in the bowl. The small children in the neighbourhood used to bring crusts of bread to feed her. She was a great show-off and would gallop up the trunk of a fallen tree in our vacant block right to the top, which was some distance off the ground, stop dead, then look around as much as to say: 'See how clever I am!'

I rigged up a chain to tether her, securing the end around a round galvanised thimble through which a steel spike was pushed into the ground. This gave her a radius of about 15 feet to graze on. If any of the local dogs barked at her when she was tethered on the road verge in front, she would respond by charging at them but would never go to the limit of her chain. They would run away and this would go on for some time until Gypsy had lured them near enough – then she would make her rush and really butt them, till they went off yelping! Very sadly, we had to get rid of her eventually. We suggested to Adrian that he should try and raffle her at Leederville Technical College, which he was then attending, but he could not sell even one ticket for a shilling! So we had to get the RSPCA man to do the job and I buried her on our vacant block. We did miss her.

Chapter Twelve

Another World War

THE NAVAL TRAINING DEPOT, FREMANTLE, IN THOSE DAYS was situated in Cliff Street, in what used to be the old Fremantle Post Office before the harbour was opened at the turn of the century. The Depot faced Croke and Mouat Streets, where we had a large drill hall with lecture rooms on the ground and first floors. My special job was to instruct in torpedoes, anti-submarines, minesweeping and seamanship. In addition to this, I was responsible for the naval boatshed, situated on the inshore side of the mole protecting the fishing boat harbour. Here we had two motorboats; two dipping-lug, 12-oared and one 12-oared, sloop-rigged cutters; and three 5-oared, single-banked whalers. The cutters were 30-foot, double-banked and the whalers were double-ended, 25-foot, single-banked boats. We also had a 10-foot, 2-oared dinghy. The pulling boats were all housed in the boatshed and were launched down the slipway, and hauled up on rollers by manpower. They were also all rigged with sails, except the dinghy. Our naval trainees were given regular training in boat-pulling and sailing. One motorboat was for general work, but the other was the district naval officer's private launch to take him to Rottnest or Garden Island, or up the Swan or Canning Rivers. On occasion I had to familiarise myself with the navigation of these waters, hence my hands were pretty full, but I enjoyed my job nonetheless.

A couple of years after our arrival in Fremantle, District Naval Officer (DNO) Commander Griffiths Bowen retired, and was succeeded by Commander Baldwin, with whom I had served in the

Canberra. He and I got on very well together. In the summer, I often had to take him over to Rottnest Island for the day and quite often he invited me to take our two little girls with me, and they thoroughly enjoyed the trips. When we got to the island, he would usually go ashore in Thompson's Bay or have me make fast astern of *Pollyanna*, a large motor yacht owned by a great friend of his named Roland Smith, who was commodore of the Royal Freshwater Bay Yacht Club.

Just after Commander Baldwin's appointment, we received a new motor launch as the DNO's boat. She was built in the naval dockyard, Sydney, and she was a beauty. She was 36 feet in length, with a Parsons petrol engine and large brass dolphins fitted on the coamings at the after end of the cabin. This was fitted out with nice curtains and cushions. For'd of the cabin, she was fitted with a washroom and toilet and had electric lighting fore and aft. In fact, she was the most elegant craft in the waters around Fremantle.

She was also a very good sea boat, which was proved in the early days of the Second World War when I had to take her to Rottnest Island every day for the first six months. This was to deliver the 'recognition signal for the day' to the officer in charge of the War Signal Station near the main island lighthouse. I used to make fast at the army jetty in Thompson's Bay and an army vehicle would take me to the Station and back.

We had some pretty rough trips, the worst being against a nor'west gale. On that particular day, we were about a quarter of a mile outside the North Mole light when Gus Jansen, in his motor launch *Thor*, who had been travelling ahead of us, taking the army paymaster to the island, turned back into the harbour. It must have been bad to make Gus turn back.

The visibility was very bad with heavy rain squalls, and we were washing down for'd. With no sight of landmarks, I had no way of knowing my distance made good against the head seas and we'd already taken three times the normal travelling time to reach the island. Then one of my crew came to the wheelhouse and said, 'Chief, there's a man aft here dying.'

I replied, so I was told, 'Let him die. Where's Philip Rock?'

Just then there was a break in the squalls and I got a sight of the Rock, my landfall at the entrance to Thompson's Bay. The lad who was 'dying' from seasickness was a relief cook for the one at Port War Signal Station, who had gone down with appendicitis. When I had a look at him after we made fast to the jetty, he certainly looked pretty bad. He had only recently joined up and he told me if he had had half an idea that life in the navy would be like this, he'd never have joined. I replied that he was very unlucky to strike such a trip, and that though he may serve for many more years, he would never get another like it. This cheered him up a little. Once he was quite recovered, he turned out to be a very good cook.

A curious thing happened one sunny day when we were halfway over to Rottnest. One of my crew, Able Seaman Lewis, a Welshman, was sitting on the foc'sle singing away, as was his wont, when he was stung by a bee. This insect must have flown at least five and a half nautical miles to have reached that spot, as the island is eleven miles from Fremantle. Whether the bee stung him because it didn't like his singing (he really had a very good voice, incidentally), or because it found itself so far from home, we would never know.

Taffy loved to take the wheel and, after leaving North Mole light, he would ask me if he could take over. I'd say, 'Yes, steer for Bathurst Point light.' I'd go and sit in the stern sheets and he'd be singing all the way to Philip Rock when I'd take over again. Welsh people are great singers.

Soon after war started in 1939, the top of Philip Rock was blasted away to give the 6-inch gun battery at the northern end of Rottnest Island a clearer view of Gage Roads and so a greater arc of fire. This made the Rock a much less obvious landmark at the entrance to Thompson's Bay. These 6-inch and 9.2-inch guns situated near the main island lighthouse were originally naval guns. The 9.2s had been taken over from the mainland by lighter a couple of years before the Second World War and the navy cooperated with the army in their transportation. When installed, they covered all the seaward approaches to Fremantle. There was, in addition to the island guns, a 6-inch battery at North Fremantle, and on occasion I had to tow a target for them to do a practice shoot in Gage Roads, for both day and night firing. For this I used our No.1 motor launch, as she was more powerful. When the telephone direct line to the Port War Signal Station was installed, it was no longer necessary for me to go over every day, and in any case I did not have the time then as my duties as acting port torpedo officer occupied so much of my day.

War was declared on 3 September 1939 when Germany refused to cease her onslaught on Poland. On the previous day, we chief petty officer instructors had been sent around Fremantle to the homes of our naval trainees to order them to report immediately for service. These men provided naval guards for the Overseas Telecommunications Station at Wireless Hill, Applecross, which was immediately taken over and remained under naval command throughout the war. We also had to provide crews for the naval inspection vessel patrolling Gage Roads, and sentries for the Naval Depot at Cliff Street. The men we were unable to contact were called up by telegram and proclamation over the radio. I well remember 'Buddo' Stevenson, one of our instructors, and I riding our push-bikes around South Fremantle, gathering up these lads. In addition to being fully kitted up with clothing, they were supplied with hammocks, mattresses (horsehair) and one blanket. Those accommodated in the drill hall had to sleep on the hammock and mattress laid out on the wooden floor.

When I saw this, I said to the CO, 'These men could be made much more comfortable than this, Sir, by sleeping in their hammocks slung on wire gantlines attached to the heavy steel upright H-bars supporting the roof structure of the drill hall.'

He replied, 'Can you rig it up, Chief?' And when I answered that I could, he said, 'Right! Go ahead and do it.'

This was where my experience in the training ship *Mercury* came to the fore: there we had slept in hammocks slung from wire gantlines stretched athwart-ships on the main deck. The big H-bars were just about the right distance apart so I set to work and spliced up 3.5-inch steel wire ropes and stretched them across the drill hall, 60 feet, and set them up with bottle screws. The lads were then able to get a much more comfortable sleep.

Another interesting job I helped with was the unloading of the underwater cable from a British freighter. It had to be manhandled from 'A' Shed on Fremantle Wharf to the large brick storage shed in the Boom Depot at the base of South Mole. This cable weighed many tons, so it was quite a job. It was subsequently used to establish telephone communication with Rottnest Island.

Soon after this was completed, I was called on to supervise the joining up of the Eastern Telegraph Cable Company's cable coming into their office on the beach at Leighton, between North Fremantle and Cottesloe. To seaward of the low water mark, about 80–100 yards out, there is a line of limestone reef called Mudurup Rocks, which drops away into deep water. So the cable, in bad weather, used to saw on this sharp edge of rock and chafe through, even though its outer diameter was about 2½ to 3 inches and is protected with a covering of ¼-inch special steel wires.

The officer in charge told me that this reef has been the cause of much trouble in the past, and in wartime it was essential for them to keep communications open. The Telegraph Company's ship found the break and secured the seaward part of the cable to a barge, which was anchored. I took two 30-foot cutters and crews, with extra hands, round from the naval boatshed under tow by our motor workboat. First of all, we picked up the inshore end of this heavy cable by hand and supported it with 44-gallon drums, then we walked it ashore onto the beach.

Among our naval trainees we had several young men who were members of Surf Lifesaving clubs and, therefore, excellent swimmers. I told them to search the beach in the vicinity of the cable station to see if they could find a break in the reef where the sand led straight out into deep water. They found such a place about 100 yards north of the station and showed it to me. I then had a yarn with the officer in charge to see if he had a spare length of cable sufficient to reach this point, and then to travel out to join up with the seaward end of the cable.

He had the extra length so, with about 100 of our lads, I manhandled this cable up the beach and, with the aid of the 44-gallon drums, out to the barge, where it was spliced. To do this, we stripped back the armouring and insulation for about 20 feet at each end, and finally reached the inner core. This was two pairs of copper wires, about ⅛-inch diameter, insulated with rubber and gutta-percha. To make the junctions, we hand-picked men specially selected because they did not perspire freely, and they were not allowed to do any manual work that might have damaged their hands. They worked under a tent erected on the deck of the big barge. Here, the insulation of the copper cores was pared back and the copper wires were soldered together so as to make a solid copper rod, which was carefully rounded; each end was then scarfed to make a perfect fit. These were then braised together, the gutta-percha applied and the various layers of insulation replaced. We then lowered the cable onto the ocean floor and the staff at the station conducted a test, which proved successful. The officer in charge was delighted with the assistance provided by the navy and sent a letter of appreciation to the Naval Board in Melbourne and to the naval officer in charge (NOIC), Western Australia. My scheme must have worked because there was no further break during the war.

Early in the war, the navy took over the Elder Building at the corner of Cliff and Phillimore Streets as the Naval Staff Offices, and I was given an office and depth-charge pistol testing room on the ground floor. This was conveniently situated for servicing ships in the harbour.

The navy also took over 'H' Shed on Victoria Quay for the use of their minesweepers. These were coal-burning fishing trawlers such as the *Bonthorpe*, which had operated out of Albany, and the *Olive Camm* and *Alfie Camm*, which had come around from Sydney. I had to train their crews in the use of depth-charges and periodically go to sea beyond the 100-fathom line to conduct live practices with them. It was sometimes perilously exciting transferring from one minesweeper to another in a 12-foot dinghy out there.

About the end of the first year of the war I was drafted to Flinders Naval Depot to undergo a refresher course with the chief torpedo and anti-submarine instructors from the other states. To bring us up to date in the latest wartime equipment, we were instructed how our ships, both naval and merchant, were to be 'degaussed' as protection against the German magnetic mine. We were shown the operation of the mine and how our ships were protected by having heavy electric cables wrapped around them on their upper decks. The current passing through them neutralised the magnetic field normally produced in any steel-built ship. This process was called degaussing.

We were also instructed in the use of magnetic sweeping for mines. This was carried out by minesweepers fitted to tow long, floating cables unreeled from very large, power-operated reels fitted near their stern. These cables were given intermittent, powerful pulses of electricity, which travelled through the surrounding seawater and activated the magnetic mines.

Another technology we were trained in was the use of Foxer gear, for the protection of ships against acoustic mines. This was accomplished by ships towing an apparatus which produced a loud noise well astern and exploded the mine at a safe distance. In addition, we were given instruction in the latest of our own mines, depth charges and explosives for demolition. At the end of the course, we were given examinations, both oral and written, and then returned by train to our various states.

Soon after the course ended, I had to go to Kalgoorlie by train to supervise the transfer of a trainload of depth charges from the Trans-Australian 4 foot 8½-inch gauge line onto a train of the Western Australian 3 foot 6-inch line. This was carried out by a team of labourers recruited in Kalgoorlie and took a couple of days, during which time I was accommodated in a hotel near the station. There were a few raised eyebrows, as may be imagined, at a sailor being engaged in an operation so far from the sea. However, the job was completed without mishap and I returned with the trainload to Fremantle.

To enable me to service ships visiting Fremantle, I was given two riggers on my staff. One had been a customs officer and had been an able seaman in the RAN Reserve and the other had been a stoker in the First World War; the first named Fraser and the latter Reeves. I had to teach them how to splice and fit the special towing wires for the 'paravanes' – anti-mine devices. This gear included special serrated wires, four-stranded, for low-speed sweeping, and special six-stranded high-speed towing wires for destroyers, as well as special seven-stranded kite wires for minesweeping. My rigging shed was in the extensive yard at the rear of the Elder Building, and most of my rigging work was done there, but some of it had to be done on board ship, such as the large converted liners used as troop carriers – *Aquitania*, *Queen Mary* and *Queen Elizabeth* – which could not enter harbour owing to their draught being too great. On a couple of occasions, I had to replace one-inch studded chain used for paravanes by these vessels. When such ships were at anchor outside Fremantle in Gage Roads, I had to organise naval auxiliary patrol vessels to patrol round the troop carriers and drop demolition charges at intervals, to prevent possible sabotage by divers wishing to attach limpet mines to these ships. These charges I fitted using TNT blocks, primers and detonators in our specially built naval magazine and fitting room at Woodman Point, about four miles south of Fremantle.

One of the most challenging jobs I had to perform was to measure up the ship and fabricate a complete outfit of paravane towing gear for the lighthouse vessel *Cape Don*. When it was completed I had to go to sea in the ship and carry out trials. We cut and spliced up all the wires, including recovery wires, took it all aboard and fitted it and then went to sea. Everything worked perfectly. I was very pleased and so was her captain.

I had working with me fitting charges a young seaman torpedoman, drafted from Adelaide Naval Depot. He was a proper know-all, who thought it was a waste of time to observe the necessary precautions when handling explosives. He wanted to use pliers instead of the proper crimping tool supplied for fitting detonators to time fuses. And he preferred standing instead of sitting on the deck when fitting detonators. Sitting was one of our major safety measures; it meant that if a detonator was accidentally dropped, it could not fall far and would land on a man's soft thighs. I told him in no uncertain terms that there were very good reasons for these precautions and that I had met men with fingers missing through mishandling detonators. For good measure, I added that, while on my staff, he'd do things my way. However, he didn't last long and was drafted back to Adelaide, though I did not organise this. He must have wangled it somehow. About a couple of months later, Lieutenant Commander Hatten, Staff Officer, Defensively Equipped Merchant Ships (DEMS), informed me he had received information from Adelaide that this young torpedoman had been killed in a premature explosion. Fortunately, he did not take anyone with him.

To facilitate the handling of gear from my rigging shed to ships in the harbour, I acquired a light hand-cart, which was most useful as it was only about 100 yards from Staff Office to the wharf between 'B' and 'C' Sheds. My office window looked straight onto the wharf, which was very convenient. I was issued with special passes to permit my staff and me to enter the wharf at all times. When the Japanese came into the war, I had a very heavy steel explosives magazine built on the wharf between 'B' and 'C' sheds to hold demolition charges, in case we had to execute a 'scorched earth' policy and destroy all ships in the harbour.

Western Australia had the unenviable distinction of being the first state in Australia to have a mine washed ashore on its coast. Near the end of the first year of war, the naval officer in charge sent for me and showed me a small snapshot taken by a pocket camera.

'What do you make of that?' he asked.

I replied: 'It looks like a mine, Sir.'

He then told me it was washed ashore on the Eleven Mile Beach, west of Esperance, in September 1940. It had been discovered by fishermen, some of whom wanted to haul it up the cliff face by wire rope, put it on a truck and cart it into Esperance to go on display in the hotel there. Fortunately one of them had been in the Naval Reserve in Fremantle and said he thought it was a mine, so they left it until it had been reported to the authorities. The Old Man said I had better go down and confirm it, so he made arrangements with the RAAF to fly me down from Pearce Air Base with a camera man to take some pictures to be sent to Naval Board, Melbourne.

So, next day off I went to Pearce in a service car and on arrival was given a parachute to wear and instructed how to operate it.

When we arrived over the airfield at Esperance, one of the aircrew said: 'There's where we land.'

'What, on that pocket handkerchief?'

'Oh, it's much bigger than it looks once you are down.'

To my surprise, we landed safely and the local policeman took us into Esperance, where we were informed that ours was the first aircraft to land on their newly constructed airfield. We were driven to Eleven Mile Beach, where we found the mine and took several photographs. It was not one of our own and I concluded it was German from the serial number: the figure seven was written in the European fashion, with a dash through the stem. During the time that had elapsed between its discovery and my arrival, someone had scratched a swastika on the lead horn at the top of the mine. To prevent a repetition of this, the policeman and I dug a hole in the sand and buried the mine. To mark its position, we placed a line of cuttlefish up the steep approach to the beach.

I was not allowed to render the mine safe because just prior to this happening, we had received a signal from Naval Board stating that no attempt should be made to render safe any mine which could not be definitely identified. We arrived back at Pearce Air Base and I was given copies of the photos, which I showed to the torpedo officers of the *Australia* and *Canberra* – both ships were in Fremantle for a couple of days. They agreed it was not one of ours and said I should wait for a Naval Board ruling as to its disposal. So the photos were sent straight away with my report, but we did not receive a reply for almost a month – when we were informed the mine was to be destroyed by demolition. Consequently, I had another air trip from Pearce, this time carrying demolition charges.

When we reached Esperance, we found the policeman had gone out to some distant part of his round. He had previously told me that he had the largest beat in Australia. It extended to the border of South Australia at Eucla. When I arrived at the beach, I found that the pieces of cuttlefish had either been blown away or removed by birds or people in the period that had elapsed while waiting for the Naval Board ruling.

I then had to scratch around in the sand with my hands, as I could not use a shovel for fear of bending or breaking the lead horn at the top of the mine, which would have activated it. Luckily, I found it before very long, and then dug a tunnel down alongside it so that I could place the demolition charge under it. I used a two-minute safety fuse, giving me plenty of time to reach a safe distance from where I could watch the explosion, which destroyed the mine. The only piece of it I could recover was the dome with the lead horn, which I brought back to Fremantle and placed in a wooden crate to send in a British merchant ship to the Navy Office, Melbourne. There was a sequel to this after the war. An officer came over from Melbourne and said they'd never received the crated mine remains, and what happened to them remains a complete mystery.

Early in the war I had the job of blasting limestone in a quarry at Beaconsfield, just south of Fremantle. The quarry had been owned by an Italian who had been interned. The stone was used to make roads and as foundations at the naval base being constructed on the Swan River at Preston Point to be known as HMAS *Leeuwin*. I used commercial explosives for this job and among my working party were a couple of lads who had worked in the quarries around Fremantle in the pre-war years.

The Naval Auxiliary Patrol was formed early in the war and consisted of motor yachts with headquarters at Freshwater Bay Yacht Club on the Swan River. Their commanding officer was Lieutenant Commander Rowland Smith. I had to instruct his crews in the handling and use of underwater demolition charges and miniature depth charges specially adapted for harbour defence work. A couple of the Naval Auxiliary Patrol craft were fitted with the full-sized depth charges like the ones carried by our minesweepers. I went to sea on all these craft to carry out live depth-charge trials and, subsequently, six-monthly live trials.

We also had depth-charge throwers installed on North Mole in line with the anti-submarine nets, which were operated by large electric motors on South Mole. Before carrying out live trials on these throwers, I suggested to the harbour master that he temporarily remove one of the navigation buoys, which would be close to the resultant explosion. He refused, saying it would be quite safe, so I carried on and the first explosion doused the light and it had to be replaced by a new buoy.

Not all of my demolition jobs had been so successful. I remember one attempted before the war, at our house in Holland Street. A frog had made its home near our front gate and in the evenings it made its mournful croaking call. This frightened Anne, so I tried to locate it under the hibiscus shrubs and hoped my attention had shifted it. But the next evening it was at it again. I promised Anne I would get rid of it by blowing it up, so I made a small charge of gelignite and placed it right on top of where I thought it was. I covered it over, lit the fuse and in a few seconds there was a loud bang. Meanwhile, the family looked on from the front verandah. I was sure that I had fixed it but almost immediately the old frog started croaking again, as loud as ever! We all collapsed with laughter, so much so that it cured Anne of her fright, meaning it wasn't a complete waste of effort.

CHAPTER THIRTEEN

The Yanks Arrive

SOON AFTER THE JAPANESE ENTERED THE WAR, BY destroying the US Pacific Fleet and their base at Pearl Harbor in a 'king hit' raid, things at Fremantle hotted up. An American cruiser was based at the port and later on a squadron of US minesweepers arrived, fitted with our gear for sweeping magnetic mines, which they didn't know how to use. The commander sent for me and told me to go to sea with them to show them how to use it. It needs considerable experience for the CO of a vessel to be able to judge when to make his turn onto an opposite course while towing several hundred yards of floating magnetic cable, without fouling the cable of his own or of the next ship in line. So I spent many days on the bridges of their ships, saying, 'No! Not yet, not yet!', when they wanted to start their turn. Eventually, they got it right.

We sometimes had a hard time handling these very heavy cables in and out of ships in Fremantle, as we had no powered winches on the dockside. I would get a working party of 100 or so men from *Leeuwin* and they would manhandle the new cable from one ship at 'H' Shed and range it along the wharf, then do the same with the defective cable from the other ship. Finally, the cable was picked up and walked slowly into the receiving ship. Had the cables been dragged along the wharf they would have been damaged, so they had to be carried. To handle the cables, these minesweepers were fitted with a very large winch in their stern below the upper deck.

I had trips by road to Geraldton and Albany to install depth-charge throwers and carry out trials, also equipping and instructing Naval Auxiliary Patrol vessels in the use of demolitions and depth charges.

Taking depth charges to Geraldton for the throwers installed on the mole turned out to be more of an adventure than I expected. We travelled in a Plymouth Utility with the depth charges and primers in the back and I carried the box of detonators on my lap in the front seat. When we got to Midland, we were pulled up by an Army Command vehicle with two young soldiers in it who asked us the way to Geraldton. They told us they were adrift as they had stayed in Perth for a dance the previous night and would be in trouble when they arrived. I told them to follow us till they got to Pearce RAAF Base, and then to carry on along the main tarred road.

We pushed on, as we could travel faster and I wanted to arrive before dark. Practically the only traffic on the road was military – there was severe petrol rationing during the war and the rarely seen civilian vehicles were those using gas producers. We got as far as New Norcia when we had a puncture in the left rear wheel. We changed to the spare and carried on until we got about half a mile past Mingenew when, travelling around a slight bend, we had a blow-out in the spare. We were hopping along at about 50 to 60 mph at the time but my driver, a young stoker who had recently joined the navy, kept the vehicle on the road and did not jam on the brakes.

We found there was no repair outfit to mend the puncture sustained at New Norcia, so I told my driver to stay with the vehicle while I walked back to obtain assistance at an army camp at Mingenew, where I explained my plight to the CO. He quickly organised a team of his men to help and they drove me back, only to find that the two young soldiers we had left at Pearce had stopped, and there they were, repairing the puncture. The spare tyre tube was chewed up and scattered along the road for about 70 yards. I found out this spare had been a retread and when I got back to Fremantle I had something to say about this.

Well, knowing these two lads were in trouble for being late, I took their names and numbers and told them I might be able to do them a good turn when I got to Geraldton, which I did. I asked the naval officer in charge to make a signal to the army CO expressing our thanks for the assistance they had given us, and hoping the delay had not caused too much inconvenience. While I was carrying out the trials, the army CO came along, introduced himself and said he was glad his men had been able to assist. A couple of days later, I met the two lads again and they told me that, instead of being punished for being adrift, they had been commended for assistance to the navy. Had we rolled over, we had the ingredients for a nice big bang with about half a ton of TNT primers and detonators.

This trip occurred in springtime and I remember vividly the magnificent display of wildflowers as we travelled north. In places around Three Springs the road is straight as far as the eye can see. In that gently undulating country, one could see for miles around and the great patches of variously coloured everlastings made a beautiful carpet over the sand plain, still uncultivated. Not so today, when all the land is planted with wheat and you only see wild flowers on the roadside, if the verge is wide enough. Tourists have to travel further north than Carnarvon, into the pastoral lands, to see fields of everlastings.

After Pearl Harbor was bombed at the end of 1941, Australia was braced for an attack by the Japanese. It wasn't long in coming. On 19 February 1942, Japan unleashed its bombers on the northern city of Darwin, where the busy dockyard was a vital drop-off point for the navy and the air force.

A force of 242 bombers, dive-bombers and fighter planes attacked in two waves, killing at least 238 people and injuring several hundred others. There have been numerous claims in the intervening years that the number of dead was in fact much higher. Five merchant ships and three warships, including one US destroyer, were sunk. Another 13 vessels were damaged. The Royal Australian Air Force base was wrecked, as were 23 aircraft, along with the civil airport and numerous homes.

Mitsuo Fuchido, a bomber pilot with the Imperial Japanese Navy, led the blitz, as he had done at Pearl Harbor a few weeks before.

Although Prime Minister John Curtin announced the raid on radio, wartime censorship meant the casualty figures were kept from the public at large. Nor was anyone told about the looting of supplies from the dock, which one journalist described as 'on such a scale that the soldiery openly consigned goods by ship to their home addresses in the south'. The goods included furniture, radios, refrigerators, cameras, pianos, clothes and toys.

Meanwhile, the surviving population of Darwin headed inland in panicked flight. The same journalist, Douglas Lockwood, observed: 'There had never been greater loss of life in a single day in Australia nor, in some respects, a day of greater ignominy.'

It was the largest raid by Japan – or indeed any foreign force – against Australia, but it wasn't the last. Darwin was bombed at least a further 60 times between March 1942 and November 1943. But by this time its naval capacity had been moved to Fremantle, Brisbane and other smaller ports, so the impact of the raids was lessened.

A report into the initial raid on Darwin, released much later, revealed that intelligence about a possible raid was ignored, as were early warnings given about the approaching Japanese flight formation. When it was finally released in 1972 – although not in full – the report painted a picture of chaos in Darwin amid inadequate defences, poor training, a breakdown in the civil administration, a stampede for the safety of the bush led by airforce personnel and a tide of drunken looting led by the military police.

However, it turned out that fears the air strike was a precursor to full-scale invasion proved ill-founded. The Japanese were planning an invasion of Timor and attacked Australia to hinder any potential for Allied defences of the island.

As my work increased, so did my staff, and I was given an old hand rigger named McGuire, who had joined as a stoker. One day we were working very late preparing minesweeping wires for one of our destroyers, which was under orders to sail early next morning. We had loaded the wires into a truck to take us to 'C' Shed, so I said to my three riggers, 'Hop on the truck.'

McGuire refused. The other two were already on board, so I told him, 'I'm giving you a direct order. Hop on the truck.' And still he refused. So I told him to report to the Police Office at *Leeuwin* at 7.30 the following morning, where I took him before the first lieutenant as a defaulter for direct disobedience of an order.

After hearing the case, Jimmy the One took me aside and had a yarn with me, asking me not to press the charge, which would mean 90 days in prison, as McGuire was a married man with children. This I already knew and I agreed to drop the charge providing McGuire was given an immediate draft to sea. I wanted to make sure that he would not come near me for the duration of the war. This was agreed and from then on I did not have the slightest trouble with my staff even though we sometimes had to work very late. If we were unloading explosives from a ship, we often had to work right through the night. McGuire came to see me after the war when he was in *Leeuwin* for his discharge from the Service and thanked me for not pressing charges against him. He told me he had not been in trouble since and we parted good friends.

Early in 1942, the US navy established a submarine base in Fremantle on North Wharf. Not long after this, the Naval Officer in Charge, Commodore Sir John Collins, sent for me and asked how many TNT demolition charges I had. When I said that I had several hundred, he told me to go aboard the US navy submarine parent ship and show its crew how to fit our demolition charges. Then I was to supply them with whatever quantity they required for their submarines so that they could 'self-destruct' in case of danger of falling into enemy hands.

Off I went across the harbour to the USS *Holland*, where I was taken into the wardroom and introduced to their torpedo commander, who had a look at our equipment. I asked what they used. He sent for their chief torpedo instructor, who produced a square container sealed with solder, looking rather like an old-fashioned cocoa tin; it held about half to one-quarter pound of explosive and what looked like a commercial detonator and fuse. When I asked how they fitted the charge, he plunged a slender marlin-spike into the top of the tin, making a hole to receive the detonator. I nearly had a fit at this crude gear and procedure. I showed him our specially tested steel, sealed container with its block of TNT primer and detonator all made to fit exactly.

'How long has your navy had special demolition charges?' he wanted to know.

'Since sailing-ship days, when they had charges to fit on the end

169

of a "bearing out spar" carried by a 12-oared cutter under muffled oars to an enemy ship at night. When the end of the spar touched the enemy ship's side, the charge was fired, hopefully destroying her or causing some damage.'

They were astounded.

I then showed them how to fit our charges to their torpedo warheads.

Later, at lunch, I was served with a thick steak which covered half the plate, and for sweet as much tinned fruit and ice cream as one could wish. It was much more than the men in our navy received.

Next day I took over all the charges they required.

Quite early in the war, I went down to Safety Bay, where a fisherman had reported a depth charge washed ashore on Penguin Island. He pulled me across in his dinghy and we walked across the island to find the depth charge was a 'dummy' that had been fired in practice from one of our ships. Later on in the war there were several reports of mines washed ashore on metropolitan beaches. However, these proved to be our own sand-filled mines, which had been laid in a dummy minefield off Fremantle to exercise our own minesweepers and had broken adrift from their moorings in stormy weather.

On another occasion, we had a report of a torpedo washed ashore near the mouth of the Moore River. I went up in a Naval Auxiliary Patrol launch accompanied by their CO, Lieutenant Commander Rowland Smith, only to find it was a paravane. This had been badly damaged on the reefs offshore and was nearly buried in the sand, so we completely buried it and left it on what was then a deserted stretch of coastline.

Soon after the fall of Singapore to the Japanese, we had a report of an enemy submarine in Gage Roads. The naval officer in charge sent for me, gave me a fix by cross-bearings and told me to go out in one of the largest Naval Auxiliary Patrol launches, the *Hiawatha*, which carried two 250-lb depth charges. I was to drop both charges at the position he had specified. I did this using the minimum-depth setting of 50 feet on the pistols, owing to the depth of water. We searched the area afterwards but all we found were some dead fish. *Hiawatha* got a fair shake up though.

There was another scare when it was thought a Japanese invasion fleet was leaving the Dutch East Indies (now Indonesia), bound for an attack on Western Australia. As a precaution, the submarine parent ships and other naval craft left Fremantle and went to Albany. Meanwhile, I placed depth charges in each of the merchant ships left in the harbour, ready to sink them alongside. I also placed a depth charge at each oil tank in the Anglo-Iranian tank area just east of the Fremantle Monument, so that these could be destroyed if we adopted a scorched earth policy. The naval officer in charge had warned me, 'If you have to carry out these orders, you will probably be the last man to leave Fremantle!'

A cheerful prospect. But, thank God, it wasn't necessary. In the years that followed, my family often had a laugh about the image of me being the last man out of Fremantle, pedalling away on my bike before the charges went off. Even so, it certainly wasn't very funny at the time.

Early in 1943, a torpedo officer was appointed to Fremantle. He was Lieutenant Commander Sullivan, a RAN reserve officer with a degree in Electrical Engineering from Sydney, who had been serving in ships escorting convoys across the Atlantic. He was given an office in Cliff Street and he and I got on very well together. I still had my office and testing room in Staff Office with my rigging shed at the rear, though my staff was increased as at this time there was more work for our ships, both naval and merchant. I was also given the job of testing the depth-charge pistols for the RAAF at their base at Pearce.

I had the rather stressful job of dealing with depth charges aboard ships whose main charges had become unstable due to climatic conditions. These depth charges had to be taken ashore very carefully and then the main charge had to be 'boiled out' to make it safe. We used boiling water to do it.

Our work was not always unpleasant, though. I also had the job of replacing the high-speed minesweeping wires aboard our own destroyers. This was a most satisfying occupation, which kept my riggers and me right up to scratch in our wire-splicing ability.

CHAPTER FOURTEEN

Kimberley Frontline

TOWARDS THE END OF 1943, THE *KING BAY*, AN AUXILIARY schooner, was prepared to proceed north to Broome to clear the anchorage of aircraft sunk there by the Japanese. These were 15 large flying boats that had carried refugees from the East Indies. The day after they had landed for refuelling, the Japanese attacked them from the air and sank them at their moorings. I was sent with a large quantity of explosives to carry out any demolition work necessary. We took with us a diving officer and three divers from among our ship's company with all their gear. The ship was fitted with a special winch to lift parts of blown-up wreckage. We sailed from Fremantle on 15 November 1943 and we were up at Broome for three months through the worst of the wet season.

Most of the sunken aircraft could be seen at low tide, as the tides at Broome rise and fall up to 30 feet. It is quite an experience for a ship to go alongside the jetty and make fast at high tide and then, six hours later, find the tide has ebbed, leaving her high and dry with the nearest water some hundreds of yards beyond the end of the jetty. The bottom of Roebuck Bay is caked mud and sand, firm enough for one to walk on at low tide, and this mud had filled the aircraft in the intervening period.

Our divers found great difficulty in the task they faced as they were perpetually being carried along by the rushing tide and everything underwater was murky. I had to use demolitions to break up the aircraft so that we could lift the pieces with our winch. We often had parts of the wrecked aircraft dumped on top of the hatch-covers over the hold, which was our mess deck, sometimes for several days until we could go out to sea and dump the fractured metal in deep water.

We tried to lift one aircraft intact by placing two steel wire ropes under it. We made the wires fast to bollards on each side of the ship and, as it rose on the tide, we hoped the ship would lift the aircraft from the mud. There was much moaning and groaning by the ship as it began to take the strain. Then the wires sliced through the fuselage, depositing the wreckage back on the bottom of the sea. So that didn't work, which meant more demolitions.

We had only been there a couple of days when our diving officer, the only active service officer aboard, went sick and was flown south by the RAAF, leaving only two RAN Reserve warrant officers, one of whom was the CO, and very unpopular to boot. What with air-raid warnings, thunderstorms and cyclones, our stay was anything but comfortable.

A couple of days before Christmas that year, there was a cyclone warning and the CO took the ship as far as possible up a mangrove creek at high tide, made her fast, then went ashore to the RAAF Base. We were left there for several days – he didn't even come aboard on Christmas Day. It is customary in our navy for the CO to go round the mess decks at dinnertime and wish everyone a Happy Christmas. This bloke had probably never heard of it. If we wanted to go ashore, we had to carry our shoes and shorts round our necks and wade through the mangrove mud to the nearest water tap in Chinatown, wash off the mud above our knees then dress ourselves.

We got to know many of the army and air force personnel up there, as the only civilians who remained after the Japanese raids were the mayor, the postmaster and Mrs Locke, the owner of the Continental Hotel. When they wanted to evacuate her, I believe she said: 'I was born here and have lived here ever since and I'll die here. If you want me out you'll have to give me an anaesthetic!' So they left her, the only woman in the town.

We had our diversions, with Japanese reconnaissance planes

coming over regularly in search of our large RAAF base at Noonkanbah Station, which lay about 180 miles east of Broome and 50 miles west of Fitzroy Crossing as the crow flies. Our big bomber aircraft flew out from here to carry out raids on Japanese-held territory in the Dutch East Indies.

The soldiers driving the trucks carrying stores to Noonkanbah were told never to use the same route on their journeys, but to travel by compass, so that the Japanese planes could not follow their tracks to the airfield. When they came over Broome, we would get a yellow alert but our RAAF fighters would not go up to intercept as this might have given the Japanese a clue as to where the big bombers were based. Luckily, they never found it. Had they raided Broome again, we would have been sitting ducks, as we were often left high and dry at low tide and our only armament was one Bren gun.

When we were made fast to the jetty, I often used to walk over to the hut of Lorenzo, a Filipino fisherman who owned a fish trap. The fish was cheap and it made a welcome change from our tins of 'meat and veg' rations. His hut was very hot, being made of galvanised iron sheets and tucked in amongst the vegetation.

One day, as a friendly gesture, we took him a tin of 'meat and veg' and a tin of fruit. The next day, when we went to visit him at low tide, he was not to be seen at the fish trap, so we continued on to his hut, where he was in bed with bad pains in his stomach. It turned out that he had left some for the next day in the tin. His tongue was black, which meant he had ptomaine poisoning. I left the 'bunting tosser' (signalman) sitting with him and I went back on board to fetch the chlorodyne from the first aid kit. It was a long walk down that long jetty in a temperature around 115°F (46°C) with great humidity. The chlorodyne did the trick and he reckoned I was a very 'good doctor' and after that he wouldn't let us pay for our fish. As a protection for his legs when he went to clear his fish trap, he wore the bottom half of a diver's suit. He had been a pearl diver in his early days.

That same signalman, Con Beasley, probably saved us from being blown to kingdom come by the Dutch cruiser *Tromp* on our journey from Broome to Port Hedland. The cruiser had suddenly loomed up and made the challenge; for some time, our CO could not find the recognition signal for the day but when he did our 'Bunting Con' rapped it out to her by Aldis Lamp very promptly. 'It's a wonder the *Tromp* didn't let us have it,' said Bill Sykes, and I agreed with him.

One day, I was called to a conference with the CO of the Air Force Station at Cape Leveque, Flight Lieutenant Carmody. He asked me if I could help by blasting gun emplacements on the cliff top at the Cape. I enquired if he had crowbars, picks and shovels. When he said he did, I said I could certainly help and next day we set off in an Army Command vehicle with a skilled driver, carrying a good supply of explosives.

The road was not good and in many places flooded by wet-season rains. Our first call was the Beagle Bay Mission, run by Roman Catholic priests who gave us refreshments. We pressed on to the Lombadina Mission, where we were met several miles out by a large group of Aboriginal children, who crowded onto our vehicle or ran alongside. At the mission, we were greeted by a venerable Father who had been there for many, many years. The nuns insisted that we should have a meal. After we had eaten, the children were assembled under a shady tree to sing for us old-time songs such as 'Barbara Allen' and 'Where the Bee Sucks'. They harmonised without accompaniment. After the singing, Carmody distributed sweets to the boys, and strips of bright material to the girls. The sweets he had bought from the RAAF canteen and the material from Streeter and Male's shop in Broome. No wonder he was popular at the mission. Their buildings were thatched and clad with large slabs of thick paperbark, a most effective material.

At Cape Leveque, I stayed with the lighthouse-keeper and his wife, who made me very welcome for the next week. The gun emplacements on the clifftop were to defend a large radar station and airfield which were being constructed here. The Cape was the nearest inhabited land in Western Australia to Japanese-occupied territory in the Dutch East Indies.

Carmody took me back to Broome where I rejoined the ship and carried on the good work of clearing the plane wrecks. This was necessary to prepare the area for Catalina flying boat moorings.

The powers-that-be were sure that, in the event of an invasion by the Japanese, they would come in through Broome, hence the preparations.

On one occasion I had laid a 175-lb TNT charge under one of the wrecks, and had run the 1,000-foot electric firing cable back to the ship ready to fire when there was sufficient water over the wreck, when a severe thunderstorm hit us. It suddenly got dark, as it was late in the day and the ship had just about become waterborne. I wanted to fire the charge but the CO would not let me, as he was not sure where the wreck was. I therefore had to recover the charge using our only boat, a 12-foot clinker-built dinghy. I was furious, but he was adamant.

He told me I could take whoever I liked with me, and so I took our best able seaman, Jackie Mulligan, who was almost my age and had spent all his working life in the merchant service. I had insulated the inboard ends of the cable and left them triced up to the rigging with a sentry to see that no one touched them till my return.

Jackie and I set off to under-run the cable back to the wreck. We had almost reached it when Jackie piped up, 'Do you know where I'd like to be now, Chief?'

'No, Jackie, where?'

'On the lee side of Mum's bum with both anchors down.'

I had to smile, even though the lightning was almost incessant and it was blowing a gale.

We recovered the charge and returned to the ship, which was bumping badly as she became waterborne. Her rudder was damaged but that was quickly repaired next day.

Our clearing work was interrupted by our being ordered to go to Port Hedland. Our job was to attempt to refloat a freighter, which had run aground on entering the harbour. We nearly suffered the same fate. On our approach, the CO was steering straight for a reef. The harbour master made us a signal by Aldis Lamp to alter course, which our signalman was smart enough to see, so we got in all right. We went alongside the freighter and transferred much of her cargo to the wharf and discharged it. When the next spring tides arrived, she was able to float off and make fast to the wharf. We returned to Roebuck Bay to complete our work there towards the end of February 1944.

The man in charge of our engines in the *King Bay* was Chief ERA (engine room artificer) Harry Sykes, who we called 'Bill' after the famous (or infamous) character, Bill Sykes. He and I became great pals. He had a very good bass voice and when we were allowed shore leave, we would gather round the piano in the Continental Hotel to sing sea shanties and other old songs, accompanied by one of our divers, who could play the piano by ear.

On one occasion when we went to see Lorenzo, he had a very big groper in his fish trap. It took the three of us to take it out and up the beach, where we loaded it onto a horse and cart for transport to the Continental Hotel. Mrs Locke invited us all to have dinner at the hotel that evening. We accepted with pleasure and had a very good meal of curried groper prepared by her Chinese chef.

Our cook on board, Syddie Bull, had been a Salvation Army captain prior to the war and had only joined for the duration. Syddie was not much good at camouflaging 'meat and veg' from tins, but he became a dab hand at cooking fish. We had to watch our drinking water very closely, as we only had a small tank down in the forepeak. The water piped to the jetty was bore water, which was quite hot and, being very full of minerals, very hard and difficult to wash clothes in.

When our task in Roebuck Bay was completed, we were flown from Broome to Perth by the RAAF, having first turned the ship over to the Army Water Transport men. There were no seats in the aircraft, only some building materials, including timber, on which we sat. Our first port of call was Noonkanbah Station. When we hopped out of the plane to stretch our legs, it was like stepping into an oven; the plane was not sealed and we had been up pretty high dressed in tropical rig. The whole airbase was pretty well camouflaged and the Japanese reconnaissance planes never found it. Needless to say, we were not long in boarding the plane again and were very pleased to be away from that tropical humidity of the northern wet season, returning to the much more salubrious climate of Fremantle.

Chapter Fifteen

Fremantle at War

WE NEARLY HAD A VERY SERIOUS ACCIDENT, A CATASTROPHE, in fact, in the port of Fremantle during the war. It was a near-miss.

Two Dutch destroyers (N Class), given to them by the British navy, were stationed there. My two riggers and I were working on board one of them, the *Tjerk Hiddes*, lying alongside at 'B' Shed. We were replacing the wire purchase for the torpedo tubes. All through the forenoon her compressors had been running, charging up the air pressure in her torpedoes, alongside which we were working. The compressor was still working when we left the ship at lunchtime.

That afternoon, as I was drawing stores from the Naval Store in High Street, I heard a loud explosion. The next minute the phone rang to say a car would be there immediately to return me to Staff Office. I had hardly put down the phone when a car did arrive, the commodore's own personal car, with the number plate RAN 1, with his WRAN driver, who told me there had been an explosion on the *Tjerk Hiddes*.

When we arrived at Staff Office, I was ordered to go aboard the Dutch ship and vent the pressure from the air vessels of all her torpedoes. RAN 1 took me to 'B' shed, where I found that the air vessel in one of her torpedoes had burst – and all her torpedomen were ashore on leave. I vented the air vessels and then I had to clean up the mess that had been created. When the air vessel burst under the extreme pressure, the forward door had been blown out. This had blown off the warhead, which had been forced down onto the steel deck by the lip of the tube, which had shattered on impact.

Fortunately, it did not explode.

The rest of the torpedo had been impelled through the steel rear door of the tube and gone overboard, doing considerable damage on the way and seriously injuring two shore-side fitters working on her ready-use Oerlikon gun magazine nearby. I found the torpedo pistol on the after Oerlikon gun platform and there were pieces of TNT from the warhead all around. Some pieces, as big as my fist, had been blown right through the weatherboard side of B shed. After all the explosive had been swept up, I had to take it in baskets out to sea in one of our Naval Auxiliary Patrol vessels and dump it.

The pressure in that air vessel must have been tremendous to have caused such damage. It was gross inefficiency on the part of the ship's torpedo department for this over-charging to have occurred. Had that warhead exploded, it would have detonated the warheads in the other torpedoes alongside it. This, in turn, would have detonated the ship's magazines and she would have been blown to smithereens, destroying a considerable part of Fremantle in the process.

I suppose the reason our people did not jump on the Dutchmen was the fact that these ships had been given to the Netherlands navy by the British government. It was a shame when one realised that our lads were battling along with old destroyers from the First World War, such as the *Waterhen* and *Vendetta*, and the leader, *Stuart*. These ships had been tearing around in the North Sea with the Grand Fleet in that war and they certainly made a name for themselves, despite the fact that we used to reckon they were held together with bits of spun yarn.

As it happened, I did help destroy a Dutch vessel, a submarine. It was damaged beyond repair, so we blew it up. That was at Woodman Point, south of Fremantle, on 12 February 1944.

Fremantle became the headquarters for the training of the now famous Z Force that attacked Japanese shipping at Singapore. Their base was near the Newmarket Hotel in Beaconsfield, very hush-hush and hidden away. It was under the command of an RN commander and their instructors were young RN lieutenants who had been engaged in one-man submarine attacks on the German battleship *Tirpitz* in its Norwegian fjord. Their training area was in and around Careening Bay on Garden Island, where they were trained in the use of limpet mines carried in kayaks and also in the use of one-man submarines. It was sometimes called the Special Boat School. These volunteers, drawn from all three Services but mainly from the navy, were sworn to secrecy regarding their work and their location.

On a night exercise with these tiny submarines, one of their members panicked and bailed out of his craft, which sank and could not be found. A signal was sent to Sydney, requesting that they fly over to Western Australia and do a magnetic sweep, to try to locate the missing sub. I was sent to Garden Island to carry out the search and was accommodated in one of the tents at the RN commander's headquarters.

I was there for a week, sweeping the waters of Careening Bay. We found all sorts of things such as old anchors, pieces of chain cable and wire ropes, old paint and cargo drums and even an old ship's galley stove. This was a time-consuming job and needed much concentration. I had to watch the galvanometer constantly and each time we had a strike, a diver in an aqualung would go down while both boats were stopped. This continued for a week, during which time we had covered practically the whole of Careening Bay. Then we received a signal that the sweep, the only one in Australia, was to be flown back to Sydney, where it was required urgently.

A few days after we ended the search, we received word from the Z Force that the missing submarine had been found in shallow water, by one of the kayaks, quite a long way from where we had been told to search.

I learnt a lot from the Z Force instructors. Their commander was a delight to be with and he and I had some long yarns together. It was most exciting to watch the men in their kayaks and mini-subs during their night exercises – they were so silent, it seemed unreal. It was weird to stand on board the British submarine, which was acting as the enemy, and watch the men in their one-man submarines travelling along, with only their heads showing above the surface and perfectly silent. They were propelled by electric batteries and appeared just like dolphins cruising along.

Their first raid on Singapore were very successful, sinking much Japanese shipping, but the later raid was discovered and our men were taken prisoner and executed just before the end of the war. The old island fishing craft *Krait* came to Fremantle to be prepared for her raids on the Japanese and I had the job of supplying her with demolition charges. Her mission was top secret and she made several very successful raids among the islands. At the end of the war, she was put in a state of preservation in the Eastern States for posterity.

Early in the Second World War, Britain created the Special Operations Executive, a secret group that would frequently function from behind enemy lines. Its twin specialties were espionage and sabotage.

By 1942, there came approval for an Australian offshoot to come into being. It was known by a number of titles including the Inter-Allied Services Department, or ISD, and comprised servicemen from Australia, New Zealand, Britain and the Dutch East Indies. It soon divided into two sections. One branch, M Special Unit, placed coast-watchers behind enemy lines monitoring Japanese shipping and radioing-in the information. Although it lacked the edgy excitement attached to some wartime missions, it nonetheless took a courageous man to volunteer for the task. Anyone discovered by the Japanese doing this kind of work was summarily executed.

Other personnel were categorised as Z Special Unit, or, inaccurately, Z Force. Its commandos were trained at bases across Australia.

Having been humiliated by the fall of Singapore, the British were particularly keen to strike back at the Japanese parked in Singapore harbour. That desire eventually manifested itself in the ambitious Operation Jaywick. On 2 September 1943, eleven Australians and four Britons of Z Special Unit left Exmouth Gulf, Western Australia, in a former Japanese coastal vessel once called the Kofuku Maru *and now known as the* Krait. *The men had dyed hair and skin and wore sarongs, so as to resemble Indonesian fishermen.*

After making a base in a cave on an island near Singapore where the Krait *was anchored in relative safety, six men embarked on their covert mission on 26 September. They kayaked into the harbour under cover of darkness and placed limpet mines on the unsuspecting Japanese ships. There was no alarm raised, even though two of the saboteurs later reported seeing someone staring at them out of a porthole above while they worked. Four ships were sunk or seriously damaged, while the men laid low at their hideout until a storm of Japanese fury had died down. All the men were back in Australia by the middle of October.*

Not all outings by Z Special Unit were so successful, however. A year later, commandos were hoping to repeat the success of Operation Jaywick in Singapore harbour. Six veterans of Jaywick were recruited alongside sixteen others. Rather than risk the Krait *for a second time, the men earmarked for the expedition arrived in a submarine, HMS* Porpoise, *and commandeered a Malayan junk,* Mutika, *to sail into Singaporean waters. Afterwards, the plan was to paddle into the main harbour in 'sleeping beauties', electrically powered submersible boats that were stowed aboard the junk. Unfortunately, before that could happen, the fishing boat was challenged by a Japanese patrol vessel and there followed a firefight. Although the plan was aborted, it is thought that some of the men managed to complete their objective by blowing up three ships in Singapore harbour. However, none of the 22 men involved in Operation Rimau came home so it's impossible to know exactly what happened in their last hours of freedom. When an Allied rescue mission turned up on the island of Merapas to bring back the commandos, there was no sign of life, although some of the supplies stashed there had been used. It looked as if the men who had reached Merapas left in a hurry. Now it is believed that a dozen were killed in action after the whereabouts of their base was betrayed and ten men were beheaded after being taken prisoner by the Japanese.*

Members of Z Special Unit were also sent into Borneo, which was under occupation by 37,000 Japanese servicemen. The most famous was Jack Wong Sue, who died in 2009. Having been sent a white feather – the symbol of cowardice – at the start of the war, when he was aged only 16, Sue forged his birth certificate and his parents' signatures in order to sign up for the Norwegian merchant navy. In the middle of the war, he tried to join the RAN but was rejected, probably because of his Chinese heritage. Instead, he joined the Royal Australian Air Force and from there became part of Z Special Unit. He was particularly valuable as a commando for his skills in Chinese languages helped him infiltrate communities and secure intelligence.

Mr Sue spent months behind enemy lines in Borneo and, in his memoirs, claimed Z Special Unit commandos in Borneo killed 1,700 Japanese and trained 6,000 guerrillas. He also wrote about the plight of Australian and other Allied prisoners of war who were treated appallingly at prisoner of war camps on Borneo. Ultimately, few survived.

On one occasion, he saw skeletal prisoners being force-marched by Japanese guards in the jungle. Although his instinct was to shoot the guards and liberate the men, his training told him to lay low. Nonetheless, he was haunted by the scene for years afterwards. He himself returned to Borneo to apologise to the family of a railway stationmaster he had threatened, having walked into the station dressed as a local under the noses of a host of Japanese guards.

With all the wartime comings and goings of ships and men in Fremantle, it was only a matter of time before I started bumping into old shipmates. It started about a month after the outbreak of the war. I was walking in Fremantle when a man came up to me and said, 'I'll bet you don't know who I am.'

I told him he'd lose his bet because I knew he was Jim Luckwell, a messmate of mine in the *Revenge* in the last war. I was right and we greeted each other most cordially. He reminded me that when the First World War broke out, King George V issued a proclamation that any deserters who volunteered were to be granted a free pardon. Jim had come out here in the squadron of RN ships which had escorted the Prince of Wales on his visit to Australia soon after the war. He had deserted from his ship in Sydney, made his way west, and was serving in the SS *Koolinda* as an able seaman. He wanted to know if George VI had issued a free pardon. If so, he said he would rejoin the navy and recover his war medals and prize money. Would I find out for him?

I approached the CO with this query and he discovered a signal saying that any deserters volunteering were still to be treated as deserters. He told Jim to stay in the *Koolinda* because they would be putting a gun aboard her soon and that as he was a gunlayer in the RN he would be captain of the gun crew aboard. He would do just as good a job there as he would back in the Service.

As it turned out, he did. Towards the end of the war, the *Koolinda* was bombed by the Japanese off the Kimberley coast. Her captain, Jack Egglestone, managed to run her ashore on a sandy beach. He then ordered 'Abandon ship' and as the last boat was leaving the ship he told Jim to hop aboard. But since Captain Jack wasn't going Jim stayed behind, saying, 'I'll go when you go!'

The two of them inspected the damage and concluded that they could plug up the holes in the hull. Then, if they could get the pumps going, they could refloat her and possibly bring her down to Fremantle to be slipped and repaired. The captain called for volunteers from among his engineers, who were camped on the beach. They returned aboard, pumped her out and got her engines going again. However, the captain was ordered by the naval authorities to take his ship north instead of south. When she reached Wyndham, she was attacked again by the Japanese and, this time, she sank.

We in the *Revenge* called Jim Luckwell 'Lucky Jim' because one time, when we were painting ship in Scapa Flow, he was on our fore t'gallant yard when he slipped and fell. The captain of the foc's'le and others who saw this expected to pick up his mangled body on deck but Jim caught the footrope of our upper signal yard and hung on. The yard was 45 feet in length and the footrope, rendering through its stirrups, acted as a spring and broke his fall. He clambered up onto the yard and instead of coming down on deck as everyone expected, he went aloft again and carried on as if nothing had happened.

On another occasion, when we were lying at anchor with the First Battle Squadron off the Golden Horn, Constantinople, a group of us were standing on the foc's'le watching the 8-knot tide rushing past the ship when someone said to Jim, 'I'll bet you wouldn't be game to walk off the end of the lower boom.'

Jim asked, 'How much?'

The reply was ten bob (shillings), quite a sum in those days. Jim promptly walked out along the 40-foot boom and dropped off the end into the Bosphorus, fully clothed. By the time he surfaced, he was nearly abreast the after gangway, which he was able to reach, being a good swimmer. On going up the gangway to the quarterdeck, he was placed in the commander's report by the officer of the watch for 'breaking out of the ship', which is always the charge against anyone leaving his ship without permission, unless he is washed overboard or falls overboard accidentally. However, he got off the charge with a caution. Jim told us he was born at sea, as his father had been a captain of sailing ships in the Merchant Navy. He was certainly a very fine sailor, one of the best ever to ship a pair of bell-bottomed trousers, as we used to say.

Another of my old shipmates from HMS *Eagle*, Taffy Jones, came to see me at the Naval Depot early in the Second World War. A former able seaman, he told me he had been a rigger in the mines at Kalgoorlie and had come down to volunteer for war service. He said he remembered me because 'Snowy' Mitchell and I used to dive off the flying deck when they piped 'hands to bathe' in the Mediterranean.

Fremantle was visited several times towards the end of the war by HMS *London*, an 8-inch-gun cruiser. I discovered an old shipmate from the *Impregnable* aboard her. George Harvey was the chief buffer – that is, the chief bosun's mate. On one of *London*'s visits to Fremantle, they gave a children's party with all sorts of games for the kids. Ethel and I took our three children aboard and found George, who was running the coconut shy. Adrian won a coconut, which he proudly took home.

It was very exciting to meet old shipmates during the war. Another of the RN ships to visit was the destroyer HMS *Whelp* and her chief yeoman of signals was an old shipmate of mine from HMS *Impregnable*. I went aboard to visit him and we were invited into the wardroom for a drink. Her first lieutenant was Prince Philip of Battenberg, who was engaged to Princess Elizabeth and became the Duke of Edinburgh, the husband of our Queen. He was very popular on the *Whelp* and later on became the captain of a destroyer. Some titled officers in the RN have not been so popular.

Thanks to her geographic isolation, Australia was an ideal venue for Allied prisoner of war camps. Italians, some Germans, Koreans, Indonesians and hundreds of Japanese were housed behind barbed wire across the continent.

As far as the 15,000 Italians were concerned, the majority were so peaceable that many were permitted to work unguarded on farms as labourers, living with Australian families.

The same could not be said of the 2,200 Japanese, who were restive. Traditionally, Japanese warriors lived by the code of 'Bushido', a web of morality with numerous aspects, one of which meant they were compelled to commit suicide at the first opportunity to escape the shame of being a prisoner. By the same token, they construed humane treatment by their Australian guards as a sign of weakness.

Almost half of the Japanese contingent was held at Cowra, in a remote part of New South Wales. When there was a strong rumour of a planned mass breakout, the authorities decided to move the men below the rank of corporal to a different camp. In accordance with the Geneva Convention governing treatment of prisoners of war, on 4 August 1944 the Japanese were given 24 hours' notice of their departure.

Early the following morning, a lone Japanese prisoner ran towards the sentries in one of the six 30-foot high observation towers, shouting at the top of his voice. Moments later, there was the sound of a bugle followed with a charge by three mobs yelling 'Banzai.' The guards fired warning shots. Then, as the determination of the prisoners became apparent, the soldiers tried to stem the tide of escaping Japanese by shooting them.

The prisoners used blankets to protect themselves on the 8-foot high barbed-wire entanglements. They were armed with improvised weapons, including sharpened mess knives, studded wooden clubs, baseball bats and garroting wire.

A group of four hundred breached the fence, killed two soldiers and turned the guns on other sentries. They melted into an empty countryside, cloaked with darkness. Meanwhile, remaining prisoners set fire to their huts and a number committed suicide.

Most of the escapees were rounded up within 24 hours, largely without offering resistance, by a combination of soldiers and the police. Some had committed suicide by hanging themselves in the trees rather than be taken prisoner once more.

At the end of the episode, 234 Japanese men were dead and a further 108 were injured. Four Australian soldiers were also killed. A military court of inquiry to investigate the incident found that conditions at the camp were fully in accordance with the standards laid down by the Geneva Convention; that there had been no complaint from the Japanese about their treatment; that the breakout was premeditated; that the actions of the Australian soldiers were a proportionate response to actions of the prisoners; and that many of the Japanese died by suicide, or were killed by other prisoners, within the boundaries of the prison camp.

It did not escape the notice of Australians that the Japanese prisoners of war were being well treated, while Australians who had fallen into the hands of the Empire of the Rising Sun were being underfed and overworked.

As I was walking out of Staff Office one afternoon towards the end of the war, a commander was entering, and when I saluted him he returned my salute with the greeting, 'Good afternoon, Chief T.I. We have been old shipmates, haven't we?'

I replied, 'Yes, Sir, in the *Revenge* in the last war. You were a young sub-lieutenant and I was a boy.'

We agreed to meet up after his meeting with the commodore and I showed him where my office and testing room were. He came along at about 1600 and asked if I was free in the dog watches, which I was, so he took me to the Fremantle Hotel in Cliff Street for a couple of drinks and a good old yarn. He was serving on HMS *Maidstone*, the RN submarine parent ship stationed at North Wharf. He had been the second-in-command of the boys' division in the *Revenge* under Lieutenant Commander Drew. These meetings I had with old shipmates during the war made me think what a small world it is.

Like everyone else, I was relieved and pleased when the war finally came to an end. As I used to tell my children, war was very tedious, punctuated by moments of extreme danger. I never particularly celebrated the armistice after the First World War or the end of the Second. I don't like to glorify war.

After VE Day in Europe in June 1945, we were visited at Fremantle by several RN ships, including their latest battleship, HMS *Anson*, and quite a few of their aircraft carriers. These ships required very little from us except food, water and fuel. They were mostly self-contained and self-supporting, but one of them, which I seem to recall as being the aircraft carrier HMS *Implacable*, required considerable help. She had struck very bad weather in the Great Australian Bight and several steel plates had been peeled back on her bow. It was amazing to see this and to realise it had been caused by the power of the sea. However, while she lay alongside at 'H' Shed of Victoria Quay, she was lightened for'd by pumping oil fuel to the aft tanks and shifting any moveable weights aft so as to bring her bow up. Then, with the assistance of our divers and engineers, satisfactory repairs were carried out.

On another occasion, one of our destroyers, HMAS *Nizam,* was severely damaged rounding Cape Leeuwin. It happened at night and the ship was travelling at fairly high speed when she was flung onto her beam ends by a very high sea and ten ratings, including the lookout on the wing of the bridge, were swept overboard and lost. Her motorboat was torn out of its davits and lost overboard. I went aboard her in Fremantle and was shown where the footprints of the torpedoman on watch in the low power room had walked up the vertical bulkhead to get to the hatchway, indicating that the ship had rolled to 90 degrees or very near it. The motorboat's davits were twisted as though they were made of rubber. I was told that the chief ERA in charge in the engine room, realising what had happened, had stopped his engines for a few seconds. Otherwise, the ship might have continued her roll and gone right over! He had done this without any order from the bridge, realising that everyone up there would have been flung off their feet anyway, and so had saved his ship.

The war in the Pacific drew to a close in August 1945. There was much rejoicing in the metropolitan areas of Perth and Fremantle. Ships in the harbour sounded their sirens almost continually and sailors, soldiers and airmen danced with girls in the streets. In the navy, sailors dressed up in their officers' uniforms and vice versa, according to an old custom. And the order was given to 'Splice the main brace' – that is, serve an extra tot of rum to all hands. It reminded me of the rejoicing in the Grand Fleet at the end of the First World War, when I was serving in the *Revenge* and the fleet was at Rosyth in the Firth of Forth, Scotland. Then the officers had danced with the men and boys on the quarterdecks of our ships. It was an unforgettable tale to tell the people ashore when we got home on leave

CHAPTER SIXTEEN

Peace

AFTER THE WAR WAS OVER, WE HAD THE JOB OF converting things back onto a peacetime footing. This work included removing the depth-charge throwers from the harbours of Fremantle and Geraldton and returning them to the naval magazines at Byford. We had to take the ammunition out of all the Naval Auxiliary Patrol vessels at Freshwater Bay Yacht Club, and also remove the demolition charges from Fremantle Wharf and the radar station at Arthur's Head. The two latter jobs entailed removing the heavy steel lockers I had established for the reception of the charges.

Then there was the return of all the explosives from our magazine at Woodman Point and the handing over of the magazine to the State Explosive Authority. Later on, the Naval Stores staff at Byford were sending explosives out to sea in barges, to be dumped beyond the 100-fathom line over the edge of the continental shelf. Among these were some limpet mines, as used by midget submarines. These mines were supposed to sink when dumped, but one of them failed to do so and could not be recovered by the barge's crew.

This was reported to the naval officer in charge, who ordered the boom defence vessel HMAS *Karangi* to go to sea and search for it. I went too and spent a week combing the dumping ground. The ship's CO, Lieutenant Commander J.C. Elley, and I were on the bridge every day with binoculars but the most exciting thing we saw was a number of migrating sperm whales. Searching for a solitary mine under these conditions was like looking for the proverbial needle in a haystack.

In late 1947 the mine eventually washed ashore near Lancelin Island and I had the job of destroying it by demolition. We drove to Gingin, where we picked up a policeman, who took us through a desolate tract of country out to the coast. The mine was filled with 750 lb of Torpex, our latest high explosive, and made a crater in the beach large enough to accommodate a fair-sized tug. I was commended for this work in a signal from the naval officer in charge WA to Naval Board, of which I was given a copy for my own record.

One of the most interesting jobs I had during my naval career was the demolition of the concrete dolphin on the north side of the Fremantle Harbour. It had been knocked over by the ship MV *Columbia Star* as she entered the harbour during bad weather. The dolphin was in effect a concrete block measuring 16 x 12 feet and 8 feet thick, reinforced with steel rods all through. It was lying in 30 feet of water on the northern edge of the swept channel. The dolphin's role had been to carry the huge leading blocks for the 4.5-inch steel wire ropes that hauled the anti-submarine and torpedo nets across the swept channel from the South Mole during the war. There was no floating crane in Fremantle Harbour capable of lifting such a weight, so it had to be broken up by demolition and removed piecemeal by HMAS *Karangi* under the command of 'Knocker' White, a RAN reserve warrant officer who had been one of my trainees pre-war.

I was given the services of the boom defence diving team plus two motorboats, one with compressors for the divers and the other to ferry explosives and gear across the harbour. I was restricted to a maximum charge of 25 lb of TNT on account of possible damage to harbour navigation lights, installations and shipping. If I could have used a 250-lb TNT depth charge placed under the head, my work would have been very much simpler. As it was, the job proved very difficult. Nevertheless, it was one of the most intriguing operations I ever had to perform. It took a month to complete and we only lost a couple of days due to bad weather.

One thing I discovered was that fish, in some manner, are able to tell that an explosion has taken place in a certain area and they do not go near there for some considerable time. For on the day we fired the first charge, we killed and stunned a large number of fish of many kinds, mainly silver bream and skipjack trevally. But on succeeding days, the only fish we killed were pelagic fish, such as blue mackerel, travelling in and out of the harbour. On that first day we collected stunned fish for the boats' crews, the divers and myself to take home a good feed. But after that, we did not see one silver bream or skippy.

In 1950, I was asked by Commander Shaw if I would like to transfer into the Permanent Naval Dockyard Police, which was just being formed, with himself as head. I had served under him pre-war, when he was second-in-command of the staff at the RAN Reserve Training Depot, Fremantle. This transfer would enable me to serve for a further five years in the RAN. He told me I would have to go to Sydney for a course in firefighting, law, police work and atomic warfare. My chances of promotion would depend on the results of exams on completion of the course. I accepted and went to Sydney for three months. It proved very interesting, as we were taught about the effects of atomic fallout and nerve gas. We attended various courts to learn procedures and precautions. Soon after returning to Fremantle, I was promoted to sergeant and remained so until I retired in 1956.

We were responsible for the security of naval establishments such as magazines, oil tanks, naval stores, the shore base HMAS *Leeuwin* and Naval Staff Office, Cliff Street. Our posts were manned 24 hours a day, which meant a change of shift every week. It came a bit harder than ship's routine, where one worked a four-hour watch, especially the night shift of eight hours.

Soon after this promotion, I was called in to see the naval officer in charge. He informed me that there was a mine reported washed ashore near Wedge Island, and asked if I felt happy about dealing with it. Of course I did, so he arranged for me to use a Land-Rover driven by a very experienced able seaman. Wedge Island is about 100 miles up the coast from Fremantle and, in those days, it was quite remote. Our first task, therefore, was to get to the town of Moora, where the police sergeant provided me with an Aboriginal guide.

He took us to the spot on this wild stretch of coast. It was fortunate we had a four-wheel-drive vehicle, otherwise we would never have reached the site through the extensive and lofty sand hills. The weapon proved to be a German moored mine that had broken adrift. I destroyed it by demolition, there being no habitation within miles. It was gratifying to know that my specialist skill was still in demand.

My most memorable job in the Naval Dockyard Police was on the occasion of Her Majesty the Queen's visit to Western Australia in late March 1954, in the Royal Yacht *Gothic*. This was a Shaw, Savill & Albion liner that had been requisitioned and fitted out especially for the royal visit to Australia.

There was a polio epidemic in Western Australia at that time and very strict precautions were in force to ensure that the Queen would not be exposed to the disease and transmit it to her children. The *Gothic* was secured alongside Victoria Quay with naval craft patrolling the harbour to ensure that no one approached the monarch. There were also very strict precautions enforced on the shore side. The security arrangements were placed in the hands of the Naval Dockyard Police and I was put in charge during the night watches for the duration of her stay. I was on duty at 11 p.m. until 7 a.m. and I had a special sentry box at the foot of the royal gangway, with a direct telephone line to Victoria Quay and to Police Headquarters in Fremantle. The only people allowed to use this gangway were Her Majesty, Prince Philip and the royal equerries.

At this time, Adrian, our son, was doing his National Service training in the Australian Military Forces and he was selected as one of the young men to be in attendance at Government House, Perth, as Queen's Messengers. This was quite an honour and ensured that our family was well represented in the army of people looking after the Queen during her stay in Western Australia. Towards the end of that year I was awarded the Queen's Coronation Medal, which I prize very much.

Throughout Claude's working life in Australia, two scandals were unfolding with the mistreatment of children at their heart. Both were probably happening below the radar of ordinary working people like Claude, who clearly delighted in the company of children. Nonetheless, countless thousands of youngsters saw their childhood sacrificed on a pyre of social engineering constructed by misguided do-gooders. The result in both cases was children deprived of love and support and, all too often, used as slave labour to bolster the Australian economy.

In the first outrage, the Australian government sanctioned the practice of parting young, fair-skinned Aboriginal or Torres Strait Islander children from their parents. Usually, the child had an Aboriginal or Torres Strait Islander mother and a white father.

Supporters of the scheme believed it helped in the process of assimilation between Australia's white- and brown-skinned inhabitants. Critics say it was nothing short of cultural genocide. The lengthy episode is now termed 'the Stolen Generations'.

The Aborigines Protection Act of 1909 permitted welfare officers to take children from Aboriginal families without necessarily having a reason to do so. It was widely thought at the time that Aboriginal children would be better off in white institutions or with white families, where they would receive good educations and better health care. Unfortunately, it didn't always prove to be the case.

The children were often subject to sexual, psychological and physical abuse. They were punished if they spoke their native language and were encouraged to fear or despise Aboriginal traditions. Education given to the Stolen Generations was often rudimentary and most were destined to work as either domestic servants or farm hands.

The forcible removal of children from their mothers continued at least until 1969. Although it is not known the exact number of children involved, some estimates claim every Aboriginal family was affected. Not until 1997, with the publication of a report called 'Bringing them Home', was the scandal highlighted. Since then, hundreds of stories have been revealed, including that of Zita Wallace, who was taken in 1947, at the age of seven.

As an adult, Zita put on the record how nuns from a Catholic-run mission enticed her and four other girls on a supposed 'shopping trip'.

'They put us in the back of a truck but we never went near any shop,' she recalled. 'They took us to the telegraph station which was the holding centre for half-caste children from all over central Australia.'

She ended up in an institution for 200 children, run by the Catholic Church, hundreds of miles away in the Tiwi Islands, about 50 miles north of Darwin, and remained there until the age of 19.

'We got belted for speaking our language. We were called pagans and heathens and spawn of the devil. We cooked for the nuns, we washed their big bloomers, we cleaned their rooms. We got just enough education to read and write. The brighter, fairer kids were sent away to colleges or to be adopted into white families but I didn't get selected.'

After the report emerged, each of Australia's states issued an apology but the government remained reticent, preferring to issue a 'statement of regret and motion of reconciliation'.

The arguments against an apology covered a broad spectrum of points. Welfare workers at the time genuinely believed they were acting in the best interests of the children, it was claimed. Many children were removed at the express request of their white fathers. Other people declared the problem was exaggerated beyond all proportion, stating that in fact very few Aboriginal children were stolen from their mothers.

However, a groundswell of support in favour of a public apology finally encouraged Prime Minister Kevin Rudd to say sorry in 2008, in order to expunge 'a blight on the nation's soul'. These are the words he used:

> *Today we honour the indigenous peoples of this land, the oldest continuing cultures in human history.*
>
> *We reflect on their past mistreatment.*
>
> *We reflect in particular on the mistreatment of those who were Stolen Generations – this blemished chapter in our nation's history.*
>
> *The time has now come for the nation to turn a new page in Australia's history by righting the wrongs of the past and so moving forward with confidence to the future.*
>
> *We apologise for the laws and policies of successive parliaments and governments that have inflicted profound grief, suffering and loss on these, our fellow Australians.*
>
> *We apologise especially for the removal of Aboriginal and Torres Strait Islander children from their families, their communities and their country.*
>
> *For the pain, suffering and hurt of these Stolen Generations, their descendants and for their families left behind, we say sorry.*

To the mothers and the fathers, the brothers and the sisters, for the breaking up of families and communities, we say sorry.

And for the indignity and degradation thus inflicted on a proud people and a proud culture, we say sorry.

We the Parliament of Australia respectfully request that this apology be received in the spirit in which it is offered as part of the healing of the nation.

For the future we take heart; resolving that this new page in the history of our great continent can now be written.

We today take this first step by acknowledging the past and laying claim to a future that embraces all Australians.

A future where this Parliament resolves that the injustices of the past must never, never happen again.

A future where we harness the determination of all Australians, indigenous and non-indigenous, to close the gap that lies between us in life expectancy, educational achievement and economic opportunity.

A future where we embrace the possibility of new solutions to enduring problems where old approaches have failed.

A future based on mutual respect, mutual resolve and mutual responsibility.

A future where all Australians, whatever their origins, are truly equal partners, with equal opportunities and with an equal stake in shaping the next chapter in the history of this great country, Australia.

The ripple effects of the Stolen Generations are still being felt today. Many believe it has substantially contributed to a downward spiral in Aboriginal wellbeing. Australia's original inhabitants, who number 450,000 in a population of 21 million, remain the poorest ethnic group and are the most likely to be jailed, unemployed, illiterate and suffer from poor health. Their life expectancy is 17 years shorter than that of other Australians.

The second scandal also resulted in a public apology by Mr Rudd, this time issued in 2009. The children involved were British, shipped out to Australia as 'good, white stock' to help people the vast, empty territories. On the face of it a move to Australia would provide enhanced opportunities for deprived youngsters from Britain's orphanages. Of course, it also relieved the financial burden on the British government and often led to slave labour, and even abuse.

In fact, the British government had been orchestrating organised child migration since at least 1869. Children were sent to Australia, New Zealand, South Africa and Canada to start a new life.

Between 1920 and 1960, an estimated 10,000 children went to Australia from Britain, thrilled with tales of adventure and exciting prospects. They were children from impoverished backgrounds, from broken homes or with single mothers. Many had been placed into children's homes while their families struggled for survival in the Depression or during the Second World War. But they were by no means all without parents. Perhaps worst of all, children were told of their parents' delight at their journey Down Under. In reality, parental permission was never sought.

When they arrived in Australia, it wasn't into the heart of a loving family, as many had expected, but into loveless institutions that were little better than Victorian workhouses. Many ended up doing menial jobs for scant reward. There was no one to campaign on their behalf to raise their public profile. Accordingly, they became known as the 'Forgotten Australians'.

One of the children of the era, John Hennessey, now from Campbelltown near Sydney, was a former child migrant who cooperated with a 1998 British parliamentary inquiry on the issue. He was aged just six when he was sent from a British orphanage to a boys' school run by the Catholic Christian Brothers in Western Australia.

Mr Hennessey revealed how he has spoken with a stutter since the day he received a savage beating from the Australian headmaster. The 12-year-old was stripped naked and flogged because he stole grapes from a vineyard to assuage his hunger.

Mr Rudd began his apology by acknowledging the treatment of British migrant children was an 'ugly chapter' in Australian history:

> *[I] say to you, the Forgotten Australians, and those who were sent to our shores as children without your consent, that we are sorry.*
>
> *Sorry – that as children you were taken from your families and placed in institutions where so often you were abused.*
>
> *Sorry – for the physical suffering, the emotional starvation and the cold absence of love, of tenderness, of care.*
>
> *Sorry – for the tragedy, the absolute tragedy, of childhoods lost – childhoods spent instead in austere and authoritarian places, where names*

*were replaced by numbers, spontaneous play by regimented routine, the joy
of learning by the repetitive drudgery of menial work.*

*Sorry – for all these injustices to you, as children, who were placed in
our care.*

*Sandra Hill was also six when she arrived in Australia in 1950. She was
pleased to hear the apology broadcast in Australia and now awaits a similar
declaration from the British government. 'I feel our rights were taken away from
us when we were deported. We have suffered all our lives [because of it],' she
said in a tearful interview with the BBC.*

I retired from the Service on reaching the age of 55, in March 1956,
having served a total of 41 years, all my working life thus far. Soon
after this, we had a new house built on the ocean front at Safety
Bay and sold our old home at Holland Street, together with the
adjoining vacant block, to West Australian Newspapers. The house
there was much too big for us; Daphne and Anne were both married
and Adrian was away teaching in the country. We had planned our
move to Safety Bay many years previously, and the manager of
West Australian Newspapers told us that we could live in our house
in Holland Street rent-free for as long as we wished, or until they
required the land. The house was empty for a couple of years before
they demolished it.

Chapter Seventeen

Gone Crayfishing

OUR HOUSE AT SAFETY BAY WAS RED BRICK AND BUILT to our own design on a block of just over one-third of an acre. The front door opened into the living room and there was plenty of space for our children and grandchildren. It was situated on the ocean front, facing south-south-west – we only had to cross the road and we were on the white, sandy beach.

Life in Western Australia in the decades that unfolded after the war seemed something of an ideal and its reputation of being on the edge of Australian life was beginning to work in its favour. In New South Wales, traditionally a more popular destination, there was an escalating gambling problem that cast a shadow on the neighbouring states of Queensland and Victoria. Professor Jan McMillen, sociologist and director of the Australian National University Centre for Gambling Research at Canberra, explains it as a 'historical accident':

> *It stems back to the end of the First World War when Australia started to develop a vibrant economy largely built on the migration wave from Europe. We've been a nation of migrants right from day one but in those post-war years Australia opened its door to migrants – firstly from northern Europe and then the Mediterranean. That period also brought a lot of affluence, with soldiers coming back from the war, getting jobs and firing up the economy again. Drinking became a major problem. These guys had money to spare and particularly around NSW and Sydney the pubs were a goldmine and alcohol consumption went through the roof. It was all very*

male dominated – women were absolutely forbidden from drinking in hotels; it was a real bloke's domain.

Professor McMillen recalls from her own childhood the existence of what was commonly called 'the six o'clock swill':

A few minutes before the pubs closed at 6 p.m., the blokes would line up six or seven drinks and down the lot, get pushed out the door, create disorder on the streets and then head home to beat up their wives. There was a move by some very progressive social policy reformers to civilise Australia's drinking habits. The [gambling] machines were it. They were allowed into social, football and golf clubs to create a revenue source so that clubs could provide meals for men and women to eat together in a civilised environment. It was a cash cow to end a social problem.

The government also wanted to deter illegal gambling. From the late 1920s rudimentary mechanical slot machines were being imported from America and played illegally in peoples' back rooms. They weren't widespread but when the police had nothing else to do they'd run around and smash up a few machines.

Australians love gambling full-stop. We will gamble on anything. This is where we differ from Britain and the US. To explain that difference you need to look at historical origins. The United States was settled by the Pilgrim Fathers who were escaping from the immorality of Georgian England. They wanted a moral, upright, vice-free society and that meant no gambling.

Australia was settled – by accident – by the immoral people Georgian Society didn't want.

For his part, Claude was more suited to the natural advantages of Western Australia, while his children enjoyed the buoyancy of its major city, Perth. 'Perth is where the Australian dream comes true. Now, like a suddenly created beauty outshining her ugly sisters, Perth is surging ahead of all rivals. The informal friendliness of Brisbane, the surf-soaked leisure of Sydney, the financial enterprise of Melbourne, the horticultural beauty of Canberra, the environmental and cultural grace of Adelaide; all are distilled in the capital of Western Australia,' wrote English journalist Jonathan Aitken in 1971.

At Safety Bay, we soon became friendly with a crayfisherman named 'Spud' Ward. His proper name was Lindsay Gordon but everyone called him Spud. He hailed from Victoria, where he had been a dingo trapper, but he had fallen in love with Western Australia whilst serving in the army during the war. He made his home at Long Point at the southern extremity of Warnbro Sound. Safety Bay township is at the northern end of the Sound. To reach his home, Spud had to travel through about five miles of bush track from Safety Bay using his short-wheelbase Land-Rover, which he brought over from Victoria and which was probably one of the first of its kind in Western Australia.

Spud and his wife Edna had two daughters, Adeline and Virginia. At the time we moved to Safety Bay, Virginia was about eight years old. Spud and Edna had built themselves a kitchen-living room and a bedroom, and the girls had a caravan as their quarters.

Spud started off fishing for crayfish with only a 12-foot dinghy, using sails and a small outboard engine. He made his craypots himself from old fencing wire and the roots of the coast wattle, which are very long and strong. He could not afford to buy the ¼-inch steel rod and cane that was the recognised method of craypot construction. At one time, he thought he would have to look for a job as he could not make a living from crayfishing. But things brightened up as he learnt more about the work and was able to obtain an 18-foot boat with a 5 hp Simplex marine engine. This allowed him to go further afield and to purchase ¼-inch galvanised steel rod and cane to make his pots, though for the body of his pots he used tea-tree sticks that grow in thickets in swampy areas in coastal regions thereabouts. The cane was only used for the neck, apron and base of the pot. He had to steam the tea-tree sticks to make them pliable enough to bend around the pot.

Soon after we arrived at Safety Bay, I arranged to work with Spud for a season to learn the crayfishing game. He was anxious to buy a new 26-foot craft built of marine ply which was being constructed in Rockingham. We lent him £1,000, interest-free, to help make the purchase. I also assisted him in laying his moorings for this crayboat in front of our house, where she would be in more sheltered water than at Long Point.

She was very staunchly built, with an auxiliary engine, a twin-cylinder Simplex. The wheelhouse was for'ard and she had a self-draining deck abaft, which is a great advantage in a crayboat, so much water is brought inboard with the pots and ropes and floats. She was awkward in operation, as she had too much freeboard for'd owing to the high foc'sle and wheelhouse. I suggested Spud get the sailmaker in Fremantle to supply a very strong nylon triangular storm sail and rig this on a small mizzen mast stepped about three feet for'd of the transom and sheeted in hard amidships by means of sheets led to cleats fitted on each quarter. He did this and it proved very successful. When brought head to wind in picking up a pot, the boat would remain there very nicely, and the sail also reduced the roll with wind and sea abeam. The steering wheel was wrongly positioned for single-man operation, so we worked out a new site for it. I provided him with a length of well-seasoned jarrah of 10-inch diameter to form a drum that would carry his wheel ropes of one-inch flexible steel wire rope. We rigged up PVC sheaves to act as leading blocks and carry the wheel ropes aft to his tiller and I spliced the wire rope to shackle them to the end of the tiller. On trials, this proved very successful, as Spud was a dyed-in-the-wool loner.

Our arrangement for pay was the usual: one-third the value of the catch to the boat, one-third to the skipper and one-third to the crew. I received one-third during the 'white season', the time of maximum catch. We had a good season and I learnt enough, as I thought, to be able to start on my own, so I kept a lookout for a likely craft.

I eventually bought an 18-foot fishing boat, carvel-built, sail with an auxiliary engine, a single-cylinder Simplex marine engine, petrol driven. Spud showed me how to make craypots and made me up a base to mount on a post about hip high to construct the neck of the pot, and another to transfer the neck so as to construct the remainder of the pot. The first pot that I made, with the assistance of my wife, I gave to Spud. It was constructed entirely of cane and was too high. Spud called it his beehive. He used it for several seasons and assured us that it caught better than any of his other pots! The next one we made also turned out a peculiar shape; Ethel christened it our

Grecian urn, because that is what it resembled. But it caught very well, in practice.

We used to go out into the swampy country around Baldivis and Wellard in our four-wheel-drive Land-Rover and cut tea-tree sticks to use in pot-making. These sticks had to be made pliable, so I rigged up a steamer at the back of the house where there was plenty of room on our block. The fuel for this was collected in the bush where we found a good supply – there was also enough for our household use. I purchased a one-man crosscut saw, which could be converted into a two-man saw. It was four feet in length, big enough to cut through quite big logs.

On these trips into the bush, we liked to make a day of it, taking lunch and a thermos of tea. When our children and grandchildren were with us, they would come along and we had some great times picnicking in the bush together. Daphne's family had a holiday home, 'Rock Cod Retreat', on the north-east of Garden Island; Anne's family had one on the beachfront at Waikiki. We loved to spend holidays together as often as we could. After Adrian moved to the metropolitan area, he and his family could visit us much more often at Safety Bay.

We gave both our daughters' families sailing dinghies and, having taught Adrian's children to pull a pair of oars in our small plywood dinghy, we gave his family a 13-foot aluminium boat and outboard.

Garden Island was a wonderful place for fishing and beachcombing. On one holiday there, Anne's family discovered a baby fairy penguin and its mother. Both were smothered in fuel oil. The mother was dead but they brought the young one back to Daphne's house, where we washed it in warm water and detergent to remove the oil from its feathers. Ethel wrapped it in an old jumper and nursed it in the warm sun until it was dry. Then we tried to feed it, even going to the trouble of chewing small strips of fresh fish and offering these, to simulate the mother's regurgitated fish that it would have previously known. Nothing worked. The boys and I rode down on our bicycles to Careening Bay at the south end of the island, a journey of eight miles each way, to buy some cod liver oil, and we managed to feed the baby penguin a little of this from an eye-dropper.

For its sleeping quarters, we made up a bed in a cardboard carton lined with old woollens, but in the early morning it would get out and peck at the lamp glasses of the kerosene fridge. I would then turn out and reheat the hot-water bottle we put in its box. At first we christened it Petula but soon discovered it was a male, so it became Pecksy the Penguin.

My granddaughter Louise had a light nylon collar and lead, which she would put on Pecksy, then take him for walks in the bush. He looked so quaint. One day she took him down to the water's edge and let him go. Away he went, without a backward glance. He headed straight out to sea until he was almost out of sight, with all of us calling his name from the shoreline. We thought we had lost him but after a couple of hundred yards, he turned round and swam back. Granny was there, ready to dry him off and sit him in the sun to warm up again. After a couple of nights of having to reheat the hot-water bottle, I thought of putting his bed on the warm brickwork of the kitchen stove and he remained snug all night from then on. He fully accepted us as his family and was a wonderful pet. Once he had settled, we used to chew up fish to feed him and he seemed quite happy with this, till he found the burley tin and proceeded to eat the remains. (Burley is a mixture of bran, pollard and whale oil.) At the end of the holidays, he was still with us and had not swum back to Carnac Island to join the colony there, so Daphne took him to Perth Zoo to join their collection of penguins.

Another pet Daphne had on the island was a carpet snake, or children's python – not poisonous, of course. It took up its abode under the house and would come to her call when they arrived for another stay. The children loved to show it off to their friends and allow them to handle it – if they were careful.

Australia boasts some treacherous wildlife. It has more venomous snakes than harmless ones. The most dangerous are the taipan, the tiger snake, death adders, copperheads, brown snakes and red-bellied black snakes. There are two varieties of crocodile: the saltwater crocodile is particularly dangerous, its smaller, freshwater cousin less aggressive. Some Australian spiders are also killers. The redback spider and the funnel-web both have a potentially lethal bite. In the

*seas off Australia there are sharks, including the infamous Great White. In
2009 there were an estimated 30 incidents involving sharks and water sports
enthusiasts around the Australian coast, some more serious than others. Although
there were no deaths, swimmers and surfers were probably mindful of the fate of
snorkeller Brian Guest, who died in December 2008 at Port Kennedy in Western
Australia. The predator was a giant Great White Shark.*

Not long after Ethel and I started going out crayfishing together, we
passed a fellow fisherman named Katunarich, whose boat engine
had broken down. I offered a tow, which he gladly accepted. There
was a fairly heavy sea running and consequently a considerable
amount of 'snatch' between the two craft. On one extra-strong jerk,
Ethel was flung against the combing and suffered a couple of broken
ribs. However, once we got inside Passage Rock, locally called Tub
Rock, the going was easy and we towed him to his mooring without
further incident.

I used to keep a log showing where we had placed our pots and
recording our catch for each area daily. To assist in this, I used the
old chart of 1875, which gave much more detail of the region than
the latest version. When we left the bay close to the southern side
of the group of rocks called The Sisters, we would see Spud's *Irene
II*, instantly recognisable by the white trysail he carried aft as a
steadying sail.

The maximum number of pots we used was forty, though we were
allowed fifty-four, which meant three pots for each foot of length of
our boat, an 18-footer. We did not have a tipper, which meant we
had to lift the pot from the surface onto the topsides of the boat
manually. This required a great deal more effort and time than if we
had had a tipper. When we had a full pot, we would sometimes have
to wait for the roll of the boat to help us lift it. Once, a sea came
aboard and Ethel caught it. She was drenched.

During my season of craying with Spud Ward, there were reports
of crayfishermen bringing in large numbers of undersized crayfish.
The new district fisheries inspector, Munro, was said to be very
strict. As we were loading our catch into the Land-Rover one day,
a bloke came up to us, introduced himself and requested a look at

our catch. Munro then felt over the bags, which were all sewn up. He could tell from the feel if the crays were undersized. He then asked what we had in the sugar bag and we told him it contained a few to take home to our families. Having checked it, he said he was pleased to meet fishermen who took appropriately sized crays for home consumption.

Not long after this, he nabbed a fisherman taking home a bag of undersize crays. Munro said, 'I'll give you two choices. You either empty them back into the sea or I run you in. Which is it to be?'

Naturally the fisherman chose the first option. Munro told him to start walking and wait to empty the bag when he gave the signal. The fisherman, wearing sea boots and heavy fishing gear, waded out until he was up to his waist in water but Munro ignored his beseeching look and told him to keep going. Only when the water was up to the fellow's mouth did Munro sing out, 'Now!'

Munro stopped a lot of people taking undersize crays but some fishermen were entrenched in their ways. I remember chatting with a Slav fisherman at his home when a policeman came to the front door with his seventh summons for catching undersize crays. It amazed me that he was so blasé not only about the summonses but also about the long-term implications of his own behaviour not just for himself but also for future generations.

Crayfish poisoning is not uncommon among crayfishermen and, in my experience, very painful. In different attacks, I have had it in both index fingers, in my right knee and in my left thumb. I believe that skin punctures inflicted by the spikes of the crays as they were removed from the pots put us at risk of bacterial infection from the cow hocks, which we used as bait, and which were often none too fresh. I also used fish for bait. My fish trap, which I made out of plastic-covered wire netting and baited with fried bread, daily attracted several dozen fish, mainly trumpeters. We found the occasional carpet shark in the pots, some so big that it was hard to credit how they'd managed to get in. I would have great difficulty in removing them, first having to kill the shark, which we kept for bait.

Seahorses, delightful little creatures, would cling to the pot ropes as they came up. On one occasion, I found a big baler shell in one of the pots, so I placed it on deck upside down, intending to take it ashore. We carried on with our work, when suddenly we heard a plop – it had managed to turn itself over and crawl to the edge of the boat and launch itself over the side.

Our boat was carvel-built of one-inch timber, that below the waterline being jarrah and that above, larch. *Madeline* was very staunchly built. She had the simplest, most effective bilge pump I have ever seen: made from two-inch copper pipe about five feet in length, it had a T-piece braised in near the upper end, which was open; the lower end was plugged with wood drilled out to about 1¼ inches and this opening was closed with a leather disc secured at one side by copper tacks and weighted with lead on its top side. The plunger consisted of a broom handle with a rubber disc secured at its lower end and, to pump out, the lower end was placed in the bilge and the T-piece was placed over the combing aft and the handle operated up and down. She would fill a bucket in about four or five strokes – magic!

I rigged a cover for the open part of the boat abaft the cabin for the winter rains. This saved a lot of trips to pump out but I also put out a stern anchor when winter gales were imminent, using an Admiralty pattern anchor with 20 fathoms of 2½-inch manila rope. This enabled us to sleep easy when it was blowing a gale.

Another item I put on the *Madeline* was a barometer, which I secured on a bracket fitted on the for'd bulkhead, just under the deck head. There were no doors on our cabin and, very soon after we became owners, a couple of welcome swallows came and built their nest on this bracket and they very soon became quite tame. When they had their young, they would come out to sea to feed them when we were out craying, and after feeding them they would rest on the sailing-horse just abaft Ethel, chirping away, before setting out again for the mainland to collect another mouthful of flies. We felt they were complaining about having to come so far to feed their babies. I used to stroke the little ones as they grew up and they got quite used to us being around. Some of the hatchlings, when they were starting to fly, would come ashore with us in the dinghy, taking little flights and then having a spell on the gunwale or transom, encouraged by their parents. They had a great time flipping around while we were unloading the dinghy but then they would find that they were not strong enough to return to *Madeline* and I would have to take them back in the dinghy. After a few more days they would gain strength enough to look after themselves.

I remember one time we were due to go on the slipway and we had young swallows in the nest. The Safety Bay slip was fully booked, so I had to go on Ces Marchant's slip at Rockingham. Ethel and I realised that if we took the young ones round there, the old birds wouldn't be able to find them and they would die, so we decided to leave them in the dinghy on *Madeline*'s mooring. I went ashore and shaped a piece of 4 x 3-inch jarrah with the adze, to fit under the after thwart of the dinghy, then I unscrewed the bracket from the cabin and carried it with the young ones in their nest, and placed it under the thwart on the platform I had provided. This prevented the seagulls from getting at them. I dropped the dinghy astern of *Madeline* and we watched until the old birds went into the nest to feed their young, before casting off *Madeline* and taking her out round Penguin Island and then north and in through South Passage to Rockingham. A couple of days later, after cleaning and painting, we returned *Madeline* to her mooring, and there were our swallows quite safe and happy. All I had to do was reverse the procedure and put them back in the cabin, and we were back to normal.

Our cabin was open aft but we were never broken into. Some kids did once pull the swallows' nest down before they had laid their eggs but they built again and still brought out their young. I laid sacking on the deck below their nest to catch their droppings, so that did not bother me when I went in to swing the fly wheel to start our engine.

Towards the end of summer, *Madeline* would be festooned with swallows – scores of them, on the shrouds, on the boom, and on the horse and any other place they could get a foothold. All, except our own two, would scatter when we went alongside. We think this was a built-in memory of theirs to congregate in large numbers, as they do in Britain prior to migrating to North Africa to spend the northern winter.

In their *Handbook of the Birds of Western Australia*, D.L. Serventy and H.M. Whittell report a similar instance of swallows nesting on a boat used for station work at Point Cloates, near Ningaloo Reef. The birds followed that boat for a distance of 35 miles and back when they had eggs or young in the nest.

We had the birds as companions for the ten years we were craying. After we sold her, *Madeline* carried on as a crayboat and we hoped our swallows were still allowed aboard. When we gave up crayfishing, we moved to Palmyra, where we lived happily in a duplex shared with our daughter Anne and her family.

At Palmyra, Ethel and I always enjoyed a good yarn about our crayfishing days. One of the more amusing anecdotes we shared was of an incident that occurred a couple of miles outside the line of reefs enclosing Safety Bay. I was busy packing crayfish when Ethel put the helm over suddenly and the boat gave a lurch. I looked up and asked what was wrong. She said there was a reef just ahead. I was unaware of one in the vicinity.

'There, where the water's boiling!' she insisted, pointing.

So I took the tiller and steered in that direction.

It turned out the turbulence was being caused by a large green turtle asleep on the surface. We got right alongside before he woke up and dived down out of sight.

Ethel did the right thing, though. In certain weather conditions, the water would 'boil' over rocks near the surface. The story of the 'turtle reef' always gave us a good laugh, though.

In *Madeline*, Ethel acted as my coxswain. She made a jolly good fist of being a sailor, though I must admit I did not give her sufficient initial training, which led to a peculiar incident. We had finished our day's work and were returning to our mooring under sail. As usual, on rounding up, I cast off the main sheet then went for'd to pick up the rope securing the dinghy to the mooring chain and lift the chain from the sandy bottom. However, the main sheet fouled on something in the stern sheets and failed to run clear. Consequently, the mainsail was still filled with wind and *Madeline* tried to sail away, with me trying to hang on to the mooring.

I sang out to Ethel in a very urgent voice, 'Let go the main sheet!'

She replied in similar tone, 'I haven't got hold of the so-and-so main sheet!'

'Free it, then!' I yelled.

Which she did, so I didn't have to go for a swim.

APPENDIX

Claude Choules' Ships
and Shore Bases

HMS *Impregnable*

Impregnable was a collection of ships which gathered at Devonport after the first training ship was established there in 1855. Although the first was called HMS *Implacable*, those that came afterwards were all known as *Impregnable*. The ships provided accommodation and classroom space, a tailor-made environment to learn practical seamanship. The students wore naval uniform, or similar, and the daily routine mirrored that of the navy. Boys were given a good grounding in academic subjects as well as a thorough training in seamanship and shipboard discipline. They practised parade ground drill, rifle drill and small-arms shooting, and became proficient in a variety of sports and skills that would see them through a career in the navy. However, there was no commitment required from the boys to actually join the Service.

Corporal punishment was common but it was usually meted out swiftly rather than sadistically. *Impregnable* finally fell victim to cost-cutting measures made after the Depression of the 1920s. Its final intake left on the first day of 1929, leaving HMS *Ganges* at Shotley the primary training base for boys.

HMS *Revenge*

HMS *Revenge* was the ninth Royal Navy vessel to bear the name and Claude Choules was one of almost 1,000 crew on board. She was launched in 1915 and commissioned the following year, in time to see action at the Battle of Jutland. At 28,000 tons packed into a 624-ft long frame, *Revenge* was an impressive sight as she scythed through the open seas. Her weapons, including eight 15-inch guns and four underwater torpedo tubes, were primed for action. Although she engaged the enemy for an hour and a half, she emerged unscathed. As hostilities ended in the First World War, and immediately prior to the surrender of the Grand Fleet, Queen Mary took tea in the *Revenge*. Within hours, *Revenge* was taking part in 'Operation ZZ'. On 21 November 1918, 60 Allied battleships escorted 11 battleships, 5 battlecruisers, 8 cruisers and 48 destroyers of the High Seas Fleet into captivity at Scapa Flow.

Between the wars, *Revenge* had two lengthy refits but spent most of her time at sea in or around the Mediterranean.

Although she was already old and outdated by the onset of the Second World War, she was nonetheless still useful and was attached to the North Atlantic Escort Force. On her first trip to Halifax, she was carrying the exotic cargo of gold bullion. She was also used in the English Channel as part of the force intended to deter Hitler's planned invasion. *Revenge* was one of the ships to escort Australian soldiers back to the Pacific to defend their homeland from the threat of Japanese invasion.

By late 1943 her age was beginning to show and she was reduced to the ranks of being a stoker's training ship. However, Prime Minister Winston Churchill himself stepped in to stop this ignominy, choosing the vessel for one leg of the passage to the Tehran Conference that year. Her military assets were stripped before the invasion of Normandy in 1944 to improve the viability of other ships in the armada sent to recapture Europe from the Third Reich. She was sold for scrap in 1948.

HMS *Defiance*

With the profile of ships' weaponry changing, the Royal Navy realised a need for a torpedo school ship specialising in latest techniques. As it happened, the HMS *Defiance* was a ship launched in 1861 that was outmoded before she even saw service. Lacking the metal cladding that had become essential for warships, in 1884 she was dispatched to Devonport to host the new school. Largely stripped of her internal machinery, she was anchored on the Hamoaze just below Saltash.

Inside *Defiance*, there were lecture rooms on the upper deck in purpose-built classrooms. There was also a gymnasium on the deck. Other facilities included a galley, a drying room and officers' accommodation. The ship's company lived on the lower deck.

Below this, in what is known as the cockpit in an old line of battleship, there was on one side a row of different patterns of above-water discharge apparatus for the 'Whitehead' torpedo used for teaching classes. Below this deck was a recreation room for the men, with a billiard table, papers and magazines. The ship was equipped with two boilers and a dynamo, and an air-compressing plant was later installed.

Subsequent ships that joined the *Defiance* as part of the school were HMS *Perseus* (which became HMS *Defiance II*), HMS *Spartan* (*Defiance III*) and HMS *Cleopatra* (*Defiance IV*). The *Perseus* was used almost entirely for training in mine warfare and had the facility for sailors to assemble and disassemble mines and to launch and recover them. In 1896, Captain Henry Jackson became known for his pioneering use of radio messaging from aboard the *Defiance*.

All the above ships were replaced in 1931 in the form of HMS *Inconstant*, HMS *Andromeda* – previously part of the *Impregnable* school – and HMS *Vulcan*.

Memories of *Defiance* were broadcast in a BBC programme in which Len Mason recalled:

> The classroom was hot and stuffy in summer or freezing in
> winter and those sketches kept on coming down and going
> up again at a rapid rate.

Just for strangers to that excellent ship, it comprised three old tubs lashed together with gangways between – HMS *Andromeda*, which originally had sails as well as engines, she was a prize from the French sometime in the 1800s – HMS *Inconstant*, steel-hulled – HMS *Vulcan* with a wooden bottom which used to be copper-sheathed until it was discovered with salt water they had a battery between the two ships, so they took the copper off. All three were hardly sea-going because, being anchored for years, they had become settled in mud. This meant you didn't get rocked to sleep.

Theory instruction was dispensed by officers, practical work by chiefs. We learned maths, electrical principles, RN history (official and unofficial), how torpedoes worked, trimming gyros, sound-powered telephones, Y-dischargers, depth charges, machine shop practice, fitting skills and other bits and pieces. The best bit of fun was firefighting and use of breathing apparatus in smoke-filled ships.

In 1955, the school became shore-based at Portsmouth and the ships were towed away from Devonport and scrapped. The torpedo school was finally closed in 1959.

HMS *Vivid*

When Claude Choules joined the barracks at Devonport, it was known as HMS *Vivid*. Although the dockyard itself dated from the seventeenth century, the barracks were not built until the last half of the nineteenth century, on what had been fields and market gardens. Until they were built, accommodation for serving seamen tended to be in unappealing hulks of redundant ships parked up at river- or harboursides. The limestone buildings clad in Portland Stone cost £250,000 and consisted of two accommodation blocks for five thousand men, a drill shed and a commodore's house. It was occupied for the first time in June 1889 and seamen shared their quarters with pigeons used for communication purposes. The clocktower was added in 1896 and included semaphore arms which could be seen from headquarters at Mount Wise. This was soon obsolete, however, with the introduction of electrical communication.

Two years later, the site was further extended with an officers' wardroom and further rooms for another 1,000 men. Gunnery training took place there from 1907. In 1934, it was renamed HMS *Drake*.

Like the rest of Plymouth, Devonport was a target during the Second World War and was hit during a heavy raid on the night of 21 April 1941. Sailors stationed at the barracks helped to clear the rubble at Devonport and throughout the city. After 1961, Devonport barracks was used solely for accommodation and accounting. A number of ships were renamed HMS *Vivid* whilst serving as depot ships for the base:

> The Royal Naval Barracks at Devonport consist of a fine and substantially built group of stone buildings, and as viewed from the higher ground on the right of the road by which they are approached, present a pleasing picture. Anyone not acquainted with the locality would search in vain for the barracks in Devonport; as a matter of fact they lie at the present extremity of Keyham Dockyard which, however, is in the process of being considerably extended, the ground between the barracks and the harbour being just now – and likely to be for a few years to come – a wilderness given over to the tender mercies of the inexorable contractor whose plant and crazy-looking little wagons are much in evidence. These works have already encroached considerably on the barracks premises, the old cricket ground and golf links having been swallowed up, and further confiscations being possibly in prospect.

Others took Claude's view and were less impressed by the facilities. In June 1892, when the barracks had been inspected by The Lords of the Admiralty, the First Sea Lord Admiral Sir Anthony Hoskins snorted that he 'had never seen such a wicked waste of money as the barracks'.

HMS *Valiant*

During the First World War, *Valiant* was a state-of-the-art vessel. Laid down in January 1913, she was completed in February 1916 at a cost of £2,537,037. During the Battle of Jutland, she fired 288 15-inch rounds and sustained comparatively slight splinter damage, when one crewman was injured. On 24 August 1916, *Valiant* collided with HMS *Warspite* and remained under repair until September 1916.

Valiant was rebuilt twice between the wars. In the second rebuild, HMS *Queen Elizabeth* and HMS *Valiant* remained almost identical sister ships, the difference being HMS *Queen Elizabeth* had a tripod mainmast, HMS *Valiant* a pole mainmast. There were considerable improvements made to her guns and their elevation. To accommodate three aircraft, an athwartships catapult was added. Subsequently, there were a considerable number of changes made to the anti-aircraft weapons.

In the Second World War, she began a sustained period of active service by taking part in operations off Norway in April 1940. In the Mediterranean in 1941, *Valiant* participated in the Battle of Cape Matapan against the Italian fleet, was bombed off Crete and received serious damage from a daring Italian underwater commando raid at Alexandria, Egypt.

During 1943, she supported the invasions of Sicily and Salerno, twice bombarding enemy forces ashore during the latter operation. She also escorted the Italian Fleet into Malta after Italy had agreed to Allied terms.

In August 1944, she was damaged in a drydock accident at Trincomalee, Ceylon (Sri Lanka), requiring her to return to England for extensive repairs that lasted into 1946.

After final service as a training ship, HMS *Valiant* was sold for scrapping in March 1948.

HMS *Eagle*

HMS *Eagle* was launched in 1918, although she wasn't converted to an aircraft carrier until 1924. After that she was capable of carrying 40 aircraft. The ship's motto was 'soaring to the sun'.

In 1929, Major Ramon Franco, brother of Spanish dictator General Franco, was fished out of the ocean by the crew of *Eagle*. Major Franco was something of a celebrity in Spain, where he was a pioneer of the national air force. He was trying to repeat a trip between Spain and Argentina when his Dornier flying boat ditched. Pilots from *Eagle* found him and three crew after they had been drifting without food or water for six days. The search was on the point of being abandoned when they were found. Following the rescue, King Alfonso XIII awarded *Eagle*'s captain and senior officers the Spanish Order of Merit and presented the ship with a magnificent silver eagle.

At the outbreak of the Second World War, *Eagle* was in Singapore and became involved in the hunt for the German pocket battleship *Admiral Graf Spee*. In March 1940, while *Eagle* was escorting troop transports in the Indian Ocean, an internal explosion killed 13 and put the ship out of commission. After repairs were finished, *Eagle* joined the Mediterranean fleet and soon her aircraft were involved in a devastating attack on Italian ships at Tobruk, the start of a successful campaign against Italian shipping that included the attacks on Taranto.

After refitting in the UK, she returned to the Mediterranean in 1942, helping to keep the supply lines open for beleaguered Malta. On 11 August 1942, while guarding a convoy bound for Malta, *Eagle* was holed by four torpedoes fired by the German submarine *U-73* and sank in eight minutes. Although one hundred and sixty men were lost, some nine hundred were saved by two destroyers and HMS *Jaunty*, a tug. *Eagle* sank about 70 nautical miles off the coast of Majorca, still carrying the silver eagle presented by the Spanish king just over a decade previously. *U-73* was sunk in December 1943 by depth charges and gunfire from two US ships. Sixteen of its crew died and thirty-four were saved.

HMS *Vernon*

Another of the Royal Navy's torpedo schools, this one was based in Portsmouth and began functioning in 1876. Its centrepiece was a 50-gun, 176-ft long wooden frigate which was on active service during the mid-nineteenth century.

Schooling took place on the beached hulk of *Vernon* while accommodation was on the former HMS *Ariadne*. Ten years on and the *Vernon* was replaced by HMS *Donegal,* which provided more space. However, it was known as *Vernon,* along with all the other vessels used.

Vernon proved its worth during the First World War when it became devoted to developing anti-submarine devices and electrical technology mines, adding considerably to the expertise of the Royal Navy in those crucial years.

In 1923, the torpedo school was considered sufficiently essential to the Royal Navy as to become a stone frigate, giving it an improved degree of permanence. Consequently, it moved into several buildings in Portsmouth, all of which were known as *Vernon*.

During the Second World War, *Vernon* became a centre of excellence in the science of mines. It had an early success when its servicemen defused a new type of magnetic mine being used by Germany after one washed ashore at Shoeburyness.

In 1940, a German booby trap inside a mine being examined at *Vernon* exploded, killing five people. Afterwards mines were taken to a nearby quarry for analysis to improve safety for handlers.

The bombing raids over Portsmouth further disrupted work at *Vernon*. Soon its departments were dispersed across southern England. Nonetheless, its work continued with some success. By 1945, the Royal Navy's diving school was also incorporated into *Vernon* and moved to Portsmouth with the rest of the scattered departments at the end of hostilities.

Although its profile changed, *Vernon* continued to function in the same way until 31 March 1986, when it was renamed HMS *Nelson*. It was briefly the headquarters for the commandant general of the Royal Marines. Mine warfare became the prerogative of the School of Maritime Operations at HMS *Dryad,* while the diving operation switched to Horsea Island. Although *Vernon* then ceased to exist, the figurehead from the original nineteenth century ship was preserved at Portsmouth.

SS *Jervis Bay*

Launched in 1922, the SS *Jervis Bay* was an Aberdeen & Commonwealth Line steamer often used to ferry immigrants from Britain to Australia. It was named for a bay in Australia.

In 1939, she was taken over by the Royal Navy, one of more than 50 liners commandeered for naval defences against Germany. Having been furnished with some guns dating from the First World War era, she was sent first to the South Atlantic as an armed merchant cruiser and then on convoy duty. Her term of duty was to be tragically short.

On 28 October 1940, HMS *Jervis Bay* began shepherding a convoy from Halifax, Nova Scotia, the 84th of its kind. The hazards were immense. Convoys like this, laden with goods to fortify Great Britain, were targets of German ships, U-boats and aircraft. There were mines scattered in the ocean, silently waiting to claim a kill. Then there was the weather, which could erupt with autumn gales at any moment. Nonetheless, despite the dangers, the close escort turned back for Canada and the convoy ships headed out resolutely into the Atlantic. The responsibility for the ships now lay with HMS *Jervis Bay* and its crew of Royal Navy, Royal Naval Reserve and Merchant Navy sailors.

As twilight fell, tensions began to run high on the *Jervis Bay* when an unknown ship was spotted on the skyline. Captain Edward Fegen flashed an enquiry across the waves: 'What ship?' There was no reply. The British hope was that it was a departing escort vessel.

But as darkness closed in, so did the ship. It was the *Admiral Scheer*, one of three German warships roaming the Atlantic looking for prey. The *Admiral Scheer* turned broadside at a range of a few miles when the convoy ships were well within range of its 11-inch guns. Soon its shells rained down.

Captain Fegen instantly ordered the convoy to scatter. Then he turned his own ship towards the enemy, while knowing his own 6-inch guns were no match. He began by disguising his trail with smoke then ordered his men to open fire.

As Fegen hoped, the *Admiral Scheer* responded by focusing all its firepower on the ship bearing down on it. Quickly its gunners found the range and the *Jervis Bay* was savagely damaged. Although it sustained deadly strikes, the *Jervis Bay* continued on its collision course despite terrible injuries to its crew. Captain Fegen himself resumed his post at the bridge after losing an arm. In a subsequent shell strike he was killed.

Within moments the *Jervis Bay* buckled under the firepower and toppled into the water, taking with her the bodies of 187 crew members.

If sailors on the *Admiral Scheer* were jubilant about the victory, or astonished at the gallantry of the armed merchant cruiser, such emotions were momentary. They realised the convoy had indeed scattered as ordered by Fegen and were now heading as swiftly as possible away from them in various directions.

Admiral Scheer set off in pursuit, using star shells and searchlights to identify *Beaverford*, *Kenbane Head*, *Maidean*, *Trewelland* and *Vigaland*. But although the convoy took losses it was far from decimated and this was thanks to the blind courage of the SS *Jervis Bay* and her crew. As the cruiser steamed on her futile mission towards the Admiral Scheer, she bought the rest of the convoy at least 20 minutes to make a getaway. It also cost the German ship 335 shells which its captain might have chosen to keep for more fruitful targets.

Captain Fegen was awarded a posthumous Victoria Cross with a citation that read: 'Valour in challenging hopeless odds and giving his life to save the many ships it was his duty to protect.'

HMAS *Canberra*

Canberra was one of the prestigious ships ordered for an infant navy. It was one of two 10,000-ton county-class heavy cruisers upon which a five-year naval development programme launched by the Australian government in 1924 was pinned.

It took two years to build the *Canberra* at John Brown & Co Ltd, Clydebank in Scotland. She was commissioned in 1928, two months after her sister ship, HMAS *Australia*. Several British ships were in the same class, including HMS *Kent, Cornwall, Cumberland* and *Suffolk*.

After spending some time in British home waters she finally struck out for Australia, arriving in Fremantle on 29 January 1929. En route she had visited Gibraltar, Freetown, Lagos, Cape Town, Simonstown – the British naval station in South Africa – and Durban.

In September 1931, *Canberra* cruised to New Caledonia and Fiji; before the outbreak of the Second World War, she had twice visited the China Station and three times gone to New Zealand.

After 1939, the defence of Australia seemed something of a straightforward affair. Germany's naval forces were unlikely to crop up in numbers in the Pacific, given their interest in isolating Britain by gaining control of the Atlantic. *Canberra* initially had a quiet time in Australian waters, then a more challenging period in the Indian Ocean on the lookout for German raiders that threatened to terrorise British merchant ships in the region. During 1941, *Canberra* was also involved in the hunt for the *Admiral Scheer*, the German battleship that sank HMS *Jervis Bay*. However, it didn't face its annihilation despite the carnage taking place elsewhere on the world's oceans.

But the war for Australia in general, and HMAS *Canberra* in particular, took on a more urgent perspective after Japan entered the war in December 1941, following its air raid on Pearl Harbor. The Pacific War brought conflict virtually to Australia's doorstep for the first time. Now convoy duties in the southern seas were considerably more treacherous. *Canberra* also took troops to New Guinea, where there followed a bitter struggle for control on an island that formed a bulwark against the enemy for Australia.

There was even danger in home waters. *Canberra* was anchored close to the American cruiser USS *Chicago* in Sydney harbour when a Japanese midget submarine attempted an attack on the night of 31 May 1942.

Three midget submarines evaded anti-submarine measures partially protecting Sydney harbour and caused havoc. Each was 80 feet long and carried two 18-inch torpedoes. The crew of two inside were huddled in a space no bigger than that of a telephone box.

Despite confirmed sightings of the rogue subs in the vicinity of the harbour, some high-ranking officers simply refused to believe an attack was under way. Although damage was restricted to HMAS *Kittabul*, a converted ferry, and the loss of life a comparatively modest 21 sailors, it showed how vulnerable Australia might be. The targets of the Japanese submarines were the USS *Chicago* as well as *Canberra*. All three midget submarines were lost in the operation, one scuttling itself before firing a shot, having got tangled up in netting at the harbour entrance. The attack took place after a reconnaissance flight by the Japanese had gone undetected the day before. Despite the immediate loss of the midget submarines, the danger facing Australia wasn't yet over.

The full-sized submarines that had transported the midget subs to their target stayed in Australian waters and picked off merchant vessels at will for almost a month until they returned to base for supplies. Two of the submarines launched attacks on mainland Australia during this period. Sydney and Newcastle were shelled, although only minimal damage was caused by these audacious operations.

In August 1942 *Canberra* was part of the Allied force that sought to take back Guadalcanal from the Japanese occupiers. During the Battle of Savo Island, she was holed by two torpedoes on the starboard side and sprayed with 8-inch shellfire. As she listed helplessly, the wounded and surviving sailors were transferred to two American ships, USS *Patterson* and USS *Blue*. When it was clear the *Canberra* could not be saved, she was sunk by USS *Ellet*. Eighty-four of the ship's company, including Captain Frank E. Gedding, perished while many more were wounded. So many ships and aircraft followed her to the bottom of the sea at this junction of waterways that it was eventually named 'Ironbottom Sound' by the Allies.

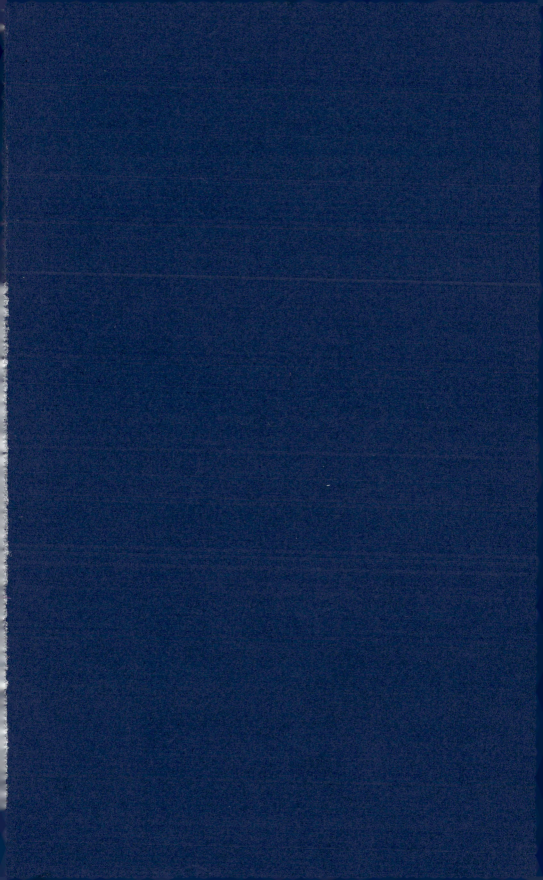